Structured
CONCURRENT PROGRAMMING
with
Operating Systems Applications

D0251733

R.C.Holt
G.S.Graham
E.D.Lazowska
M.A.Scott

University of Toronto,
Computer Systems Research Group
Toronto, Ontario

ADDISON-WESLEY
PUBLISHING COMPANY
Reading, Massachusetts
Menlo Park, California · London · Amsterdam
Don Mills, Ontario · Sydney

This book is in the
ADDISON-WESLEY SERIES IN COMPUTER SCIENCE

Consulting Editor
M. A. Harrison

The cover and diagrams in this book were prepared by the Media Centre,
University of Toronto.

Reproduced by Addison-Wesley from camera-ready copy prepared by the authors.

ISBN 0-201-02937-5
 EFGHIJKLM-MA-89876543210

PREFACE

   This book introduces the art of concurrent programming. This
particular type of computer programming, with several activities
progressing in parallel, is intellectually intriguing and is
essential in the design of operating systems.

   Concurrent programming has been used for many years in
writing parts of operating systems, such as device managers. But
it is only recently that convenient, high-level constructs have
been developed to handle these problems well. This book surveys
the older, low-level concurrency mechanisms, such as semaphores
and interrupts, and then concentrates on a structured approach to
concurrent programming based on monitors.

   The only background required of the reader is a knowledge of
some high-level language such as Fortran, PL/I, Algol or Cobol.
The example programs in this book are written in Concurrent SP/k
(or CSP/k), which is the SP/k subset of PL/I extended with
concurrency constructs.   These programs can be easily
transliterated to other recently developed concurrent programming
languages such as Concurrent Pascal. A CSP/k compiler that runs
on the IBM System 360/370 is available from the SP/k Distribution
Manager, Computer Systems Research Group, 216C Sandford Fleming
Building, University of Toronto, Toronto, Ontario, M5S 1A4,
Canada.

   This book can serve as the basis of a unit on concurrency
within a larger course on operating systems, systems programming
or programming languages, or as the sole text for a specialized
course. The material presented concerning the design of an
operating system allows the reader to build a spooling,
multiprogramming, paging system in CSP/k. Programs that simulate
the hardware for this system are given in appendices and are
available with the CSP/k compiler. This type of project gives
invaluable insight into production system software.

Much material presented in this book has been developed at the University of Toronto in conjunction with the authors' colleagues. The following people have helped in essential ways: David Barnard, Philip Bernstein, Shirley Cain, Jim Cordy, Bryon Czarnik, Ira Greenblatt, Reinhard Menzel, Hugh Redelmeier, Rosanna Reid, Kenneth Sevcik, Henry Spencer, Dionysios Tsichritzis, and Inge Weber.

The support by the National Research Council of Canada for the work leading to this book is gratefully acknowledged.

Computer Systems Research Group
University of Toronto

R.C. Holt
G.S. Graham
E.D. Lazowska
M.A. Scott

CONTENTS

CHAPTER 1

CONCURRENT PROGRAMMING AND OPERATING SYSTEMS

Concurrent programming means writing programs that have several parts in execution at a given time. The concept of concurrent or parallel execution is intellectually intriguing and is essential in the design of computer operating systems. This book covers the fundamentals of concurrent programming using structured techniques. After an introduction to the need for concurrent programming and its basic concepts, a notation called monitors is presented and used for solving problems involving asynchronous program interactions. Monitors have been added to the SP/k subset of PL/I and the concurrent algorithms in the book are presented in this extended version of SP/k, called Concurrent SP/k or CSP/k.

Two chapters are devoted to the design of a model operating system that supports spooling, multiprogramming and paging. The reader may choose to complete the implementation of this operating system; since the model system's hardware is specified by CSP/k programs, the implemented operating system can be executed (in a simulated mode) using the CSP/k compiler. The last chapter explains how monitors can be implemented on actual computer systems.

After giving examples of concurrency, this chapter concentrates on operating systems. Operating systems implement concurrent programming by sharing CPU time among several programs and use concurrent programming to control resources and serve users.

EXAMPLES OF CONCURRENCY

In programming, and in other activities, concurrency problems can arise when an activity involves several people, processes or machines proceeding in parallel. We will give several examples of concurrency, beginning with one that does not involve computers.

An example: activities in a large project. A large project such as the construction of a building is accomplished by many workers carrying out different tasks. These tasks must be scheduled, and one method of doing this uses precedence charts, as shown here.

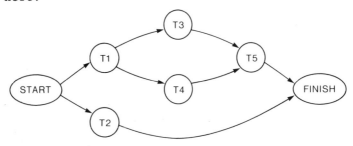

This example chart shows that in the beginning, tasks T1 and T2 can both be started. After T1 is done, T3 and T4 can be started, and when both of them are done, T5 can be started. The whole project is finished when T2 and T5 are done. As the next example will show, precedence charts can be used to specify concurrency in computer programs.

There are two main reasons for using parallel tasks in this example. First, there are many workers available and they must be allowed to work at the same time (in parallel). Second, the project can be completed in less elapsed time if tasks are allowed to overlap. In computer systems, analogous reasons (many asynchronous devices and the need to shorten elapsed time) may result in concurrent programming.

An example: independent program parts. Precedence charts can describe possible concurrency in a computation. The expression (2*A)+((C-D)/3) can be evaluated sequentially (one operation at a time) by finding the product, difference, quotient and sum, in that order. But parallelism is possible, because some parts of the expression are independent, as is shown in this precedence chart.

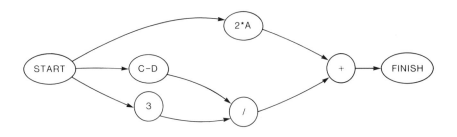

Groups of statements, as well as expressions, may have independent parts that can be executed in parallel. For example, the following loop determines if 'JONES' is in a list by testing NAME(1) then NAME(2) and so on.

```
DO I=1 TO SIZE;
    IF NAME(I)='JONES' THEN
        FOUND=TRUE;
    END;
```

This loop could be executed by checking all of the names at the same time, because the tests are independent. For a large computation, parallelism such as this can minimize the elapsed time for completion.

As computing elements such as microprocessors become cheaper, it becomes more and more attractive to split programs into several parallel tasks. In the future we may find that computers are built as huge collections of tiny processing elements, analogous to building an elephant out of a swarm of mosquitoes or bees, and we will need to know how to program such contraptions.

An example: simulations. Sometimes programs are written to simulate parallel activities. For example, a program might simulate boats entering a harbor; this program could predict the effects of increased boat traffic. A good way to program this simulation is to have an asynchronous program activity (a process) corresponding to each simulated activity (each boat). Each process mimics its boat, and the interaction of these processes models the interaction of boats entering the harbor. Programming the simulation is done by writing the constituent concurrent programs.

An example: control of external activities. Special purpose computer systems are used to control chemical processes such as the manufacture of cement. Sensors transmit signals to the computer to report temperature, pressure, rate of flow, etc. The computer in turn transmits signals that set valves, control speeds, sound alarms, etc. The computer system also keeps a log of its actions and prints reports. A computer system such as this keeps track of many interrelated concurrent activities. One good way to program such a system is to have a concurrent software process in the computer for each external activity. A software process tracks its corresponding activity; it is

responsible for sending and receiving signals to and from the
activity. Programming this computer system is done by writing
the concurrent programs that observe and control the activities.

These examples have given various practical uses of
concurrency. But the most important examples of concurrent
programming arise in operating systems. The next sections
explain why this concurrency arises and how it is handled.

OPERATING SYSTEMS

Modern computer installations have many asynchronous hardware
components, such as operator consoles, card readers, printers,
disk drives, tape drives and CPUs. The operating system must
ensure that these components are used efficiently and that they
provide convenient service for the users.

An operating system consists of a collection of software
modules. These modules receive requests from users (for example,
to run jobs) and must schedule the system's components to satisfy
these requests.

The operating system may support multiprogramming, that is,
it may allow more than one user's program to be in execution at a
given time. To support multiprogramming, the operating system
must share the system's resources among the executing programs.
Some resources, such as tape drives, are exclusively allocated to
a program, until the program terminates or no longer needs the
resource. Other resources, such as the CPU, are shared
dynamically, in a way that gives the appearance that each program
has its own virtual resource. For example, the operating system
may allocate a "slice" of CPU time to one program, then to
another program, and so on. This is called time slicing and
gives the appearance that each program has a virtual CPU, which
is like the physical CPU but somewhat slower. As a second
example, the operating system may provide each program with a
virtual memory. This is done with the help of special hardware
(for "paging" or "segmenting") that allows the operating system
to allocate physical memory only to the active parts of programs.

There are two basic reasons why multiprogramming is needed in
computer systems. The first is for efficient use of hardware
resources and the second is for quick response to users'
requests. First we will consider efficiency. The system's
hardware components run in parallel at vastly different speeds.
For example, the time to process a single character may vary from
a tenth of a second for a console, to a thousandth of a second
for a card reader, to a millionth of a second for a CPU.
Clearly, the CPU should not be forced to waste time (100,000 of
its operations) while a console transmits a character. While a
user is typing messages to a running job, another job should be
given the CPU. If a job is I/O bound, spending most of its time
waiting for input/output devices, the spare CPU time can be used

by a <u>compute bound</u> job, which spends most of its time using the CPU. If the system has a variety of equipment, a job that uses only a few of the devices should not prevent concurrent use of other devices. These examples show how multiprogramming provides more efficient use of computer equipment.

Apart from efficiency, multiprogramming allows the computer system to respond quickly to users' needs. Suppose a user has a short, urgent job but a long-running job is already in the system. With multiprogramming, the short job can run in parallel with the long one and can finish hours before it. In interactive systems, a form of multiprogramming is necessary, with one program for each user. The system is shared among the interactive users and their programs so that each receives good response; this is called <u>time sharing</u>. These examples show how multiprogramming allows prompt attention to users' needs.

COMMUNICATION IN OPERATING SYSTEMS

Operating systems must be organized so as to control hardware devices and run users' programs. This section gives a simplified model of how communication occurs among the devices, the operating system and the users' programs; the next two sections describe how operating systems are organized to handle this communication.

An operating system controls an I/O device by sending it a <u>start I/O command</u>. If the device is a reader, the command causes it to read a card, putting the card's characters into main memory. When the device has carried out the command, it can send an <u>interrupt</u> signal back to the CPU indicating that it is free to carry out another operation. This signal can switch the CPU from a user's job to the operating system; this allows the operating system to send another command before returning the CPU to a user's job.

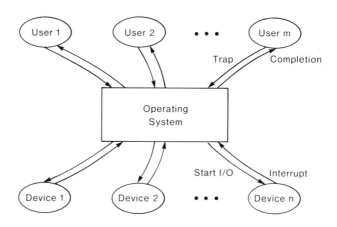

Meanwhile, each user's job occasionally makes requests to the operating system, for example, to read a card or to write a disk track. The job makes a request by a <u>trap</u> or a <u>supervisor call</u> instruction; this instruction is like a subroutine call and transfers control from the user to the operating system. Having received such a request, the system blocks the job (gives it no more CPU time) until the requested action has been completed. Then the job is unblocked and allowed to continue executing.

There is usually an <u>interrupting clock</u>; it occasionally sends an interrupt signal that transfers control from a user's job to the operating system. This allows the system to implement time slicing and pass the CPU from user to user, and to cancel a user's job that is using excessive CPU time. Without the interrupting clock, an infinite loop in one user's job could prevent other users (and the operating system) from using the CPU.

When a program is actually using the CPU, we say it is <u>running</u>. When it is waiting for a request to be serviced, we say it is <u>blocked</u>. When a program would be running except that the CPU is allocated to another program, we say it is <u>ready</u>. The operating system maintains a queue of the programs that are ready. This transition diagram shows how the states of a program change:

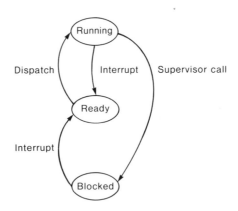

We say the operating system <u>dispatches</u> a program when it lets it run, by giving it the CPU.

A trap generally causes a program to be blocked; however in some instances (not shown in the diagram) if the operating system can immediately satisfy the request, the user program is again dispatched and no blocking occurs. Other than by a trap, the only way a running program loses the CPU is by an interrupt. A clock interrupt may signal the end of the program's time slice, or an I/O interrupt may allow another program to run. In a system with only one CPU, at most one program can be in the

running state, but with several CPUs there can be as many
simultaneously running programs as there are CPUs.

BASING AN OPERATING SYSTEM ON A MONOLITHIC MONITOR

There is a particularly simple method of handling
asynchronism, and of building operating systems, based on the
concept of a monolithic monitor. Essentially this technique
implies that the users' programs and the devices do not
communicate directly and that all their interactions are passed
through an operating system that cannot be interrupted. We will
now explain this idea in more detail.

The interrupt signals are provided by hardware; they allow
the operating system to give immediate attention to changes in
device status so the devices can be kept usefully active. When
the operating system is engaged in some critical activity, for
example, updating the queue of ready programs, it must not be
interrupted, because the interruption might cause another update
of the half-updated queue. The result could be a hopelessly
tangled set of pointers and subsequently a system crash. To
handle these critical situations, a CPU usually provides a method
of disabling or masking interrupt signals. When interrupts are
disabled the hardware holds the signals pending until interrupts
are again enabled.

The monolithic monitor approach uses disabling/enabling in
the following way. Every trap (from the user to the operating
system) and every interrupt (from a device or the clock to the
operating system) immediately disables interrupts. This means
that whenever the operating system begins executing, interrupts
have been masked. They remain masked until the operating system
dispatches a user program. As a result the operating system is
never interrupted, and it gives up control only by handing the
CPU to a user program (by dispatching).

The beauty of this approach lies in its simplicity and in the
straightforward handling of asynchronism. It is quite easy to
build a very small operating system on this basis that correctly
schedules devices and manages users. But a monolithic monitor is
not suitable for most operating systems because of two
fundamental problems.

The first is that activity in any part of the operating
system disables interrupts from all devices. This means that
devices are held up waiting for new commands. For computer
systems of any appreciable size, this loss of response to devices
can not be tolerated. For certain devices, information is lost
if the response is too slow. Inevitably some method must be
introduced to allow parts of the operating system to be
interrupted, although with great care to avoid scrambling
critical data.

The second problem is that tables must be maintained in the monolithic monitor to record the status of each and every device. For example, if a user requests a disk read, the system must know from its tables whether the disk is busy. The size and complexity of these tables can become excessive.

The concept of a monolithic monitor underlies a variety of operating systems. In too many cases the system has outgrown the concept; to improve performance more and more activity is moved outside of the uninterrupted monitor. This gradual evolution of an operating system tends to lead to system errors, as ad hoc tricks are used to try to maintain the consistency of critical shared data. These problems suggest that the responsibility for the various devices should be decentralized and moved out of the monolithic monitor in the initial design.

There is an alternate approach that recognizes these difficulties; it minimizes the system's uninterrupted activities and concentrates these in a module called the kernel.

BASING AN OPERATING SYSTEM ON A KERNEL

The alternative to a monolithic monitor moves the various activities in an operating system out into asynchronous, interruptable software entities called processes. Each process is similar to a user's program in a multiprogramming system, in that it shares the CPU's time and is in one of the states: running, ready, or blocked.

One elegant way to structure the operating system is to have a software process (a device manager) corresponding to each device. This manager process has sole responsibility for starting the device and observing when the device becomes free; this means the software process tracks the hardware device. This approach simplifies the operating system's tables because the status of a device is implicitly given by the status of its manager process. For example, a card reader device is busy exactly when its manager has sent it a command and has not yet been notified of the completion.

Each user's program can be managed and executed by a process. When the user has an I/O request, it is sent by the user's process to the corresponding manager process. The user's process must then be blocked until the manager notifies it that the I/O has been performed.

Of course there must be mechanisms for interprocess communication, so the users' processes can transmit requests and wait for completions. There must also be a mechanism for a device manager to start up its device and to wait for its interrupt, and a mechanism to share CPU time among all the software processes. All these responsibilities are absorbed by a fundamental operating system module called the kernel.

The kernel can be implemented like a very small monolithic monitor, which schedules the CPU among the processes, receives I/O interrupts and transmits them to device manager processes, and supports interprocess communication. The kernel uses clock interrupts to help it share CPU time among the processes.

Outside the kernel all interrupts are <u>invisible</u> and do not affect the logical progress of the processes. An interrupt can slow down a process by causing its CPU to be temporarily removed, but this is the only effect on the process. The device manager processes observe I/O interrupts, but these appear to the managers as synchronous replies from queries to the kernel, not as asynchronous signals.

The kernel gives each process the appearance of having its own CPU. Each of these <u>virtual</u> CPUs behaves like a real CPU except that it has a variable rate of progress. This rate is determined by interrupts, the kernel's CPU scheduling policy, and the use of CPU time by other processes.

The kernel's responsibilities can be implemented by hardware or microprogramming, with the efficiency advantage of making interprocess communication and process/device communication quite fast. Such an implementation has the structural advantage of making asynchronous interrupts invisible to all software modules; this simplifies system design.

Two extremes in organizing operating systems are a huge monolithic monitor versus a minimal kernel that supports only one type of process. Many variations lie between these extremes, and these are greatly influenced by the specific nature of the computer's architecture. Often the processes that manage devices are quite different from those that execute user jobs; on CDC 6000 systems the device managers do not even run on the CPU - they use special "peripheral processors". Use of multiple CPUs, called <u>multiprocessing</u> for historical reasons, does not necessarily cause difficulties. In the case of a monolithic monitor, the only additional complication of multiple CPUs is guaranteeing that only one CPU at a time can enter the monitor. Since the kernel in a kernel-based system is implemented as a very small monolithic monitor, the same technique (limiting entry into the kernel to one CPU at a time) applies. Processes (and user programs) outside of the monitor or kernel have their own virtual CPUs, so the presence of multiple CPUs should speed up execution without affecting system correctness.

AN EXAMPLE OPERATING SYSTEM

The T.H.E. operating system nicely illustrates a system based on a kernel. It is a small system that multiprograms several users' Algol programs. It has a hierarchical organization with five levels. The lowest level is the kernel, which implements the concept of processes. In the T.H.E. system, the kernel provides interprocess communication by operations on "semaphores". These operations, called <u>synchronization primitives</u>, give each process the ability to block itself and wake up other processes, and the means to guarantee mutually exclusive access to data shared among processes. Semaphore operations will be discussed in detail in the next chapter.

This table lists the functions of the levels in the T.H.E. system:

Level 5	Job managers	Read control language and execute users' programs
Level 4	Device managers	Handle devices and provide buffering
Level 3	Console Manager	Implements virtual consoles for the above processes
Level 2	Page Manager	Implements virtual memories for the above processes
Level 1	Kernel	Implements a virtual CPU for each process

Level 2 of the T.H.E. system is a process that manages a drum and implements automatic paging for all the other processes. After level 2 each process has a large virtual memory which is implemented by automatically moving pages between main memory and the drum.

Level 3 is a process that manages the system console and enables processes on higher levels to communicate with the operator. Level 4 consists of one process per remaining I/O device; there are manager processes for each of the system's readers, printers, plotters and so on.

Finally, level 5 consists of one process per allowed user program. Each of these processes is a job manager. When a job manager completes a user job it searches for a reader that is not occupied. It then reads the control language for another job from the reader and proceeds to execute that user's job. Typically this means compiling the user's program and running it. The job manager is responsible for reserving any I/O devices needed by the job and eventually releasing them.

PROCESSES, PROCESSORS AND PROCEDURES

We have presented operating system structures to demonstrate the necessity of concurrent programming. The concept of a kernel allows us to use concurrent processes even though there is only one CPU (or only a few CPUs). Before going further, we should define precisely some of the basic terminology of concurrent programming.

   Process. A process is an asynchronous activity. It can be thought of as the execution of a program by a CPU. However, the CPU may actually be a virtual CPU that is implemented by multiplexing one or more physical CPUs among many processes. A process is, in general, guaranteed to progress through its computation unless it is explicitly blocked. However, its rate of progress may vary considerably.

   Processor. A processor is a physical (hardware) mechanism that executes instructions, proceeding from instruction to instruction. A CPU is the prime example of a processor. Some computer systems have special I/O processors (or channels) whose responsibility is to pass commands to devices.

   Procedure. Procedures are sequences of instructions that direct the execution of a processor. Procedures are sometimes called programs. Generally we can separate the data used by a procedure from the procedure itself (the code). If this separation allows the procedure to be executed by more than one process at a time, by setting up a separate data area for each process, we say the procedure is reentrant (or pure). This is analogous to having two cooks simultaneously using the same cookbook (procedure) but using separate pots and ingredients (data).

   These three definitions are fundamental to the understanding of both concurrent programming and operating systems. The next chapter will begin by giving language features for specifying with a program that several processes are to be executed concurrently.

CHAPTER 1 SUMMARY

   This chapter gave several examples of concurrency. Then it presented reasons for using concurrent programming and methods of supporting it. The following important vocabulary was introduced.

Process - an asynchronous activity such as the execution of a program by CPU.

Processor - a hardware mechanism, such as a CPU, that executes instructions, one after another.

Procedure - a sequence of instructions to be executed by a processor; sometimes called code.

Reentrant procedure – a procedure that can be executed by several processes at the same time. It consists of pure code (no writeable data) and each process provides its own data area.

Precedence chart – a diagram that gives the required ordering of several activities.

Multiprogramming – having several programs active at the same time in a computer system. (Each of these activities is a process.)

Time slicing – sharing CPU time among several processes by alternately giving each a short time interval (a slice) of time.

Compute bound – a job that does little input/output but uses a lot of CPU time; an I/O bound job does the opposite.

Start I/O command – a command sent from a CPU (or other processor) to request an operation by a device.

Interrupt – a signal sent from a device to a CPU (or other processor) to indicate that a requested operation is complete. A clock may also send an interrupt to a CPU. An interrupt causes the CPU to switch to execute the operating system.

Trap or supervisor call – a special instruction that a program can execute to switch control to the operating system, for example, when requesting the next input.

Dispatching – giving the CPU to a job so the job can run.

Disabling and enabling interrupts – when a CPU has interrupts disabled, it can not receive interrupts; they remain pending (queued by the hardware) until the CPU is again enabled.

Running, ready and blocked – a process (or job) is running when it is actually using a CPU, ready when it would be using a CPU but none is available, and blocked when it can not use a CPU because the process is waiting, for example, for an I/O completion.

Monolithic monitor – a method of implementing an operating system; all interrupts are disabled whenever any part of the operating system is active. The operating system handles all input/output.

Kernel – a module that implements processes and provides them with a mechanism for interprocess communication. If the kernel is implemented by hardware or microprogramming then the software may not need to deal with interrupts, because device starting/completion is done by the interprocess communication mechanism.

CHAPTER 1 BIBLIOGRAPHY

Hoare gives an excellent brief survey of the function of operating systems. Dijkstra's description of the organization of the T.H.E. system is a classic, well worth reading. Holt's survey of program structures provides a catalog of software structuring mechanisms, including monolithic monitors and kernels.

Dijkstra, E.W. The structure of the T.H.E. multiprogramming system. Comm. ACM 11,5 (May 1968), 341-346.

Hoare, C.A.R. Operating systems: their purpose, objectives, functions and scope. In Operating Systems Techniques (C.A.R. Hoare and R.H. Perrott, editors), Academic Press (1972), 11-19.

Holt, R.C. Structure of computer programs: a survey. Proceedings of the IEEE 63,6 (June 1975), 876-893.

CHAPTER 1 EXERCISES

1. Give a precedence chart that specifies the maximum concurrency for the following program segment. Allow each subexpression to be computed separately. Be careful not to allow a variable to be assigned a value before its old value is used.

```
K=I+7;
J=7-(5+(3*I));
I=J+(5*K);
```

2. Suppose a multiprogramming system is running one compute bound job and one I/O bound job. Which of the jobs should be given priority for using the CPU? Explain why.

3. In certain situations, the throughput of a computer system can be maximized by avoiding multiprogramming and running only one user job at a time. Characterize these situations, taking into consideration the job mix, types of jobs, types and number of peripherals and use of files.

4. As processors (microprocessors in particular) become cheaper, it becomes desirable to decentralize certain operating system responsibilities, moving them away from the CPU and out into channels, devices and terminals. Characterize the types of computational responsibilities that can be moved into each of those locations.

5. Consider a computer system that supports two types of processes: system processes and job processes. Each job process is controlled by a system process. This manager process can suspend (put to sleep) and reactivate (re-awaken) its job

process. This results in a new process state that a suspended job process enters, besides the usual three states (running, ready and blocked). Draw the transition diagram showing how job processes can change states.

6. Characterize the sorts of systems in which a monolithic monitor would or would not serve as a good basis for an operating system.

7. Make a list of the visible and invisible interrupts that an executing user job experiences.

8. In the T.H.E. system, if there is a hardware error in reading a memory page, it is impossible for the page manager to notify the operator. Explain why. The solution to this problem seems to be to switch the console manager to level 2 and the page manager to level 3. Explain why such a switch would have a heavy efficiency penalty.

9. Some procedures are "serially reusable" but not reentrant. This means that the procedure cannot be used by two processes at once, but can be re-used after a completed execution without refreshing the procedure. Give examples of program constructs that cause this situation.

10. In Chapter 5 you will be introduced to the problem of the dining philosophers, a well known synchronization problem in which a group of philosophers must cooperatively share forks in an attempt to consume spaghetti. In the following problems we shall consider a more elegant gastronomic enterprise, the Snooty Clam seafood restaurant.

(a) We begin our study of the Snooty Clam restaurant in the kitchen. Earlier in this chapter, we showed how a pair of cooks can be viewed as two processes sharing a common procedure (a recipe). Kitchen facilities (such as the oven) and utensils (such as spoons) can be viewed as resources.

After spending a fortune to create the proper atmosphere in the dining room, the owners of the Snooty Clam found themselves so strapped for cash that they were only able to buy a single saucepan and wire whip. This, of course, means that only one chef at a time can make sauce. The problem is compounded by the arrangement of the kitchen. All pots and pans are hung against one wall, and all stirring implements against another. So in order to acquire the resources required to make a sauce, a chef must visit first one wall, then the other.

Consider the problems that might arise if two chefs simultaneously decide to make sauce, but head for opposite walls in their quest for resources. (Chefs are notoriously temperamental, and refuse to relinquish an acquired resource until they have finished using it.) Devise an allocation policy for the saucepan and wire whip that will prevent the problem you have observed.

(b) The wine cellar in the Snooty Clam lies at the end of a long, narrow tunnel which, unfortunately, is not illuminated. After a recent collision that resulted in three broken bottles, the manager decided that only one of the restaurant's four wine stewards should be allowed in the tunnel at a time, although several can simultaneously use the cellar given that they enter it via the tunnel at different times.

To implement this policy, the manager installed red lights above the entrances at both ends of the tunnel. At each entrance is a switch that turns on or off all these lights. Before entering the tunnel, a wine steward checks to see that the light is off. If so, he first switches it on and enters the tunnel. Upon emerging at the opposite end, he switches the light off.

The manager was very proud of this rather ingenious solution. Unfortunately, though, during its second day of operation a collision occurred in the tunnel. How?

(c) The Snooty Clam restaurant does not take reservations. The dining room contains a single table seating twenty patrons. When space becomes free, parties are seated in the order in which they arrived, except that a party that cannot be seated in the available space is passed over.

What is the effect of this seating policy on large parties? If parties are seated strictly in the order in which they arrive, how will this affect the utilization of the tables?

CHAPTER 2

CONCURRENCY PROBLEMS AND LANGUAGE FEATURES

To solve problems in concurrent programming, we need a good notation for concurrent algorithms. This chapter presents a number of basic concurrency problems and gives programming language features for dealing with them.

SPECIFYING CONCURRENT EXECUTION

To use parallelism in programming we need to be able to specify two or more concurrent activities. The following language feature is sometimes used.

```
COBEGIN;
    Stmt 1;
    Stmt 2;
    •••
    Stmt n;
COEND;
```

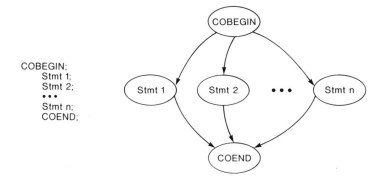

This specifies that the constituent statements can be executed in parallel, as shown in the corresponding precedence chart. Of course, each of these statements may actually be groups of statements. We can think of the cobegin/end construct as creating n concurrent processes, each of which must execute to completion before the creating process is allowed to continue.

There is another notation that can be used to initiate a new activity (a process). It has this form:

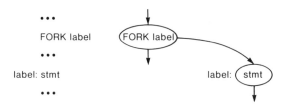

Essentially, the FORK statement is a GOTO statement which simultaneously branches and continues on, as shown in the precedence chart. FORK can be thought of as COBEGIN without COEND. There are additional statements called QUIT and JOIN that allow the two branches of activity to merge. The newly created activity which started at the specified label executes a QUIT statement when it has completed its work.

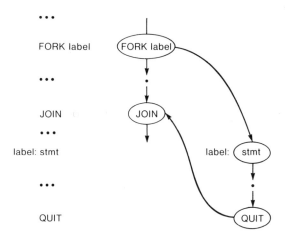

When the original activity, proceeding from the FORK, needs to wait until the created activity is complete, it executes a JOIN statement. The process executing JOIN is blocked until the QUIT has been executed.

We can use FORK, JOIN and QUIT to simulate cobegin/end, just as IF and GOTO can simulate a WHILE loop. But cobegin/end is preferred because it is better structured and leads to more understandable algorithms.

DISJOINT AND OVERLAPPING PROCESSES

When concurrent processes use no common data, they are said to be disjoint (or independent). Here is a concurrent program to find the maximum of A, B, C and D.

```
1   COBEGIN;
2       M1=MAX(A,B);
3       M2=MAX(C,D);
4       COEND;
5   M=MAX(M1,M2);
```

Since statements 2 and 3 are disjoint, we have no difficulty understanding the program.

When the parallel statements have overlapping data that is changed, things can get confusing. Here statements 3 and 4 are not disjoint.

```
1   J=10;
2   COBEGIN;
3       Print J;
4       J=1000;
5       COEND;
```

At first it appears that statement 3 will print 10, because J is set to 10 in statement 1. But a closer inspection reveals that statement 4 changes J to 1000. If statements 3 and 4 are to be done simultaneously, will J be printed as 10, or as 1000, or maybe as some other value? This presents a problem: just what does parallelism mean when some processes change a variable while others are using it?

The unfortunate answer to this question is that the results depend on relative speeds, and in general we can not predict the speeds of processes. Constructs such as cobegin/end make no guarantee about speeds. Kernels that share time among processes do not control the precise timing of interrupt signals. Hardware processors do not in general execute at precisely defined rates. Even if we could determine the speed of a process for a given execution, each successive execution might be different.

When the outcome of a computation depends on the speeds of processes, we say there is a race condition, and that parts of the computation are time critical. Operating systems use concurrency to maximize throughput and convenience; but they must be carefully designed to prevent race conditions that could destroy the system or the results of users' programs.

We will give two more examples of processes with overlapping data to illustrate the danger of race conditions. Suppose one process, called the observer, is responsible for observing and counting certain events; for example, it may observe the number of jobs submitted to a computer center. It executes this program:

```
OBSERVER: DO FOREVER;
            Observe an event;
            COUNT=COUNT+1;
            END;
```

Another process, called the reporter, occasionally prints reports about the observed events. The reporter executes this program:

```
REPORTER: DO FOREVER;
            Print COUNT;
            COUNT=0;
            END;
```

As soon as the reporter prints the count of events, it sets the count to zero, because the events have been reported.

The observer and reporter are overlapping in that they both use the variable called COUNT. This overlap causes a problem. Suppose that the observer has increased COUNT to 6 and the reporter prints 6. Suppose that before the reporter sets COUNT to zero, the observer increases COUNT to 7. Now suppose the reporter continues and changes COUNT from 7 to 0; the unfortunate result is that an event goes unreported. In general, the reporter may fail to report any number of events because increments to COUNT may occur between printing COUNT and setting it to zero.

There is another problem in this example that is less obvious, and has to do with the statement that increments COUNT. An implementation of the statement COUNT=COUNT+1 may involve more than one machine instruction, such as:

```
LOAD   COUNT     (Put COUNT in accumulator)
ADD    1         (Add 1 to accumulator)
STORE  COUNT     (Store accumulator into COUNT)
```

When the observer process is executing this sequence, it may be overtaken by the reporter. Suppose COUNT is 15, and this value is loaded into the accumulator. Then the reporter may print 15 and set COUNT to zero. Next the observer adds 1 to its accumulator and stores the result 16 into COUNT. The unfortunate result is that 15 events were reported, but COUNT is left indicating that 16 events are yet to be reported.

From this example we conclude that when processes update shared data, the results can be unpredictable and not at all what is desired. In the next section we will show how to deal with this problem, but first we will give another typical example of race conditions.

In operating systems there are often queues, for example, queues of processes ready to use the CPU. Consider a singly linked queue:

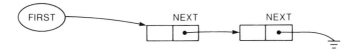

As shown this queue has two elements. To insert a new element E into the queue, the following is executed:

```
NEXT(E)=FIRST;
FIRST=E;
```

This changes the queue to the following:

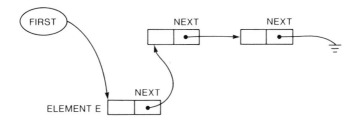

Suppose that while E is being inserted, another process is trying to insert element F by executing

```
NEXT(F)=FIRST;
FIRST=F;
```

Suppose the two processes simultaneously set NEXT(E) and NEXT(F) to FIRST. Now suppose FIRST is set to F by one process and then immediately re-set to E by the other. The resulting messed-up queue has this form:

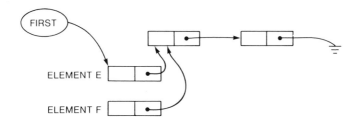

Unfortunately, element F has been lost; it cannot be found by following links from FIRST. This would be disastrous if, for example, element F represented a job to be executed.

The race conditions given in these examples have the same disastrous results whether the processes execute "physically" or "logically" in parallel. By physically parallel we mean that each process has a processor (CPU) and these are simultaneously running. When processes are implemented by time slicing of a single CPU and only one process at a time can be running, the processes execute logically in parallel. In the case of time slicing, race conditions occur as a result of the unpredictable transfer of the CPU from one process to another.

The solution to these race conditions is to make sure that only one process at a time gains access to the shared data that is updated. Each of these accesses occurs in a part of the program called a "critical section"; we will now discuss methods of guaranteeing "mutually exclusive" access to these sections.

CRITICAL SECTIONS

As we have seen, when a process is updating variables, it is generally unreasonable to allow any other process to access the same variables. The required control of access can be accomplished by the mutexbegin/end construct, as illustrated here:

```
Process P1:                      Process P2:
   Do until finished;               Do until finished;
      Compute;                         Compute;
      MUTEXBEGIN;                      MUTEXBEGIN;
         Access shared variables;         Access shared variables;
         MUTEXEND;                        MUTEXEND;
      Compute;                         Compute;
      END;                             END;
```

The mutexbegin/end construct, with its brackets MUTEXBEGIN and MUTEXEND, guarantees that a process will have mutually exclusive access to the sections of programs within the brackets. At a particular time, P1 or P2, but not both, are allowed to execute the part of their program, called a critical section, within the brackets. A process is allowed to use several mutexbegin/end constructs, but these can not be nested.

A generalization of mutexbegin/end would have a parameter specifying a particular collection of shared variables. For example, we could have:

```
   MUTEXBEGIN(V);
      Access to shared variables in collection V;
      MUTEXEND(V);
```

But we will keep this discussion simple by ignoring the parameterized construct.

One of the fundamental problems in concurrent programming is how to implement mutexbegin/end. Its two brackets must accomplish the following:

MUTEXBEGIN. Must determine if there is any other process in a critical section: has another passed a MUTEXBEGIN but not the corresponding MUTEXEND? If so, the entering process must wait. When no other process is in a critical section, the process proceeds beyond MUTEXBEGIN, setting an indicator so that other processes reaching a MUTEXBEGIN will wait.

MUTEXEND. Must allow a waiting process, if there is one, to enter its critical section.

It seems easy enough to implement MUTEXBEGIN and MUTEXEND. A flag called OCCUPIED can be initialized to false to indicate that no process is in a critical section. Then MUTEXBEGIN can be written as:

```
1  DO WHILE(OCCUPIED);
2     END;
3  OCCUPIED=TRUE;
```

The flag called OCCUPIED is repeatedly tested until found to be false, then it is set true and the process enters its critical section. MUTEXEND can be written as:

```
OCCUPIED=FALSE;
```

These implementations seem to accomplish our goal of allowing only one process at a time into a critical section. But appearances are deceiving in concurrent programming.

Our implementation is just plain wrong. Suppose process P1 tests OCCUPIED in statement 1 and finds that it is false. At the same time, or very shortly before or after, P2 may make the same test. Both processes, executing in parallel, will conclude that OCCUPIED is false, will proceed to execute statement 3, and will enter their critical sections at the same time. In the next section we will be more careful when we try to develop a solution for the mutual exclusion problem.

MUTUAL EXCLUSION BY BUSY WAITING

In computer systems with more than one (hardware) processor, the processors may need to have mutually exclusive access to certain data. When one processor is using the data, another processor wanting to use the data must wait; this waiting can be accomplished by repeated execution of a test to see when the critical section can be entered. This repeated testing is called a busy wait and is clearly a waste of processor time. This can be tolerated when the critical sections are used only a small fraction of the time, say five per cent, or when processor time is not considered particularly valuable.

Sometimes busy waiting is necessary; one of the prime examples is in a multiple CPU system. In such a system there is usually a set of queues, including the ready queue, that maintains the status of processes. The kernel manages these queues, and to keep the queues from becoming tangled, only one CPU at a time should enter the kernel. The kernel should be designed to be very fast so that a negligible amount of processor time is lost via busy waiting. In the rest of this section we show how busy waiting and a property of memory called "interlock" can be used to guarantee mutual exclusion.

There is special circuitry that controls the accessing of the memory by processors. This circuitry makes the memory act like a device that receives commands from the processors to fetch and store words or bytes; this memory device carries out only one command at a time. (Systems with multiple banks of memory may support memory interleaving, in which each bank carries out only one command at a time.) This "one command at a time" access is called memory interlock.

If one processor is the CPU and the other is a channel (an input/output processor) then the channel is usually given priority by the memory circuitry; we say the channel steals cycles from the CPU because the CPU must wait (and lose memory cycles) while the channel transfers data to or from the memory.

In the absence of memory interlock we cannot be sure that concurrent execution of the assignment statements J=10 and J=1000 will leave J as either 10 or 1000; J might end up as a random bit pattern. With memory interlock, J ends up as either 10 or 1000, but we may not be able to predict which.

Given memory interlock we can implement mutexbegin/end in the following manner. We initialize a shared variable TURN to 1. We use separate local copies of MY_TURN and HIS_TURN for P1 and P2; for P1 they are initialized to 1 and 2, and for P2 to 2 and 1, respectively. MUTEXBEGIN is implemented as:

```
DO WHILE(TURN¬=MY_TURN);
    END;
```

And MUTEXEND is:

```
TURN=HIS_TURN;
```

This "solution" has an awful shortcoming; it requires that P1 enter its critical section, then P2, then P1 and so on. If P2 is ready to use its critical section first, too bad! It must wait until P1 catches up, and this strict alternation continues.

We will now give an implementation of mutexbegin/end that avoids the strict alternation, but still uses busy waiting. We

will use a shared variable called TURN that is initialized to 1,
and shared variables called NEED(1) and NEED(2) that are
initialized to false. Each process has local variables ME and
OTHER initialized to 1 and 2 for the first process and to 2 and 1
for the second. This implementation is called Dekker's
algorithm, after Dekker, the Dutch mathematician who devised it.

```
MUTEXBEGIN:
 NEED(ME)=TRUE;  /* Make known my need to enter */
 DO WHILE(NEED(OTHER));  /*My need is known; wait till his is not*/
    IF TURN¬=ME THEN
       DO;
          NEED(ME)=FALSE;  /* Temporarily retract my need */
          DO WHILE(TURN¬=ME);  /* Wait for my turn */
             END;
          NEED(ME)=TRUE;  /* Re-broadcast my need */
          END;
    END;

MUTEXEND:
 NEED(ME)=FALSE;
 TURN=OTHER;  /* Allow other to enter */
```

When critical sections are not being used heavily, MUTEXBEGIN
usually finds that NEED(OTHER) is false, signifying that the
other process has not requested entry. Entry into the critical
section is therefore immediate, with no execution of the loops.
The variable TURN is used to decide which process is to enter
first only when both processes have requested entry.

The logic of this implementation is extremely subtle and can
be appreciated by considering the many possible timings of the
processes and attempting to program a simpler solution. The
algorithm can be generalized to handle any number of processes,
but becomes even harder to understand. The main point about
Dekker's algorithm is that it demonstrates that with only memory
interlock and busy waiting, mutual exclusion can be guaranteed.
The algorithm satisfies the following requirements for mutual
exclusion.

(1) Only one process at a time is allowed in a critical
    section.

(2) A process will be allowed to enter its critical section
    if no other process is using a critical section.

(3) No set of timings can keep a process waiting indefinitely
    as it tries to enter its critical section.

(Theoretically, there are timings of the processes that can
violate the third requirement. This can occur when the first
process constantly enters and leaves its critical section. The
second process repeatedly checks NEED(OTHER) and always finds it
true because each check happens while the first process is in its

critical section. Why are these timings highly improbable in most practical systems?)

There is a much simpler implementation of mutexbegin/end, given that the processor has an instruction that both tests and sets (modifies) a word. For example, if the processor has a condition code called CODE, the operation could be:

```
1  TESTANDSET(OPERAND):
2     CODE=OPERAND;  /* Test the word */
3     OPERAND=TRUE;  /* Set the word */
```

Lines 2 and 3 must be carried out by a single, uninterruptable machine instruction. If there are multiple processors, memory interlock must prevent another processor from accessing the operand between the test (line 2) and the set (line 3). Note that each processor has its own condition code.

We use a shared variable called OCCUPIED that is initialized to false and implement mutexbegin/end as follows.

```
MUTEXBEGIN:
   TESTANDSET(OCCUPIED); /* See if OCCUPIED true; set it true */
   DO WHILE(CODE);
      TESTANDSET(OCCUPIED);
      END;
```

```
MUTEXEND:
   OCCUPIED=FALSE;
```

Even when there is no instruction called "test and set", there may be an instruction with the desired properties. For example, we could use a DECREMENT instruction which subtracts one from a word and sets the condition code if the result is negative.

In this section we used busy waiting to solve the mutual exclusion problem. We developed an unsatisfactory solution that implied strict alternation among processes entering a critical section, and two good solutions: Dekker's algorithm and the test-and-set method. We will now show how special operations called synchronization primitives can solve the problem without busy waiting.

SYNCHRONIZATION PRIMITIVES: SEMAPHORES

Constructs such as cobegin/end and mutexbegin/end can be thought of as primitive operations (or primitives) because they have a simple meaning, and because we can use them without knowing their implementation. One of the best known sets of primitive operations for process synchronization is based on special variables called semaphores.

In a programming language, we might declare a semaphore called S this way:

DECLARE(S)SEMAPHORE INITIAL(1);

The only valid operations on semaphores are P (sometimes called WAIT) and V (sometimes called SIGNAL). The two semaphore operations allow a process to block itself to wait for a certain event and then to be awakened by another process when the event occurs. P and V have the following meaning.

P(S): Wait until S>0 and then subtract 1 from S.
V(S): Add 1 to S.

Both P and V must be done indivisibly. The P operation potentially blocks the executing process and V potentially wakes up a blocked process. The process executing the V operation is not blocked and continues execution.

A semaphore can be thought of as a bowl to hold marbles. The numeric value of the semaphore corresponds to the number of marbles in the bowl. The INITIAL attribute in the semaphore's declaration gives the original number of marbles in the bowl. Each executed V operation puts a marble into the bowl. Each executed P operation attempts to remove a marble. If none is available, P causes the process to wait. The process waits until a marble is available, removes the marble, and continues execution.

If the processes share CPU time by using time slicing, the semaphore operations can be implemented by a software kernel. The kernel that supports semaphores may be implemented by microprogramming, as is done in the VENUS operating system. When a process becomes blocked by a P operation, the kernel allocates the CPU to a ready process, so busy waiting is avoided.

P and V can be implemented using a busy wait as we will now show. In the following, local (separate) variables called BLOCKED are used by each process.

```
V(S): MUTEXBEGIN;
         S=S+1;
         MUTEXEND;

P(S): BLOCKED=TRUE;
      DO WHILE(BLOCKED);   /* Busy wait */
         MUTEXBEGIN;
            IF S>0 THEN
               DO;
                  S=S-1;
                  BLOCKED=FALSE;
                  END;
            MUTEXEND;
         END;
```

Of course this implementation is practical only when busy waiting can be tolerated. Note that the test to see if S is greater than zero must be in the same critical section with the statement that decrements S; otherwise two P operations might erroneously decrement S when its value is found to be 1. This would correspond to two processes erroneously grabbing the same marble from the semaphore bowl.

Given that semaphores are available – and that we can assume they have been implemented by the kernel – we can use them for synchronizing processes. If two processes want to update the same variable without interference, they can use a semaphore which we will call MUTEX.

```
DECLARE(MUTEX)SEMAPHORE INITIAL(1);
```

Before updating the critical variable, a process executes:

```
P(MUTEX);   /* Implements MUTEXBEGIN */
```

After the update, the process executes:

```
V(MUTEX);   /* Implements MUTEXEND */
```

The semaphore called MUTEX originally "contains a single marble" because of INITIAL(1) in the declaration. The P operation removes the marble and V puts it back. When a process is updating the critical variable, the marble is gone, so any further P operations are blocked until the update is complete. Notice that this implementation shows that semaphores can be used to solve the mutual exclusion problem. If there are several independent critical variables (or critical data structures or resources) then a semaphore can be declared for each one to provide separate mutually exclusive access.

Semaphores can also be used to provide processes with the block/wakeup facility, which allows each process to wait until certain events occur. For example, suppose process R must wait until process Q has completed a certain action.

```
Q:Compute;                R:Compute;
  Wakeup process R;         Block until awakened by Q;
  Compute;                  Compute;
  ...                       ...
```

The wakeup and block operations can be supported by having a private semaphore for each process, provided by a vector PRIVSEM of semaphores initialized to zero. Each process has a distinct process number, and this is held in the process's local variable called ME. The block/wakeup operations are implemented as:

```
WAKEUP(PROCESS_NO):
  V(PRIVSEM(PROCESS_NO));
```

```
BLOCK:
    P(PRIVSEM(ME));
```

Each private semaphore corresponds to a bowl that initially has
no marbles in it. The wakeup operation deposits a marble in the
bowl, and the block operation attempts to remove a marble.
Notice that this implementation works in our example when Q does
the wakeup before R blocks and as well when R blocks before Q
does the wakeup.

We gave implementations of block/wakeup and mutexbegin/end
that use semaphores requiring only the values 0 and 1,
corresponding to zero or one marbles. Such semaphores are called
binary semaphores. They are somewhat simpler than general or
counting semaphores, whose values can be any non-negative
integer.

Block/wakeup and mutexbegin/end are sufficient by themselves
to synchronize processes in an operating system.   Since these
operations can be implemented by binary semaphores, binary
semaphores are also sufficient. Although binary semaphores are
sufficient, they are not particularly convenient or well
structured; for this reason this book will concentrate on a more
sophisticated synchronization method based on monitors. But
before introducing monitors, we will complete our discussion of
synchronization primitives such as semaphores.

To illustrate the use of binary semaphores in solving
synchronization problems, consider a set of processes that share
a resource having several identical units. The units might be,
for example, tape drives or data buffers. When a process needs a
unit (or another unit) of the resource, it executes REQUEST, and
when done with a unit, it executes RELEASE.   The REQUEST
operation blocks the process when all the units are already
allocated. To implement these operations we will use a variable
called AVAIL that is initialized to the total number of units, is
decremented by REQUEST, and is incremented by RELEASE.   Here is
the implementation:

```
REQUEST:
    MUTEXBEGIN;   /* Implemented by P(MUTEX) */
        BLOCKED=(AVAIL=0);
        IF BLOCKED THEN
            Put integer ME on queue to wait for a unit;
        ELSE
            AVAIL=AVAIL-1;
        MUTEXEND;   /* Implemented by V(MUTEX) */
    IF BLOCKED THEN
        BLOCK;   /* Implemented by P(PRIVSEM(ME)) */
```

```
RELEASE:
    MUTEXBEGIN;  /* Implemented by P(MUTEX) */
        AVAIL=AVAIL+1;
        Determine U such that process U is waiting for a unit;
        IF waiting process U exists THEN
            DO;
                Remove U from queue waiting for a unit;
                AVAIL=AVAIL-1;
                WAKEUP(U);  /* Implemented by V(PRIVSEM(U)) */
                END;
    MUTEXEND;  /* Implemented by V(MUTEX) */
```

This implementation can clearly be done with binary semaphores because the only synchronization operations used are for mutexbegin/end and block/wakeup. Interestingly enough, this implementation demonstrates that counting semaphores can be provided using binary semaphores; this follows from the observation that REQUEST and RELEASE behave just like P and V and the value of AVAIL corresponds to the value of a counting semaphore. If we had counting semaphores available, the REQUEST and RELEASE operations could be implemented simply as P(R) and V(R) where R is a semaphore initialized to the total number of units.

OTHER SYNCHRONIZATION PRIMITIVES

There are other primitive operations, besides P and V, that have roughly the same capabilities. For example, the lock and unlock primitives are used in some systems to guarantee mutually exclusive access to a particular object or data structure. A programming language could provide "gates"; for example, a declaration might appear as:

    DECLARE(G)GATE;

We can consider that a shared object is surrounded by a fence with a gate in it. Before using the object, a program should lock its corresponding gate, and afterwards should unlock it:

```
    LOCK(G);    /* Similar to MUTEXBEGIN */
    UNLOCK(G);  /* Similar to MUTEXEND */
```

These two primitive operations are like the parameterized version of mutexbegin/end. A variation of lock/unlock used in IBM 360/370 operating systems is called enqueue/dequeue; these allow specification of either shared or exclusive access. Exclusive access is just what we have already discussed. Shared access means many processes at a time can access the object, typically for read-only usage. Enqueue/dequeue prevent overlap of shared and exclusive access.

Lock/unlock and enqueue/dequeue provide a generalized version of mutexbegin/end. Other primitives provide a facility similar to block/wakeup. These are often based on synchronization variables called "events", which are declared in PL/I as:

DECLARE(E)EVENT; /* Implicitly initializes E to false */

In PL/I the following primitives operate on events.

WAIT(E); /* Blocks process until E is true */
COMPLETION(E)=TRUE; /* Sets event E to true */
COMPLETION(E)=FALSE; /* Sets event E to false */

Events in PL/I are different from semaphores in that the wait operation does not change the value of the event; by comparison, the P semaphore operation decrements a semaphore. The lack of change of the event's value by wait is inconvenient in the common case of repeated use of an event; this situation requires explicit resetting of the event to false after the process wakes up, and this must be done with great care to avoid losing the next wakeup signal.

Events can be used in PL/I to provide a facility similar to fork/quit/join. A new process can be started up by executing:

CALL P EVENT(E);

This is like a fork operation and it starts up a new "child" process executing procedure P. The calling process can be thought of as the parent. When the child process has completed its job, it can terminate by executing an EXIT statement. This sets E to true, so the parent can wait for the completion by executing:

WAIT(E);

The child's EXIT statement corresponds to QUIT and the parent's WAIT(E) corresponds to JOIN.

We will now leave primitive synchronization operations, as typified by P and V, to consider more sophisticated interprocess communication methods such as message passing. In some operating systems a method such as message passing is directly supported by the kernel; in others, the kernel supports only primitive synchronization operations and these may be used to implement the more sophisticated operations.

MESSAGE PASSING

One of the principal uses of synchronization primitives is to allow processes to exchange information. This fact suggests that these primitives should be generalized to become communication operations that provide both synchronization and data transmission.

The SEND and RECEIVE operations are such mechanisms. A process executes SEND to pass a <u>message</u> (some information) to another process; the other process accepts the information by executing RECEIVE. For example, suppose a user process wants to have the disk manager read a certain track from the disk. The user might execute:

    SEND command to disk manager;

The command specifies the desired input/output operation. The disk manager executes this program:

    DO forever;
       RECEIVE user command; /* Wait for next command */
       Start up the disk to carry out the command;
       Wait until the disk is finished with the command;
       SEND user the status of command;
       END;

A more complicated manager might accept and queue several requests while the disk is busy. When the user program wants to wait until the command is complete, it executes:

    RECEIVE status of command;

This blocks the user until the manager sends the status.

There are many different types of send and receive operations. These differences arise from the various methods of storing messages and routing them from sender to receiver. In most systems the sender of a message continues executing after executing SEND. This implies that the message must be stored until received in some special place, and this place is called a <u>mailbox</u>. In a programming language mailboxes called C and S might be set up by:

    DECLARE(C,S)MAILBOX;

The mailbox called C could hold commands and S could hold status. Assuming each process has local variables called COMMAND and STATUS, the sends and receives of our example could be:

    SEND COMMAND TO C;   /* User puts command in mailbox C */
    RECEIVE COMMAND FROM C; /* Manager gets command */
    SEND STATUS TO S;   /* Manager puts reply in mailbox S */
    RECEIVE STATUS FROM S;   /* User gets reply */

The programming language TOPPS has constructs that are equivalent to this type of send/receive.

One of the problems with mailboxes is deciding upon an appropriate size for messages. The simplest solution is to force all messages throughout the system to have the same length. The RC4000 operating system takes this approach and uses a system-wide length of 24 characters. Messages that are shorter than 24 characters must be padded out to the required length. Some "messages", such as input/output transfers, will be too long to fit in a mailbox. This difficulty is called the large message problem; it is solved by using messages to transmit control information (such as input/output commands) and using a separate mechanism to transfer the large amount of data.

The mailbox scheme designed for the SUE/360 operating system is extremely general. It allows multiple-slot mailboxes, which can hold several messages (one per slot). Mailboxes are created dynamically and the size of a mailbox's slots are specified at creation. The slots are arranged so that messages are received in the order they are sent (first-in-first-out). Each mailbox has an input port for accepting messages, and an output port for transmitting messages. Each process has a number of input ports and a number of output ports, attached to corresponding mailbox ports. This rather elaborate scheme was never implemented. Instead, a simpler mechanism was adopted; the adopted scheme is similar to monitors, which will be presented in detail later.

The UNIX operating system provides an elegant form of mailboxes. These are called "pipes" because they provide a channel to stream data from one process to another. Suppose a person types the command "ls" on a UNIX console. The "ls" stands for "list" and causes the names of the files in the user's directory to be printed by the console. The flow of information is from the directory via the "ls" program to the console:

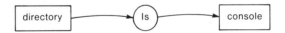

The user can specify that the list of names is to appear on the offline printer instead of the console by typing:

    ls | opr

"Opr" is a program that takes a stream of information and prints it. The symbol "|" specifies that a pipe is to channel the output of "ls" so it becomes the input to "opr". The flow of information now becomes:

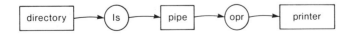

In UNIX all transmission to/from devices, files, and pipes is done by a standard set of operations called read and write. The number of bytes to be transmitted is specified in each operation. These read/write operations can be considered to be special forms of receive and send. They provide a powerful software tool by allowing software modules to be connected easily in various configurations. Each module is written without consideration of whether its input or output is to or from a device, file, or process.

Whenever one process produces a sequence of outputs that is used by another process as input, we say there is a producer/consumer relationship. In the UNIX example, the "ls" program produces lines that are consumed by the "opr" program. In general, mailboxes and message passing are used to facilitate such relationships.

There are some simplifications that can make message passing more efficient than an elaborate scheme such as that proposed for the SUE/360 operating system. For example, the system may support only single-slot mailboxes; this simplifies the administration of mailboxes, but decreases the ability of the mailboxes to provide buffering against differing speeds of the sender and receiver. Ultimately, all the slots of a mailbox can be eliminated, leaving only a "zero-slot" connection between the processes. In this arrangement if the SEND occurs first, the sender is blocked until the RECEIVE occurs; then the transmission of the message takes place and both processes are allowed to proceed. Conversely, if the RECEIVE occurs first, the receiver is blocked until the SEND occurs. Another simplification is to shorten all messages to zero characters (to null messages) and to use SEND and RECEIVE only for synchronization - not for communication. When this is done, receive and send revert to being synchronization primitives similar to P and V.

Message passing has been used as a structuring tool for handling asynchronism in various operating systems, most notably the RC4000 system. However, unless great care is taken, the send and receive operations are too slow, typically requiring execution of 100 to 1000 machine instructions each. Besides, mailboxes tend to impose a network structure on an operating system, with each process being a node connected by mailboxes to other nodes. Such a network does not encourage the hierarchical organization of an operating system. There is another method of synchronization and communication that overcomes many of these shortcomings: the monitor concept.

MONITORS

The concept of a monolithic monitor, discussed in Chapter 1, can be generalized into a programming language feature for handling synchronization. The feature is called a monitor and provides convenient facilities for guaranteeing mutual exclusion and for blocking and waking up processes. We will now give an introduction to monitors; later, in Chapter 4, we will cover monitors in detail as a feature of the language Concurrent SP/k.

Previously the lock/unlock synchronization primitives were described in terms of a fence around critical data; a gate in the fence controls access to the data. The code executed between LOCK and UNLOCK corresponds to the critical section for that particular data. A monitor can also be thought of in terms of a fence around critical data. One difference from lock/unlock is that all sequences of statements that manipulate the data are collected and moved inside the fence. The fence has several gates, one corresponding to each sequence of statements. Each of these sequences becomes a special purpose procedure called an "entry". This means that all the critical sections for a particular set of shared data are collected into one place.

Whenever one of these entries is invoked, mutually exclusive access to the shared data is automatically provided, so only one process at a time is allowed inside the enclosure. The enforcement of mutual exclusion is implicit: the programmer needs only to invoke the entry. Given that monitors are a construct in a high level language, it is up to the language translator to generate code to implement mutual exclusion.

Monitors provide a block/wakeup facility in the following way. If a process enters a monitor and finds that a required condition (such as the availability of a free resource) is not true, it executes a WAIT statement. This removes the process from the monitor, blocks its progress, and places it on a queue waiting for the condition to become true. When another process enters the monitor and finds the condition to be true, it executes a SIGNAL statement that removes a waiting process (if there is one) from the condition's queue and wakes it up.

The following illustration shows a monitor with three gates, for entries E, F and G, and two conditions, C and D. There is one process, P5, inside the enclosure; P5 has entered gate E to access the critical data. Processes P1 and P2 are blocked at gate E and P4 at gate G, waiting until no process is inside. Processes P3 and P6 have executed WAIT statements for condition C. Condition D currently has no processes waiting for it.

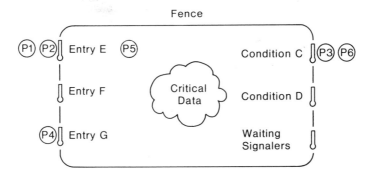

If process P5 now leaves the monitor, one of the processes P1, P2 or P4 will be allowed to enter. If, instead, P5 executes a SIGNAL statement for condition C, one process, either P3 or P6, will be allowed to enter. Assuming P3 enters, the situation changes to this:

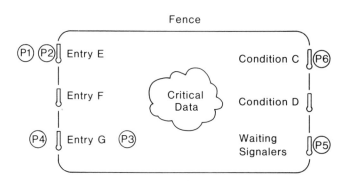

Fence

We are assuming that P3 was in entry G when it executed a WAIT for condition C. The SIGNAL by P5 causes P3 to continue executing in entry G. Since only one process at a time is allowed inside the enclosure, P5 is forced to step outside while other processes are inside. If P3 next signals condition C, then P6 enters the enclosure and P3 steps out to join P5. If a process signals a condition that has no processes waiting for it, such as D, then nothing happens (good or bad). However, the signaling process may temporarily step out of the enclosure just as happens when there are waiting processes.

In Hoare's formal definition of monitors, he assumes that the critical data for each monitor has associated with it a consistency criterion. This criterion is called an invariant, or I for short, and means that the data should be accurate and up-to-date. For example, the critical data used in allocating a particular resource should accurately represent the current status of the resource. A process enters the monitor to test or update the critical data, but must always leave the data so it corresponds to the resource's current status. When the monitor is created, the initial status of the resource is recorded in the critical data, so the invariant I is initially true. Before a process leaves an entry or signals a condition, it must make sure that the critical data is consistent and up-to-date, so I is left true. As a result, any process that enters the monitor knows that I is true, and can use the critical data knowing that it is consistent and up-to-date. The requirement for consistent critical data is easy to attain with monitors, and consequently monitors are a useful and understandable mechanism for dealing with concurrency. Later chapters contain many examples of monitors, so we will not cover them in any more detail here.

Monitors have been used as the basis of the SUE/11 operating system; this is a small special purpose system that is used to run PL/I subset (SP/k) jobs on a PDP-11 minicomputer. Compilers have been implemented that support the Pascal language augmented by monitors. The most notable extended versions of Pascal are called Concurrent Pascal and Modula. Interesting special purpose operating systems have been written in Concurrent Pascal and used on PDP-11 minicomputers.

We have discussed mutual exclusion, the block/wakeup facility, and message passing as fundamental problems and constructs in concurrent programming. We will now consider another fundamental concurrency problem: deadlock.

THE DEADLOCK PROBLEM

In concurrent programming, a process sometimes must wait until a particular event occurs. If the event takes place and the waiting process is awakened, then there is no problem. But if the event never occurs, the process will be blocked forever! We say a process is <u>deadlocked</u> when it is waiting for an event that can never occur.

A simple example of deadlock can occur in a system with two processes, P1 and P2, and two resources, R1 and R2. Suppose process P1 acquires resource R1 and P2 acquires R2. Then P1 requests R2. Since R2 is already allocated, P1 is blocked until R2 becomes available; presumably R2 will eventually be released by P2. But now P2 requests resource R1. Since R1 is already allocated, P2 is blocked until R1 becomes available. The situation is illustrated in this diagram.

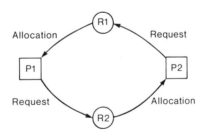

We are assuming that a resource cannot be pre-empted from a process - which means that once a resource is acquired by a process, it will not become available to another process until the acquiring process releases it. The result is that the cycle of waiting conditions illustrated in the diagram can never be satisfied. Processes P1 and P2 are deadlocked. They will remain blocked until special action is taken by an "external force" such as the operator or the operating system.

Unfortunately, not all deadlocks are as simple as this example. More complex cases can arise when there are many processes and many resources. The blocking that results in a deadlock can arise from any of the synchronization operations that allow processes to wait; for example, the semaphore P operation, the LOCK operation, the RECEIVE operation, and attempting to enter a monitor.

In operating systems, deadlocks can be expensive or disastrous. We will give two examples that are taken from production operating systems. The first example involves spooling, which means temporarily storing input and output records on disk, to provide buffering for devices such as card readers and printers. In spooling systems, deadlock can occur due to competition for disk space. The problem occurs when the space becomes completely filled with input records for jobs waiting to execute and output records for jobs not finished executing. If there is no way to recover the space from a partially executed job (and there is not in many systems), then the only way to recover from such a deadlock is to restart the system. A crude but usually effective solution to this problem is to prohibit the spooling of new jobs when too much spooling space is occupied, say, more than 80%.

The second example of deadlock can easily be caused by a hostile user, given that the system supports PL/I with multitasking (concurrent programming). The following four-line program does the trick.

```
REVENGE:PROCEDURE OPTIONS(MAIN,TASK);
   DECLARE(E)EVENT;
   WAIT(E);
   END;
```

This program does nothing but wait for an event that will never occur. The user will not be charged for CPU or I/O because the program uses neither. However, any resources allocated to this program, such as the memory it occupies, will remain idle until the deadlock is detected and removed, either by the operating system or by a keen-witted operator. The next section explains how certain types of deadlock can be automatically detected.

DETECTING DEADLOCK

In a multiprogramming system, users' jobs compete for the available resources. For example, two jobs may simultaneously need to use a tape drive. Resources such as tape drives are called reusable, because after they have been used by one process, they can be re-used by another process. In this section we will show how deadlock can be detected when processes share reusable resources. Each reusable resource has the following properties:

There is a fixed total number of identical units of the resource. Each unit of the resource is either available (not allocated) or has been acquired by (allocated to) a particular process. A particular unit of a resource can be allocated to at most one process at a time. A process can release a unit of a resource only if the process has been allocated that unit. Units cannot be pre-empted; once a process has acquired a unit, the unit will not become available until released by the process.

The physical devices of the computer system, such as memory, tape drives and disks, can be thought of as reusable resources. The number of units of some of these resources will depend on the allocation strategies of the computer system; for example, disks may be allocated in units of tracks, or cylinders or even entire disks. Certain information structures, such as files or linkage pointers for buffers, are reusable resources. The process must request, acquire and release access to these information structures to guarantee that the structure can be inspected or updated without interference from other processes. Previously, we showed that mutually exclusive access to certain data was required in critical sections; we are now pointing out that such critical data is equivalent to a reusable resource (with a single unit).

We can represent a system of processes and reusable resources by a graph having nodes for each process and resource. The units of a resource are shown by small circles inside the resource nodes, as illustrated here:

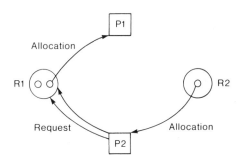

This graph shows a system with two processes and two resources. Resource R1 has two units and R2 has one unit. One of the units of R1 has been allocated to P1. P2 has acquired the unit of R2 and has requested both units of R1. P2 will be blocked until P1 releases its unit of R1.

As processes request, acquire and release units of resources, the graph changes. Suppose the system has two processes and a single resource with three units, one of which is allocated to process P2, as shown here.

Now process P1 requests two units of the resource:

Since two units are available, P1 acquires them:

Next process P1 releases one of the units:

In these graphs, an arrow is drawn from a process to a resource for each request of a unit and an arrow is drawn from a resource to a process for each allocated unit.

What we would like is a method of analyzing a graph to determine if there is a deadlock; that is, to see if some processes can never be granted their requests. It turns out that there is a relatively easy way to do this, using "graph reductions". We say a graph can be <u>reduced</u> by a process if all the process's requests for units can be granted. For example, in this graph we can reduce by process P1 because its request for a unit of R2 can be granted.

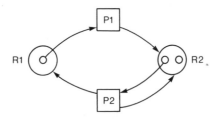

We reduce a graph by a process by deleting all arrows to or from the process. For example, when the above graph is reduced by P1, we get this graph:

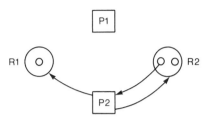

Since the requests by P2 can now be granted, we can further reduce the graph to the following:

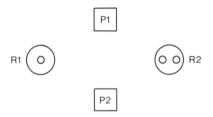

We say this graph is <u>completely</u> <u>reduced</u> because there are no more arrows and thus no more allocations or requests.

Essentially, the reductions determine whether processes can release their resources so other processes can receive their requests. The reductions will either delete all arrows, or they will leave certain processes not reduced. The processes that could not be reduced are those that are deadlocked. The following theorem can be proved:

There are no deadlocked processes if and only if the graph is completely reducible.

The order of reductions -- when different orders are possible -- is immaterial because the same final graph is obtained regardless of the order. The reason is that each reduction can allow new reductions (because new units are released), but can never prevent other reductions from taking place.

We can now give the algorithm for seeing if processes are deadlocked. The algorithm repeatedly checks to see if processes can be reduced, until none can be. Then it sees if all processes were reduced, i.e., if the graph was completely reduced. If all processes were reduced, there was no deadlock. Before the algorithm begins, each element of the logical vector REDUCED is set to false, indicating that no processes are initially reduced.

```
     /* ALGORITHM TO DETECT DEADLOCK */
1    REDUCED_PROCESSES=0;
2    REDUCTION=TRUE;
3    /* REPEAT UNTIL NO MORE REDUCTIONS ARE POSSIBLE */
4    DO WHILE(REDUCTION);
5       REDUCTION=FALSE;
6       /* TRY TO REDUCE EACH PROCESS */
7       DO P=1 TO NUMBER_OF_PROCESSES;
8          IF ¬REDUCED(P) THEN
9             DO;
10                IF process P can be reduced THEN;
11                   DO;
12                      REDUCED(P)=TRUE;
13                      REDUCED_PROCESSES=REDUCED_PROCESSES+1;
14                      REDUCTION=TRUE;
15                      Reduce by process P;
16                      END;
17                END;
18          END;
19       END;
20   COMPLETELY_REDUCED= (REDUCED_PROCESSES=NUMBER_OF_PROCESSES);
```

This algorithm is written in PL/I, except for lines 10 and 15. To write lines 10 and 15 in PL/I we must choose a data structure for the graphs. If there is only one resource, which has several units, the graph can be represented by the following variables:

REQ: a vector with a subscript range from 1 to NUMBER_OF_PROCESSES, giving the present request by each process.

ALLOC: a vector with a subscript range from 1 to NUMBER_OF_PROCESSES, giving the present allocation to each process.

AVAIL: an integer giving the present number of available units.

Assuming these are appropriately initialized before our algorithm is executed, line 10 can be written this way:

```
IF REQ(P)<=AVAIL THEN
```

Line 15 can be written as:

```
AVAIL=AVAIL+ALLOC(P);
```

If there are several resources, each with several units, then REQ, ALLOC and AVAIL must additionally be subscripted by a resource number. In this case we introduce the flag REDUCE_BY_P and replace line 10 by:

```
    REDUCE_BY_P=TRUE;
    DO R=1 TO NUMBER_OF_RESOURCES;
        IF REQ(P,R)>AVAIL(R) THEN
            REDUCE_BY_P=FALSE;
        END;
    IF REDUCE_BY_P THEN
```

Now line 15 is written as:

```
    DO R=1 TO NUMBER_OF_RESOURCES;
        AVAIL(R)=AVAIL(R)+ALLOC(P,R);
        END;
```

If the graph is represented by a linked list, different replacements for lines 10 and 15 would be required.

Our algorithm can be used each time a request is made that cannot be immediately granted. Alternatively, the algorithm might be invoked only when there is reason to suspect a deadlock, for example, when a process has been blocked for a long time. An algorithm much like this one was used in the TOPPS language processor to detect deadlocks and to remove deadlocks similar to those that occur with events in PL/I.

We have now surveyed basic problems and language features in concurrent programming. The next two chapters introduce the languages SP/k and Concurrent SP/k, and then the following chapter gives concurrent programming algorithms in CSP/k.

CHAPTER 2 SUMMARY

In this chapter we have introduced programming language features that support the following basic concurrency requirements:

- Concurrent execution (cobegin/end, fork/quit/join).

- Mutual exclusion (mutexbegin/end, lock/unlock, semaphores, monitors).

- Block/wakeup (events, semaphores, wait/signal in monitors).

- Message passing (send/receive, mailboxes, pipes).

The following additional important terms were discussed in this chapter:

Disjoint processes (independent processes) - processes that have no shared data.

Busy waiting - continual testing and re-testing of a condition until it becomes true.

Test and set instruction – an instruction that both tests and changes a value in an indivisible action; allows simple implementation of mutual exclusion via busy waiting.

Synchronization primitives – simple operations, such as P and V for semaphores, that allow processes to synchronize their activities. These can be used to implement mutual exclusion and block/wakeup.

Reusable resources – devices, files, or data structures that can be used by one process, then re-used by another, and so on. A process must request, acquire and then release such resources.

Deadlock – the situation in which one or more processes are blocked waiting for something that can never occur. Processes can become deadlocked when competing for reusable resources.

CHAPTER 2 BIBLIOGRAPHY

This chapter has referred to several operating systems, namely, UNIX [Ritchie and Thompson], RC4000 [Brinch Hansen 1970], VENUS [Liskov], SUE/11 [Greenblatt and Holt], and SUE/360 [Sevcik et al.]. The articles on UNIX and RC4000 are especially interesting. The TOPPS language is specified in detail by Czarnik et al. Hoare's article [1974] on monitors contains their formal definition along with an implementation in terms of semaphores and several interesting examples of monitors. Concurrent Pascal and Modula are described by Brinch Hansen [1975] and Wirth [1977]. More on the theory of deadlock can be found in Holt's article [1972].

Brinch Hansen, P. The nucleus of a multiprogramming system. Comm. ACM 13,4 (April 1970), 238-241, 250.

Brinch Hansen, P. The programming language Concurrent Pascal. IEEE Trans. on Software Engineering SE-1,2 (June 1975), 199-207.

Czarnik, B. (editor), Tsichritzis, D., Ballard, A.J., Dryer, M., Holt, R.C., and Weissman, L. A student project for an operating systems course. CSRG-29, Computer Systems Research Group, University of Toronto (1973).

Greenblatt, I.E. and Holt, R.C. The SUE/11 operating system. INFOR, Canadian Journal of Operational Research and Information Processing 14,3 (October 1976), 227-232.

Hoare, C.A.R. Monitors: an operating system structuring concept. Comm. ACM 17,10 (October 1974), 549-557.

Holt, R.C. Some deadlock properties of computer systems. Computing Surveys 4,3 (September 1972), 179-196.

Liskov, B.H. The design of the VENUS operating system. Comm. ACM 15,3 (March 1972), 144-149.

Ritchie, D.M. and Thompson, K. The UNIX time-sharing system. Comm. ACM 17,7 (July 1974), 365-375.

Sevcik, K.C., Atwood, J.W., Clark, B.L., Grushcow, M.S., Holt, R.C., Horning, J.J., Tsichritzis, D. Project SUE as a learning experience. Proc. FJCC 1972, Vol. 39, 331-337.

Wirth, N. MODULA: a language for modular programming. Software Practice and Experience Vol. 7,1 (January-February 1977), 3-35.

CHAPTER 2 EXERCISES

1. Generalize Dekker's algorithm to handle n processes.

2. One method of implementing semaphores has the P operation decrement the semaphore count before testing the count's value. The result is that the count is sometimes negative, and the absolute value of the negative count gives the number of processes waiting. Give such an implementation of P and V in terms of mutexbegin/end and block/wakeup.

3. The parameterized version of mutexbegin/end is very similar to lock/unlock. The difference is that MUTEXBEGIN and MUTEXEND are syntactically (statically) balanced brackets. Give the advantages and disadvantages of parameterized mutexbegin/end versus lock/unlock.

4. The parameterized version of mutexbegin/end allows separate mutual exclusion for separate collections of critical data. Show how, in certain cases, nesting of these constructs can lead to deadlock. Give a rule which a programmer can follow to prevent such deadlocks.

5. Implementing mutual exclusion by busy waiting can be very tricky. Is the following implementation correct? Explain.

```
MUTEXBEGIN:
  NEED(ME)=TRUE;
  DO WHILE(NEED(OTHER));
    END;

MUTEXEND:
  NEED(ME)=FALSE;
```

6. Implementing mutual exclusion by busy waiting can be very
tricky. Is the following implementation correct? Explain.

```
MUTEXBEGIN:
    NEED(ME)=TRUE;
    DO WHILE(NEED(OTHER));
        NEED(ME)=FALSE;
        DO WHILE(NEED(OTHER));
            END;
        NEED(ME)=TRUE;
        END;

MUTEXEND:
    NEED(ME)=FALSE;
```

7. In Dekker's algorithm it is possible for one process to wait
forever while the other repeatedly enters and leaves its critical
section. This is an example of indefinite postponement, also
known as individual starvation, effective deadlock and permanent
blocking. Give an "improved" algorithm that guarantees that
neither process can wait forever. Assume that neither process
has infinite delays inside critical sections.

8. The "banker's algorithm" is a method of preventing deadlock
due to competition for reusable resources. The method assumes
that each process has a "claim" on resources, specifying its
maximum need for resources. For example, process P1 might need
at most 2 units of resource R1 and 5 units of resource R2. The
operating system (the banker) receives requests from processes,
and temporarily blocks any requests that could lead to deadlock.
The operating system determines if a request is safe (can not
lead to deadlock) by seeing if an immediate request by all
processes for the remainder of their claims leads to deadlock.
Show how the deadlock detection algorithm given in this chapter
can be used to see if requests are safe.

9. In some operating systems, notably the RC4000 system, there
is exactly one mailbox per process. This means that messages are
sent to processes rather than to mailboxes, because mailboxes
have no separate identity. Give the advantages and disadvantages
of separating mailboxes from processes.

10. High-level concurrent programming features can be based on
the idea of resources. Essentially, a resource is anything that
a process can wait for. "Reusable resources" were described in
this chapter, and they can be used for mutual exclusion, as well
as for allocation of physical devices. "Consumable resources"
are like mailboxes; a release (send) operation to a consumable
resource gives it another unit (a message) and a request
(receive) operation retrieves a unit. Implement request/release
for reusable and consumable resources, using mutexbegin/end and
block/wakeup.

11. In some systems deadlock can be prevented by pre-arranged
conventions. One of the simplest and most effective of these is

based on ordered (or hierarchic) reusable resources. Each resource is in one of the classes 1, 2, up to n. A process must always request resources in order, from class 1 up to class n. Putting this another way, a process that holds a resource from class i is not allowed to request a resource from a lower numbered class. Prove that this convention prevents deadlock.

12. The deadlock detection algorithm in this chapter requires maximum time proportional to m times n^2, where m is the number of resources and n is the number of processes. Develop an algorithm that requires time proportional to m times n. (Hint: for each resource use a queue of processes ordered by request size.)

13. In a system with one resource type, find an algorithm to detect deadlock whose execution time is independent of the number of processes. Do not restrict requests to be for only one unit.

14. Explain why non-parameterized mutexbegin/end cannot be nested. Note that parameterized mutexbegin/end can be nested, given different parameters. Give a rule the compiler can enforce that prevents deadlock due to nested parameterized mutexbegin/end. Here is an example that can lead to such a deadlock.

```
P1: ...                        P2: ...
   MUTEXBEGIN(A);                 MUTEXBEGIN(B);
      MUTEXBEGIN(B);                 MUTEXBEGIN(A);
         ...                            ...
      MUTEXEND(B);                   MUTEXEND(A);
   MUTEXEND(A);                   MUTEXEND(B);
```

15. High in the Andes Mountains, there are two circular railroad lines. As shown in the diagram, one line is in Peru, the other in Bolivia. They share a section of track, where the lines cross a mountain pass that lies on the international border.

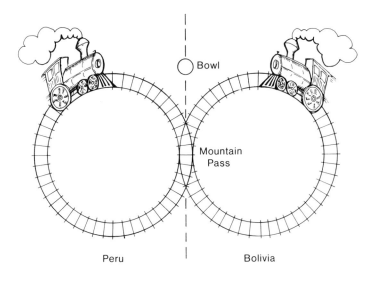

Unfortunately, the Peruvian and Bolivian trains occasionally collide when simultaneously entering the critical section of track (the mountain pass). The trouble is, alas, that the drivers of the two trains are blind and deaf, so they can neither see nor hear each other.

The two drivers agreed on the following method of preventing collisions. They set up a large bowl at the entrance to the pass. Before entering the pass, a driver must stop his train, walk over to the bowl, and reach into it to see if it contains a rock. If the bowl is empty, the driver finds a rock and drops it in the bowl, indicating that his train is entering the pass; once his train has cleared the pass, he must walk back to the bowl and remove his rock, indicating that the pass is no longer being used. Finally he walks back to the train and continues down the line. If a driver arriving at the pass finds a rock in the bowl, he leaves the rock there; he repeatedly takes a siesta and re-checks the bowl until he finds it empty. Then he drops a rock in the bowl and drives his train into the pass. A smart aleck college graduate from the University at La Paz (Bolivia) claimed that subversive train schedules made up by Peruvian officials could block the Bolivian train forever. (Explain). The Bolivian driver just laughed and said that could not be true because it never happened. (Explain). Unfortunately, one day the two trains crashed. (Explain).

Following the crash, our college graduate was called in as a consultant to ensure that no more crashes would occur. He explained that the bowl was being used in the wrong way. The Bolivian driver must wait at the entry until the bowl is empty, drive through the pass and walk back to put a rock in the bowl. The Peruvian driver must wait at the entry until the bowl contains a rock, drive through the pass and walk back to remove the rock from the bowl. Sure enough, his method prevented crashes. Prior to this arrangement, the Peruvian train ran twice a day and the Bolivian train ran once a day. The Peruvians were very unhappy with the new arrangement. (Why?)

Our college graduate was called in again and was told to prevent crashes while avoiding the problem of his previous method. He suggested that two bowls be used, one for each driver. When a driver reaches the entry, he first drops a rock in his bowl, then checks the other bowl to see if it is empty. If so, he drives his train through the pass, stops it and walks back to remove his rock. But if he finds a rock in the other bowl he goes back to his bowl and removes his rock. Then he takes a siesta, again drops a rock in his bowl and re-checks the other bowl, and so on, until he finds the other bowl empty. This method worked fine until late in May, when the two trains were simultaneously blocked at the entry for many siestas. (Explain.)

To solve this problem, a Dutch mathematician named Dekker was brought in. What did he recommend? Another Dutchman named Dijkstra said there was a better way, using a single bowl as a semaphore. What did he call the bowl?

CHAPTER 3

A SEQUENTIAL PROGRAMMING LANGUAGE: SP/k

Chapter 2 discussed many notations for expressing concurrency and synchronization. We presented the monitor approach as a convenient and structured tool. This book uses a concurrent programming language based on the monitor concept -- Concurrent SP/k, or CSP/k. CSP/k is a superset of SP/k; SP/k is a subset of the PL/I programming language. The purpose of this chapter is to introduce SP/k as a prelude to the discussion of CSP/k in the next chapter. Readers with a working knowledge of full or subset PL/I may want to skip to the SP/k program example at the end of this chapter and study the chapter summary. Appendix 1 and parts of Appendices 3 and 4 contain SP/k language and compiler details; these appendices should be useful as a reference when writing SP/k programs.

SP/k was chosen as the base for a concurrent language for many reasons. It is upwardly compatible with PL/I, a widely used programming language. SP/k programs can be run under a variety of PL/I compilers. SP/k is a high-level language, with the advantage that well-constructed and well-documented programs can be readily written and maintained. SP/k compilers for the IBM System 360/370 and for the DEC PDP-11 series of computers are very fast and reliable; the SP/k run-time systems on these machines are highly diagnostic, to aid program development.

Most importantly, the features of SP/k chosen from PL/I encourage programmers to produce well-structured programs. For large, complex programs, this is especially important. Operating systems are prime examples of large programs; they are also prime examples of concurrent programs. Thus, it is important that SP/k, the basis of CSP/k, contains features that allow the development of well-structured programs.

THE SP/k SUBSETS

The name SP/k stands for "Structured Programming subset k". SP/k is a series of subsets of the PL/I programming language, called SP/1, SP/2, and so on. SP/7 is the largest subset used in this book. Each subset is nested within the next higher one so that it is possible to learn a large programming language vocabulary gradually through a subset approach. Although SP/1 contains only a small number of PL/I language features, a programmer can actually write and run complete programs using this subset.

The subset approach is particularly useful for those learning their first language. However, because of the level of this book and its intended audience, we assume that our readers already know a high-level programming language (e.g., Fortran or Algol). We therefore will not follow the subset approach in explaining SP/k.

Our SP/k discussion will be brief, outlining only the most important features, because our major interest is CSP/k. Appendix 1 contains more details about SP/k.

VALUES AND VARIABLES

SP/k allows four data types (or attributes): fixed and float decimal values, logical values, and character string values. A fixed constant (an integer) is a sequence of decimal digits with no decimal point (such as 17). The sequence can optionally be preceded by a sign. An example of the variable COUNT being declared as a fixed decimal data type is

    DECLARE(COUNT)FIXED;

A float constant (a real number) has a mantissa and an exponent (such as 3.9E1). (In scientific notation, this number is represented as 3.9×10^1 .) An example of two variables being declared as float is

    DECLARE(DISTANCE,SPEED)FLOAT;

Operators for fixed or float arithmetic expressions include the usual binary operators: addition (+), subtraction (-), multiplication (*), and division (/); unary + and - are also allowed. Integer division produces a truncated answer (towards zero) and a warning message. Parentheses can be used to override the usual rules of arithmetic operator precedence.

A logical (or Boolean) constant has the value '0'B or '1'B, meaning false and true. An example of a variable being declared as logical is

```
DECLARE(FINISHED)BIT;
```

Relational operators on fixed or float values produce logical values; these binary operators are

<	less than	¬=	not equal
<=	less than or equal	>	greater than
=	equal	>=	greater than or equal

Logical operators work on logical values to produce logical values; these operators are & (and), | (or), and ¬ (not).

A character string constant (a literal) is a sequence of characters (letters or digits or special symbols) enclosed in single quotation marks, for example, 'OPERATING SYSTEMS'. Only varying length character string variables are allowed in SP/k; they must be declared with their maximum length, as in

```
DECLARE(JOB_NAME)CHARACTER(20)VARYING;
```

Besides the relational operators, there are three additional operators on character string values. Concatenation builds longer character strings by joining two character string values together; the operator is ||, as in

```
TITLE='STATISTICS FOR JOB '||JOB_NAME;
```

Character string values can be taken apart by selecting substrings from them. The SUBSTR built-in function has the form

```
SUBSTR(STRING,STARTING_POSITION,SUBSTRING_LENGTH)
```

This denotes the substring of STRING beginning at position STARTING_POSITION with a length of SUBSTRING_LENGTH. If the third argument of SUBSTR is omitted, the substring goes to the end of the string. The first position in a string is numbered one. The final string operation is the LENGTH built-in function for determining the length of a character string value; an example is

```
LENGTH('CONCURRENCY')
```

which, in this case, has the value 11.

In addition to scalar variables, SP/k has arrays -- structured collections of values of the same data type. The declaration of an array gives the array name, bounds information, and type attributes, as in

```
DECLARE(A(50))FIXED;
DECLARE(B(1:50))FIXED;
DECLARE(C(10,0:5))FLOAT;
```

The declarations for A and B are equivalent, declaring both to be one-dimensional arrays, indexed from 1 to 50. The third declaration creates a two-dimensional array, with the first index running from 1 to 10 and the second index from 0 to 5. Particular array elements are accessed by enclosing index values in parentheses, as in A(13) or C(1,N).

The assignment operator in SP/k is = ; the assignment statement has the form

```
variable=expression;
```

The variable on the left hand side can be either a scalar variable or an array element. If the data types of the variable and the expression are numeric and different, a type conversion will take place.

CONTROL STRUCTURES

SP/k has three kinds of control structures, apart from procedure call/return (to be discussed in the Procedures section). The first is sequential execution, represented by

```
S1;S2;S3;S4; . . .
```

This is interpreted as: execute S1, then execute S2, and so on. The second is selective execution, which tests a logical expression to select a control path flow. It is represented by the IF-THEN-ELSE statement as in

```
IF NUMBER>0 THEN
    #POSITIVE=#POSITIVE+1;
ELSE
    #NON_POSITIVE=#NON_POSITIVE+1;
```

The ELSE branch may be omitted if not needed. If more than one statement is to be executed in the THEN or ELSE branches, these statements are enclosed by a DO-END group, as in

```
IF NUM>0 THEN
    DO;
        #POSITIVE=#POSITIVE+1;
        SUM=SUM+NUM;
        END;
```

The third control structure is iterative execution, or the loop, which controls the repetitive execution of statements. There are two types of loops; one is the counted (or unconditional) DO loop. An example to add the squares of the first ten values in the array A is

```
SUM=0;
DO J=1 TO 10 BY 1;
    SUM=SUM+A(J)*A(J);
    END;
```

The expressions in the DO heading are evaluated once at the beginning of loop execution. If the BY clause is omitted, a step size of 1 is assumed. The second type of loop is the conditional DO loop. Rewriting the previous example to use a conditional loop gives

```
SUM=0;
J=1;
DO WHILE(J<=10);
    SUM=SUM+A(J)*A(J);
    J=J+1;
    END;
```

The logical expression in the DO heading may contain Boolean operators such as &; the expression is evaluated prior to each loop execution.

Notice that SP/k does not have the GO TO control structure or statement labels.

INPUT AND OUTPUT

SP/k allows two types of input/output. The first type is list input/output; it is "format free" and very simple to use. To specify list input of three values, we would use

```
GET LIST(X,Y,Z);
```

The data values for X, Y, and Z must be separated from each other on the data card by at least one blank. Character values must be enclosed in quotation marks. An example of list output is

```
PUT LIST('AVERAGE= ',TOTAL/N);
```

The PUT LIST statement fills the next available "output field" on a print line, going to a new line only when the output fields of the previous line have been filled. There are five output fields on each line.

Edit input/output allows more flexibility than the simpler list input/output. Edit input appears as

```
GET EDIT(var_1,...,var_n) (format_1,...,format_n);
```

where each format item applies to the corresponding variable and describes the location, size, and form of the data on the data card. Similarly, edit output appears as

```
PUT EDIT(exp_1,...,exp_n) (format_1,...,format_n);
```

There are many input/output formats possible for the various data types; rather than list them all here, we refer the reader to Appendix 1.

SP/k also allows input/output control statements. PUT PAGE starts a new printer page; PUT SKIP skips to the next print line.

PROCEDURES

SP/k is a block structured programming language and procedures introduce another level of scope for naming variables. Variables declared within a procedure are local (private) to that procedure; variables declared in an enclosing scope (another procedure) are global to (shared with) the enclosed procedure and may be accessed from it.

There are two types of procedures: subroutines and functions. Both have the general form

```
procedure header
    variable declarations
    other procedure definitions
    statements
    END;
```

Subroutine procedures begin with the procedure header

```
proc_name:PROCEDURE(par_1,...,par_n);
```

The parameters are declared with the local variables. A subroutine procedure is called by a statement of the form

```
CALL proc_name(par_1,...,par_n);
```

There must be an exact match between the number and types of the parameters in the CALL statement and in the procedure header (except for fixed and float data types, which can be interchanged). Each time a value is stored into a parameter during procedure execution, that value is stored into the corresponding parameter variable in the CALL statement (this is "call by reference"). Control returns from a subroutine procedure by executing either the RETURN statement or the last statement of the procedure.

Function procedures differ from subroutine procedures in that they return a value. A function procedure begins with

```
proc_name:PROCEDURE(par_1,...,par_n)RETURNS(attribute);
```

where the attribute applies to the value being returned by the procedure. That value is returned by executing the statement

```
RETURN(expression);
```

where the expression must have the specified attribute. Function procedure invocations do not use the CALL form; instead, the function name, with arguments, is treated as an expression and is

used at the point in the calling procedure where the returned
value is needed. An example using SUM_OF_SQUARES, assumed to be
a function procedure with one argument, is

```
TOTAL=TOTAL+SUM_OF_SQUARES(N);
```

Both types of SP/k procedures can be recursive (can call
themselves directly or indirectly). They do not need PL/I's
RECURSIVE keyword in their procedure headers.

FORM OF PROGRAMS

SP/k programs have the same general form as PL/I programs,
namely

```
program name:PROCEDURE OPTIONS(MAIN);
    variable declarations
    procedure definitions
    statements
    END;
```

Note that procedures are defined after the declaration of the
main procedure's variables but before any executable statements.
All variables in SP/k must be declared.

SP/k comments appear as text enclosed by a /* in front and a
*/ behind, and must appear on a single card.

Our discussion of SP/k concludes with an SP/k program that
manages queues. Queues and other data structures (see the
exercises) are used in an operating system in a variety of ways,
e.g., to store accounting information or the ready list. The
next section introduces queueing operations and illustrates many
features of SP/k.

AN EXAMPLE PROGRAM: QUEUE MANAGEMENT

This section contains an example of an SP/k program that
implements a first-in-first-out (FIFO) queue, a type of linear
list structure. This type of queue has new entries added to its
"tail"; entries are removed from its "head". If sequential
(array) allocation is used to store the entries, the head and
tail become indices into an array QUEUE. A queue with three
entries would be represented as:

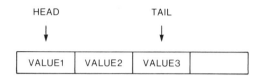

Adding an entry with a certain VALUE at the tail of the queue is done by the statements

```
TAIL=TAIL+1;
QUEUE(TAIL)=VALUE;
```

Removing an entry from the head of the queue and finding its VALUE is done by the statements

```
VALUE=QUEUE(HEAD);
HEAD=HEAD+1;
```

This SP/k code shows that entries are removed in the order they are added (hence, FIFO).

The code however fails to deal with certain issues. What happens during insertion if TAIL equals #_SLOTS, the size of the QUEUE array? It would be hasty to assume that the queue could hold no more items, because there may not be #_SLOTS entries stored in the queue. If the first position of the array (index 1) is regarded as the successor of the last position (index #_SLOTS), wraparound addressing with the MOD built-in function can be used for indexing. An index variable X would then be incremented as in

```
X=MOD(X,#_SLOTS)+1;
```

The sequence of values taken by X would be

```
..., #_SLOTS-1, #_SLOTS, 1, 2,..., #_SLOTS, 1, ...
```

Other issues are: How are an empty queue and a full queue represented? What happens if we attempt to add an entry to a full queue or remove an entry from an empty queue? The extensions to the code necessary to answer these questions are treated in the exercises.

Our SP/k solution uses wraparound addressing and assumes error-free conditions (i.e., no adding to a full queue and no removing from an empty queue). Addition and removal have been represented as subroutine procedures. They operate under the control of the main procedure, processing commands from an input data stream.

```
1 QUEUES:PROCEDURE OPTIONS(MAIN);
2     DECLARE(QUEUE(1:10),COMMAND,VALUE)CHARACTER(20)VARYING,
3        (#_SLOTS,HEAD,TAIL)FIXED;

      /* AN ITEM ENTERS THE QUEUE AT THE TAIL. */
4     INSERT:PROCEDURE(CONTENTS);
5        DECLARE(CONTENTS)CHARACTER(*)VARYING;
6        TAIL=MOD(TAIL,#_SLOTS)+1;
7        QUEUE(TAIL)=CONTENTS;
8        END /* OF INSERT */;

      /* AN ITEM LEAVES THE QUEUE FROM THE HEAD. */
9     DELETE:PROCEDURE(CONTENTS);
10       DECLARE(CONTENTS)CHARACTER(*)VARYING;
11       CONTENTS=QUEUE(HEAD);
12       HEAD=MOD(HEAD,#_SLOTS)+1;
13       END /* OF DELETE */;

      /* INITIALIZATION */
14    HEAD=1;
15    TAIL=0;
16    #_SLOTS=10;

17    GET LIST(COMMAND);
18    DO WHILE(COMMAND¬='END');
19       PUT SKIP LIST('COMMAND IS ',COMMAND);
20       IF COMMAND='INSERT' THEN
21          DO;
22             GET LIST(VALUE);
23             PUT LIST(VALUE);
24             CALL INSERT(VALUE);
25             END;
26       ELSE
27          IF COMMAND='DELETE' THEN
28             DO;
29                CALL DELETE(VALUE);
30                PUT LIST(VALUE);
31                END;
32          ELSE
33                PUT LIST('ERROR');
34       GET LIST(COMMAND);
35       END /* OF COMMAND LOOP */;

36    END /* OF QUEUES */;
```

This concludes our description of SP/k. The next chapter introduces CSP/k, a language that builds upon SP/k to provide concurrency and mutual exclusion.

CHAPTER 3 SUMMARY

In this chapter we introduced SP/k, a subset of the PL/I programming language. Here is a brief list of its main features.

Data types (or attributes) – There are four: fixed and float decimal, logical (BIT), and character string. In SP/k there is no automatic conversion among decimal, logical, and character types. However, there is automatic conversion between fixed and float.

Declarations – They establish the names and data types of variables for use in the programs. In SP/k every variable must be declared. Identifiers (names of variables) can be up to 31 characters long.

Arithmetic operators – The SP/k arithmetic operators are +, -, *, and /. When fixed and float values are combined by one of these operators, the result is float.

Relational operators (comparison operators) – The SP/k relational operators are <, <=, =, ¬=, >, and >=.

Logical operators – The SP/k logical operators are & (and), | (or), and ¬ (not).

Character string variables – These are declared as CHARACTER (maximum length) VARYING. The maximum length must be at least 1 and at most 127.

Character string operators – There are three operators: concatenation (||) for joining two strings to produce a third, the SUBSTR built-in function for taking a substring, and the LENGTH built-in function for determining the length of a string.

Arrays – They are structured collections of values of the same data type. Arrays can have multiple dimensions. Lower bounds are 1 by default but can be explicitly specified.

Assignment statement – This assigns the right-hand side value to the left-hand side variable. The assignment operator is =.

Control structures – These direct the execution of programs. There are three control structures: sequential, selective (IF-THEN-ELSE), and iterative. The iterative structures are the unconditional loop (counted DO loop) and the conditional loop (DO WHILE loop). There is no GOTO statement and there are no statement labels.

List input/output – This is format-free. For list input, the data values must be separated from each other on the data card by at least one blank. Character strings read by list input must be enclosed in quotation marks (apostrophes). For list output, the next available output field on a print line is filled. There are five equal-width output fields on a print line.

Edit input/output - Associated with each edit input/output statement is a format list which describes the location, size, and form of the data corresponding to each element of the input/output list.

Scope of a variable - This is the range of the program over which the variable can be accessed. A variable that is declared in a procedure P can be accessed inside P (and from statements inside procedures inside P), but not outside P. Each time procedure P is entered, its variables are allocated; when p is left, P's variables are deallocated and their values are lost.

Procedures - There are two types: subroutine and function. Subroutine procedures are invoked by a CALL statement giving the subroutine name; function procedures are invoked by using the function name in an expression. Function procedures return a value. Parameters are passed by reference, meaning that changing a parameter inside the procedure immediately changes the corresponding argument in the call.

In addition to SP/k, we introduced the queue as a data structure and discussed many of its features: the head index, the tail index, and the operations of inserting and deleting. We used the MOD built-in function to achieve wraparound addressing for indexing.

CHAPTER 3 BIBLIOGRAPHY

More information about SP/k can be found in the textbooks by Hume and Holt [1975] and by Conway, Gries, and Wortman [1977], and in the overview article by Holt et al. [1977]. There is a good treatment of data structures, sorting, and searching in the books by Knuth [1968, 1973]. Dijkstra's book [1976] is a good source of advanced programming problems.

Conway, R.W., Gries, D., and Wortman, D.B. Introduction to Structured Programming Using PL/I and SP/k. Winthrop of Prentice-Hall (1977).

Dijkstra, E.W. A Discipline of Programming. Prentice-Hall (1976).

Holt, R.C., Wortman, D.B., Barnard, D.T., and Cordy, J.R. SP/k: a system for teaching computer programming. Comm. ACM 20,5 (May 1977), 301-309.

Hume, J.N.P. and Holt, R.C. Structured Programming Using PL/1 and SP/k. Reston of Prentice-Hall (1975).

Knuth, D.E. The Art of Computer Programming, Volume 1 - Fundamental Algorithms. Addison-Wesley (1968).

Knuth, D.E. The Art of Computer Programming, Volume 3 - Sorting and Searching. Addison-Wesley (1973).

CHAPTER 3 EXERCISES

1. Extend the queue management example to handle error conditions (i.e., adding to a full queue and removing from an empty queue).

2. A priority queue is a special type of linear list structure. Each item in the list has a priority. Suppose the entries in the queue are in ascending order by priority. Insertions into the list maintain the sorted order. Deletions remove the element having the smallest key value; this end of the list is called the head, as it was for a queue. Write a program to do priority queue management with wraparound addressing.

3. Using a singly-linked list to represent a priority queue, solve the previous problem. Compare the two solutions. Do you need to consider wraparound addressing in this solution?

4. A stack is another special type of linear list structure. Insertions and deletions can only be made at one end, the top. Note that the stacks have a last-in-first-out behavior, as opposed to a first-in-first-out behavior. Write a program to do stack management with sequential allocation. Do you need to consider wraparound addressing?

5. A dequeue (double-ended queue) is yet another special type of linear list structure. Insertions and deletions can be made at either end of the list, the left and the right. Write a program to do dequeue management with sequential allocation.

6. Priority queues are examples of the need to maintain sorted lists. There exist numerous sorting algorithms, differing in their execution time and data storage requirements. A useful measure of execution time is the maximum number of comparisons between elements; the good algorithms need about N*log N comparisons to sort N elements. Write a sorting program using any of the good algorithms (e.g., Heapsort, Quicksort, Merge Sort) from the literature.

7. Many applications require the searching of a list of elements for a given item. To search a list of N elements, sequential searching (e.g., compare the item with the first element, the second element, ...) uses about N/2 comparisons on the average and N comparisons in the worst case. If the list is in order on a key field, a more efficient method is the binary search: compare the item with the middle element of the list; the result of this comparison will indicate which half of the list should be

searched next. Assuming ascending order, if the item is less than the middle element, the right half of the list is eliminated from consideration; if the item is greater than the middle element, the left half of the list is eliminated. The binary search uses at most about log N comparisons. Write a program to do a binary search.

8. (Dutch Flag Problem) [Dijkstra 1976] You are given a pegboard with pegs of three different colors: red, white, and blue. The pegs are lined up in a row, in arbitrary order. Write a program that reorders the pegs so that going from left to right all the red pegs precede all the white pegs which precede all the blue pegs. In addition to normal programming language constructs, you are given a "swap" operation that swaps two pegs in their respective holes. Your program should examine the color of each peg at most once.

CHAPTER 4

A CONCURRENT PROGRAMMING LANGUAGE: CSP/k

CSP/k extends the SP/k programming language by adding features that support concurrency and mutual exclusion. Concurrency is provided by processes, units of concurrent computational activity. Mutual exclusion is provided by monitors; critical data can be protected by having all accesses to the data by processes go through a monitor. In this chapter we describe the monitor and process features of CSP/k. Small examples are given to help the reader gain familiarity with the language. Larger CSP/k programs, to illustrate the concurrency features of the language in more detail, are given in the next chapter. Appendices 2-5 provide more details about the CSP/k language and compiler.

SPECIFYING CONCURRENCY

We begin by giving a small CSP/k example that illustrates concurrency. Our purpose is to show some syntactic and semantic features of processes. Monitors are not used.

The example consists of two processes, HI and HO. They are defined in the concurrent program HIHO (on the next page). Each process declares a local variable I; each instance of I represents a different variable. The processes are identical in structure, each printing a message 100 times in a counted DO loop with I as the control variable. The code of each process is preceded by a process header (process name, colon, and the keyword PROCESS) and followed by an END statement.

```
1 HIHO:PROCEDURE OPTIONS(CONCURRENT);

2    HI:PROCESS;
3       DECLARE(I)FIXED;
4       DO I=1 TO 100;
5          PUT SKIP LIST('HI');
6          END;
7       END;

8    HO:PROCESS;
9       DECLARE(I)FIXED;
10      DO I=1 TO 100;
11         PUT SKIP LIST('HO');
12         END;
13      END;

14   END;
```

The processes HI and HO operate in parallel at undefined relative speeds. An equivalent syntactic feature was used in Chapter 2 to specify this: the cobegin/end feature.

What is the output from HIHO? Because processes are doing the output, all possible orderings of 100 of each of the string values 'HI' and 'HO' are possible outputs. Each execution of HIHO may result in a different output ordering of the string values because we cannot make any assumptions about the relative progress of the processes.

This concludes our brief discussion of the HIHO program. The example showed how processes are defined in CSP/k. It also showed how the parallel execution of processes can cause difficulties in understanding the operation of a program.

REENTRANT PROCEDURES

This section builds upon the HIHO example to illustrate another language feature associated with processes -- reentrant procedures. HIHO2 (on the next page) is a concurrent program that specifies the same concurrency as HIHO; HIHO2 however uses the reentrant procedure SPEAK to group together the common code of the two processes. SPEAK is an example of a procedure global to all processes.

```
 1 HIHO2:PROCEDURE OPTIONS(CONCURRENT);

 2    SPEAK:PROCEDURE(MESSAGE);
 3       DECLARE(MESSAGE)CHARACTER(*)VARYING;
 4       DECLARE(I)FIXED;
 5       DO I=1 TO 100;
 6          PUT SKIP LIST(MESSAGE);
 7          END;
 8       END;

 9    HI2:PROCESS;
10       CALL SPEAK('HI');
11       END;

12    HO2:PROCESS;
13       CALL SPEAK('HO');
14       END;

15    END;
```

Each process calls SPEAK, giving its own message. Two instances of SPEAK are created, each with its own local variable I. Each process executes its own version of the procedure in parallel, and the output possibilities for HIHO2 are the same as those for HIHO.

Reentrant procedures are useful when several processes must execute the same code (e.g., device managers). Grouping common code into a procedure improves programming time and program understandability.

MUTUAL EXCLUSION

In Chapter 2, monitors were described as fences enclosing critical data. All code accessing the data is gathered within the fence. Processes wishing to execute the code are forced to pass through one of the gates in the fence.

CSP/k monitors are a particular notation for this fence-gate concept. The fence in CSP/k is the <u>monitor</u>; the gates are <u>monitor</u> <u>entries</u>. This section introduces monitors and entries using an example illustrating mutual exclusion.

The concurrent program COUNTING (on the next page) is a CSP/k version of an example given in Chapter 2. COUNTING has a monitor UPDATE with two entries, OBSERVE and REPORT, and two processes, OBSERVER AND REPORTER. The critical data of the monitor is the variable COUNT, declared in line 3. An equivalent syntactic feature used in Chapter 2 to protect critical data was the mutexbegin/end feature.

OBSERVER is a process that adds 1 to COUNT in the OBSERVE entry (line 8); REPORTER is a process that prints COUNT and resets it to zero in the REPORT entry (lines 11 and 12). The initial value of COUNT is set in line 5 in the monitor initialization code; this (optional) initialization code is executed before any processes begin execution.

```
1 COUNTING:PROCEDURE OPTIONS(CONCURRENT);

2     UPDATE:MONITOR;
3         DECLARE(COUNT)FIXED;
4         DO;
5             COUNT=0;
6             END;

7     OBSERVE:ENTRY;
8         COUNT=COUNT+1;
9         END;

10    REPORT:ENTRY;
11        PUT SKIP LIST(COUNT);
12        COUNT=0;
13        END;

14    END /* OF UPDATE */;

15    OBSERVER:PROCESS;
          ...
16        CALL OBSERVE;
          ...
17        END;

18    REPORTER:PROCESS;
          ...
19        CALL REPORT;
          ...
20        END;

21    END;
```

The variables declared local to a monitor (the critical data) are permanent in the sense that they retain their values from one execution in the monitor to the next. This is of course necessary to maintain the correct state of the critical data at all times. On the other hand, variables within procedures and entries are reallocated at each call and lose their values when the procedure or entry returns to its caller.

The mutual exclusion necessary for accessing the variable COUNT is provided in this example by a CSP/k monitor and its entries. More about CSP/k monitors and entries is given shortly. Before that, we continue our brief discussion of new CSP/k language features in the next section by going beyond mutual exclusion to see how CSP/k provides the block/wakeup feature.

BLOCK/WAKEUP

The block/wakeup feature introduced in Chapter 2 allowed processes to wait until certain events occurred. CSP/k provides this feature in monitors through the use of wait and signal statements on condition variables.

We use an example to illustrate these ideas. Access to a resource is protected by a monitor named RESOURCE with two entries; we assume exclusive access to the resource is desired. A process wishing to gain access to the resource calls the monitor entry ACQUIRE; a process returning control of the resource calls the monitor entry RELEASE. This situation occurs often in operating systems. For example, the resource may be a file on a peripheral device and the processes may be wanting to update it.

```
1   RESOURCE:MONITOR;
2       DECLARE(IN_USE)BIT;
3       DECLARE(AVAILABLE)CONDITION;
4       DO;
5           IN_USE=FALSE;
6           END;

7       ACQUIRE:ENTRY;
8           IF IN_USE THEN
9               WAIT(AVAILABLE);
10          IN_USE=TRUE;
11          END;

12      RELEASE:ENTRY;
13          IN_USE=FALSE;
14          SIGNAL(AVAILABLE);
15          END;

16      END;
```

IN_USE is the state indicator of the resource being used by the processes; the processes set IN_USE as they acquire and release the resource. Access to IN_USE must be controlled; as such, it is critical data in the monitor, declared in line 2 and initialized in line 5. The resource is global to the processes and is accessed directly by them in their own process code. We assume that the processes access it only by first going through the ACQUIRE entry.

The ACQUIRE entry consists of lines 7-11. A process tests IN_USE in line 8 to see if it is possible to proceed. If the resource is in use, the process suspends its execution by executing the WAIT statement in line 9. At some time later, when the condition AVAILABLE holds, the process will be resumed. It will then set IN_USE to true in line 10 and leave the monitor, having gained exclusive access to the resource.

The RELEASE entry consists of lines 12-15. The releasing process sets IN_USE to false in line 13. The process then executes a SIGNAL statement with the condition variable AVAILABLE in line 14; this allows a process waiting for the condition to continue.

A process executing in a monitor is guaranteed that it is the only process accessing the critical data at that time. From the above discussions of the ACQUIRE and RELEASE entries, we see that it is sometimes necessary for a process to step out of a monitor prior to completing its full execution in the monitor, to allow other processes to access the critical data. It is a function of the monitor to ensure that only one access to critical data is active at any one time. Once one process is allowed into a monitor entry, all subsequent requests to enter the monitor are held up until the process active in the monitor has left or "stepped out of" the monitor.

The monitor entries ACQUIRE and RELEASE cooperate to ensure the correct accessing of the resource whose state is represented by IN_USE. A process in the ACQUIRE entry finding that IN_USE is true will wait. A process returning control in the RELEASE entry will set IN_USE to false and then signal a waiting process. The signaled process will set IN_USE to true and leave the monitor with exclusive access to the resource. Until that process returns control in the RELEASE entry, all processes entering the ACQUIRE entry will find IN_USE to be false and will wait.

This completes our brief introduction to the main features of CSP/k, including monitors, entries, initialization code, WAIT and SIGNAL statements, and CONDITION variables. We will treat these topics in more detail in the next sections.

MONITORS AND ENTRIES

In this section we discuss the form of monitors. A monitor consists of a header, variable declarations, initialization code, zero or more procedures, and zero or more entries.

The monitor header is the monitor name (RESOURCE in the previous example), followed by a colon and the keyword MONITOR.

Variables declared after the monitor header are the critical data of the monitor. Because CSP/k inherits the scope rules of SP/k, the definition of these variables extends over the monitor and any enclosed procedures and entries. The scope rules allow the variables to be accessed only from inside the monitor, thus ensuring controlled access to critical data.

Monitor initialization code sets the values of monitor variables prior to the first call to a monitor entry. Before any processes begin execution, all initialization code is executed in the order in which it appears in the program. The initialization code appears after monitor variable declarations but before local procedure and entry definitions. It must be present, but it may be null, as in DO; END; .

Procedures defined in a monitor are local to the monitor. They are accessible from entries and from initialization code in the monitor, but not from processes or from entries of other monitors.

Monitor entries are optional. Monitors without entries may be used to initialize global variables (e.g., such a monitor may set the global variable FALSE to '0'B).

Monitor entries begin with an entry header that gives the entry name, followed by a colon and the keyword ENTRY. Entries may have parameters and local variables, as procedures do. An entry is accessed from a process by a subroutine CALL statement or by a function invocation, in which case the entry returns a value. Calls from inside a monitor entry to entries of the same or another monitor are prohibited. Monitor procedures and entries may access variables and procedures global to the entire program. Because such variables are not automatically protected by monitors, it is the responsibility of the programmer to ensure that they are accessed by the processes in a correct manner.

This completes our discussion of the form of monitors. We have also discussed the scope rules which help to control access to critical data. The next section explains how the WAIT and SIGNAL statements are used to block and wakeup processes.

WAIT AND SIGNAL STATEMENTS

A process wishing to access critical data calls the monitor entry which performs the desired type of access. Only one process at a time succeeds in entering the monitor; all subsequent calls to the monitor are held up until the previous call has been completed or the previous process has stepped out of the monitor. The idea of a process stepping out of a monitor comes from the WAIT and SIGNAL statements.

We will explain this idea in terms of the single resource monitor (RESOURCE) given earlier. The processes competing for exclusive access to the resource repeatedly acquire, use, and release it. The first process to enter the ACQUIRE entry will find the resource is not in use, will set IN_USE to true, and will leave the monitor with exclusive access to the resource. The next process wishing to acquire the resource will enter the monitor and find that the resource is in use. This process cannot proceed in execution but it must free (step out of) the monitor to allow the process currently having control of the resource to enter the RELEASE entry at some later time.

A WAIT statement executed in a monitor entry removes the executing process from the monitor and suspends its execution. All this is done automatically as a result of executing the WAIT statement, and we need not be concerned at this time with how this is implemented.

When a process enters the RELEASE entry to return exclusive control of the resource, it could simply reset IN_USE to false and leave the monitor. This would allow the next process entering the ACQUIRE entry to gain control of the resource. But what about the processes that have already suspended their execution waiting for the release of the resource? Their pending requests cannot be ignored, so the process in the RELEASE entry must execute a SIGNAL statement. This specifies that the awaited situation exists, and wakes up exactly one of the waiting processes.

If there is no waiting process, the signaling process continues execution, possibly after other processes execute in other monitor entries. If there is a waiting process, the monitor must be freed to allow the waiting process to continue execution after the WAIT statement; to do this, the signaling process steps out of the monitor (much as the waiting process did). This guarantees that a process unblocked after a WAIT operation will find that the awaited situation exists; no other process execution is allowed to intervene. When no other process is in the monitor, the signaling process will resume execution following its SIGNAL statement. The signaling process may resume execution immediately after the signaled process completes its monitor call, or later. In either case, the signaling process cannot in general assume that the monitor variables have not been altered by other processes.

WAIT and SIGNAL statements operate on CONDITION variables, the next topic of discussion.

CONDITION VARIABLES AND PRIORITIES

Life would be simple if there were only one reason for waiting (and thus only one reason for signaling). However, there may be several reasons for waiting and a need to distinguish among them. In a producer/consumer relationship, there are two reasons for waiting: the consumer waits for buffers to be filled, and the producer waits for buffers to be emptied.

CONDITION variables are used to represent awaited situations. These variables must be declared in a monitor. They cannot be initialized by monitor initialization code; their values are automatically initialized to "empty". Condition variables are the operands of WAIT and SIGNAL statements. No other statements may operate on them, and they cannot be passed as parameters.

Conditions are used to signal state transitions (i.e., changes in the values of critical data). Using this philosophy, we can interpret the test in the ACQUIRE entry of the single resource monitor as: if the critical data is in the "wrong state" (IN_USE is true), then wait for a state transition to the "right state". We assume that a process signals a condition only when the associated monitor state holds.

The SIGNAL statement on a condition variable obeys two basic rules. First, it should wake up exactly one of the waiting processes. Second, the scheduling policy used should be fair, i.e., it should preclude indefinite postponement of a waiting process. An example of a fair scheduling policy is the FIFO policy. Under FIFO, the longest waiting process is resumed; this is what is implemented in CSP/k. However, it is often desirable to allow an explicit form of scheduling waiting processes. In operating systems, scheduling using explicit priorities is common, e.g., in scheduling the CPU after an I/O completion interrupt.

For these purposes, CSP/k allows the optional feature PRIORITY for a condition variable. An example declaration is

DECLARE(READY)CONDITION PRIORITY;

It is used in a WAIT statement this way:

WAIT(READY,P);

where P (a nonnegative integer expression) specifies the priority value. The SIGNAL statement on a priority condition variable has the same form as one for a normal condition variable,

SIGNAL(READY);

It has the effect of resuming the waiting process with the smallest priority value; thus, O specifies top priority.

Priority condition variables provide a closer control over scheduling waiting processes than normal condition variables. This flexibility has its dangers, however. Priority scheduling does not satisfy signaling rule 2 given above; it does not preclude indefinite postponement. A process with a high-numbered priority value may be indefinitely postponed if there are too many processes with low-numbered priority values.

Finally, CSP/k provides the EMPTY built-in function. EMPTY is a function with one argument, a condition variable, and returns a Boolean value: true if there is no process waiting for the specified condition variable, and false otherwise. It has the form

EMPTY(condition variable)

This concludes the detailed discussion of CSP/k monitors. The monitor has been presented as a programming language feature which permits mutually exclusive access of critical data. The process is our next topic.

MORE ABOUT PROCESSES

Each process needs a certain amount of memory to execute. The compiler estimates this space based on static analysis of the program; however, these estimates are conservative (pessimistic). There is an alternate form of process header that specifies information to the compiler about the data space requirements of the process; a requirement of 300 bytes has the form

OBSERVER:PROCESS(300);

The data space requirements consist of the storage for local process variables and for local variables of all procedures and monitor entries that the process can call. The amount of space actually used by the process is printed after program execution.

Processes can declare local variables and procedures, and can access all monitor entries, global procedures, and global variables. All monitor and global procedure definitions must appear before any process definitions; monitor and global procedure definitions can be intermixed.

Processes begin execution after all monitor initialization code has been executed. From a conceptual viewpoint, processes begin execution at the same time and proceed in parallel. From a CSP/k implementation viewpoint, processes are linked to a ready list in a seemingly random order and execute in an interleaved manner on a single processor. Each viewpoint has its merits. However, we emphasize that all logical properties of a CSP/k program must be derived from the conceptual viewpoint without making any assumptions about the relative speeds of processes.

It is common in operating systems to talk about processes creating (or spawning) subprocesses that execute in parallel. There is no dynamic creation of processes in CSP/k, however. All processes must instead be declared statically within the program. If process P1 wishes to create a subprocess P2 dynamically in CSP/k, P1 and P2 would be defined, P2 would immediately call a monitor entry to block itself on some condition variable, and P1 would signal that condition variable in another monitor entry when it wanted to "create" P2.

This completes the discussion of CSP/k processes. The next section provides a complete CSP/k program and illustrates many of the features we have been discussing.

AN EXAMPLE PROGRAM: CIRCULAR BUFFER MANAGEMENT

In Chapter 3 we gave an SP/k program to do queue management. In that program, procedures accessed the queue data structure, doing insertions and deletions. The example did not handle the error conditions of inserting into a full queue or deleting from an empty queue.

In this section we give a similar example for circular buffer management. In this new example, two processes access the data structure, a list organized as a FIFO queue and represented by a one-dimensional array. The example is recast as a problem in buffer management in an operating system. A FIFO queue is used to represent the buffer list because it is important to remove the data in the order in which it was added (e.g., a message queue). The process wishing to insert information (fill the buffers) is a producer; it might be an input spooler transferring data from cards to disk. The process wishing to delete information (empty the buffers) is a consumer; it might be an output spooler transferring data from disk to printer.

Our new example introduces several new problems. Because the producer and consumer are concurrent units accessing the buffers, a monitor should be used to provide mutually exclusive access; the buffers then become critical data in the monitor. Also, the producer and consumer must be synchronized to ensure that the producer never accesses the buffer list when it is full and the consumer never accesses the buffer list when it is empty.

Mutually exclusive access is achieved by ensuring that all references to the buffer list and its state variables are in a monitor. The state variables are the familiar HEAD and TAIL, and a new variable representing the number of buffers (array positions) filled, #_FULL. #_FULL has a minimum value of 0 and a maximum value of the number of array positions, #_BUFFERS. #_FULL is tested by the producer and consumer to determine whether they can proceed in execution.

The producer must wait for an empty buffer whenever #_FULL=#_BUFFERS; the consumer should therefore signal whenever it has emptied a buffer. The consumer must wait for a full buffer when #_FULL=0; the producer should therefore signal when it has filled a buffer. The producer and consumer cooperate to ensure that one never gets too far ahead of the other.

A CSP/k program to do circular buffer management is given on the next page. The monitor has two entries, SPOOL for filling a buffer, and UNSPOOL for emptying a buffer. Each entry has the form: possible wait, manipulation of buffer, appropriate signal.

```
 1 MESSAGE_QUEUE:PROCEDURE OPTIONS(CONCURRENT);

 2     CIRCULAR_BUFFER:MONITOR;
 3             DECLARE(BUFFER(5))CHARACTER(80)VARYING;
 4             DECLARE(HEAD,TAIL,#_BUFFERS,#_FULL)FIXED;
 5             DECLARE(BUFFER_VACANT,BUFFER_OCCUPIED)CONDITION;
 6             DO;
 7                 HEAD=1;
 8                 TAIL=1;
 9                 #_BUFFERS=5;
10                 #_FULL=0;
11                 END;

12         SPOOL:ENTRY(CONTENTS);
13             DECLARE(CONTENTS)CHARACTER(*)VARYING;
14             IF #_FULL=#_BUFFERS THEN
15                 WAIT(BUFFER_VACANT);
16             BUFFER(TAIL)=CONTENTS;
17             TAIL=MOD(TAIL,#_BUFFERS)+1;
18             #_FULL=#_FULL+1;
19             SIGNAL(BUFFER_OCCUPIED);
20             END;

21         UNSPOOL:ENTRY(CONTENTS);
22             DECLARE(CONTENTS)CHARACTER(*)VARYING;
23             IF #_FULL=0 THEN
24                 WAIT(BUFFER_OCCUPIED);
25             CONTENTS=BUFFER(HEAD);
26             HEAD=MOD(HEAD,#_BUFFERS)+1;
27             #_FULL=#_FULL-1;
28             SIGNAL(BUFFER_VACANT);
29             END;
30         END;

31     PRODUCER:PROCESS;
32         DECLARE(CARD)CHARACTER(80)VARYING;
33         CARD='NOT EOF';
34         DO WHILE(CARD¬='EOF');
35             GET SKIP EDIT(CARD)(A(80));
36             CALL SPOOL(CARD);
37             END;
38         END;

39     CONSUMER:PROCESS;
40         DECLARE(LINE)CHARACTER(80)VARYING;
41         LINE='NOT EOF';
42         DO WHILE(LINE¬='EOF');
43             CALL UNSPOOL(LINE);
44             PUT SKIP EDIT(LINE)(A(80));
45             END;
46         END;

47     END;
```

The output of the CSP/k program is a listing of the input cards, one per printer line. An example output is

    HERE
    ARE
    SEVERAL
    DATA
    CARDS
    EOF

This concludes the discussion of the CSP/k example. The example illustrated mutual exclusion, synchronization, and processes, features not present in the SP/k example. The producer process read information and called a monitor entry; the consumer process called a monitor entry and printed information. In an actual operating system, these processes would take time to execute, even with true parallelism. In CSP/k, the timing delays associated with process execution can be provided by the BUSY statement.

THE BUSY STATEMENT

The BUSY statement is a feature that makes CSP/k a useful simulation language. To understand this feature, we first must introduce the concept of simulated time. The CSP/k run-time system maintains a clock that represents current simulated time. This clock operates ("ticks") only when a process requests timing service through the BUSY statement. The clock does not operate as a result of normal process execution (executing SP/k statements); these statements are considered to take zero time. The SIGNAL statement also takes zero time, and the WAIT statement takes time only if the process executing it becomes blocked. If blocking occurs, the time spent waiting is determined by the process that eventually does the signal.

The BUSY statement can appear in processes and in global procedures called by processes, but not in monitors. The statement has the form

    BUSY(N);

where N (a non-negative integer expression) represents the number of time units the process will be delayed. The delayed process will resume execution when the current simulated time has increased N time units.

It is only through the BUSY statement that simulated time can be increased. To help explain the BUSY statement, we outline a model of the CSP/k implementation of BUSY here; the actual details can be found in Appendix 5. A process executing a BUSY statement suspends its execution and is linked to the BUSY list in ascending order of restart time (for the previous example, this is current time + N). The CSP/k run-time system runs processes from its ready list until the ready list is empty. At that point, the system takes the first process from the BUSY list, advances current simulated time to the restart time of that process, and begins running that process.

Using the BUSY statement, we can simulate the resource usage of one of the processes accessing the single resource monitor as

```
P1:PROCESS;
    DO WHILE(TRUE);
        CALL ACQUIRE;
        BUSY(3);  /* USE THE RESOURCE FOR 3 SECONDS */
        CALL RELEASE;
        BUSY(4);  /* DO OTHER WORK FOR 4 SECONDS */
        END;
    END;
```

where we have arbitrarily set the parameters of the BUSY statements. In this example, we have assumed that the time units correspond to seconds. Other units could be used. In the circular buffer example, a BUSY statement could be inserted after the GET SKIP LIST statement in the producer to represent the delay in producing the information. A BUSY statement could be inserted before the PUT SKIP LIST statement in the consumer to represent the delay in consuming the information.

The BUSY statement is the final CSP/k language feature we introduce. We close this chapter with a discussion of process statistics.

PROCESS STATISTICS

The CSP/k run-time system controls the interleaved execution of processes and enforces mutually exclusive access of monitor data. The system also gathers statistics about process execution and prints information about the states of processes at program termination. A CSP/k program terminates when there are no processes ready to execute.

Here is an example of the printout resulting from executing a circular buffer management program.

PROCESS NUMBER	STATEMENTS EXECUTED	MEMORY USED	MEMORY CLAIMED	LAST LINE EXECUTED	STATUS	UTILIZATION IN PERCENT
1	76	244	460	DONE	TERMINATED	63
2	75	244	460	DONE	TERMINATED	57

The process number refers to the textual order in which processes were defined in the CSP/k program. The memory used is the amount of data stack (in bytes) used by the process; the memory claimed is the data stack requirement either estimated by the compiler or specified in the process header. Space can be saved by using the process header specification if the claimed space greatly exceeds the used space. If the process did not terminate execution, the number of the last line it executed is given; if it did terminate, the word DONE is given as the last line executed. The status may be one of

VIRGIN   The process never began execution.

READY   The process was linked to the ready list.

ABORTED   The process aborted due to some unrecoverable error.

BLOCKED   The process is waiting for a condition to satisfied.

TERMINATED The process terminated execution.

(The reason that BUSY is not a valid status is given in Appendix 5.) Utilization is the fraction of total system simulated time that the process was busy; it is omitted if no BUSY statement was executed by the process.

This concludes our description of CSP/k. The examples given in this chapter illustrated basic issues in mutual exclusion and synchronization. Larger examples, illustrating more complex concurrency problems such as deadlock, are given in the next chapter.

CHAPTER 4 SUMMARY

In this chapter we introduced CSP/k, a concurrent programming language that builds upon SP/k by adding features that support concurrency. Here is a brief list of its main features.

Processes – They operate in parallel at undefined relative speeds. Processes may call reentrant procedures or monitor entries. The process header can specify the data space requirements of the process.

Monitors – They are fences enclosing critical data. The variables declared in the monitor are the critical data and are permanent (retain their values between executions in the monitor). A monitor consists of a monitor header, declarations of local variables, initialization code, zero or more procedures, and zero or more entries.

Monitor initialization code – It sets the values of monitor variables prior to the first call to a monitor entry. It must be present.

Entries – Monitor entries begin with an entry header (an entry name, a colon, and the keyword ENTRY are required). An entry is accessed from a process by a subroutine CALL statement or by a function invocation, in which case the entry returns a value. Entries may have parameters and local variables, as procedures do.

WAIT statement - A WAIT statement executed in a monitor entry removes the executing process from the monitor and suspends its execution.

SIGNAL statement - A SIGNAL statement executed in a monitor entry specifies that an awaited situation exists and wakes up exactly one of the waiting processes. If there is no waiting process, the signaling process continues execution; if there is a waiting process, the signaling process suspends its execution until no other process is active in the monitor.

CONDITION variables - They are the operands of WAIT and SIGNAL statements. CONDITION variables are used to represent awaited conditions. Conditions may optionally be declared as priority conditions. In this case, the WAIT statement must also specify the priority.

EMPTY - This built-in function has one argument, a CONDITION variable, and returns a Boolean value: true if there is no process waiting for the specified condition variable, and false otherwise.

BUSY statement - It can appear in processes and in global procedures called by processes, but not in monitors. A process executing a BUSY(N) statement is delayed and will resume execution when the simulated time has increased N time units.

Process statistics - They are gathered by the CSP/k run-time system during program execution and printed after program termination.

We also gave a circular buffer example that extended the queue management example of Chapter 3 by introducing concurrency and mutual exclusion.

CHAPTER 4 BIBLIOGRAPHY

The operating system text by Brinch Hansen [1973] is a good source of material on concurrent processes. Several notations for monitors have appeared in the literature: [Brinch Hansen 1972,1977], [Hoare 1974], and [Wirth 1976]. The Hoare paper is a particularly important contribution to the area. Several systems that support concurrent processes have been implemented recently. CSP/k, the concurrent language of this book, was designed in part by Reinhard Menzel [1976], who was also responsible for its implementation. Other system are the TOPPS system by Czarnik et al. [1973], the Multiprogramming Operating System (MOS) by Shaw and Weiderman [1971], the MODULA system by Wirth [1976], and the Concurrent Pascal system by Brinch Hansen [1977].

Brinch Hansen, P. Structured multiprogramming. Comm. ACM 15,7 (July 1972), 574-577.

Brinch Hansen, P. Operating System Principles. Prentice-Hall (1973).

Brinch Hansen, P. The Architecture of Concurrent Programs. Prentice-Hall (1977).

Czarnik, B. (editor), Tsichritzis, D., Ballard, A.J., Dryer, M., Holt, R.C., and Weissman, L. A student project for an operating system course. CSRG-29, Computer Systems Research Group, University of Toronto (1973).

Hoare, C.A.R. Monitors: an operating system structuring concept. Comm. ACM 17,10 (October 1974), 549-557.

Kaubisch, W.H., Perrott, R.H., and Hoare, C.A.R. Quasiparallel programming. Software - Practice and Experience, Vol. 6 (1976), 341-356.

Menzel, R.G. Concurrent SP/k: a language supporting concurrent processes. M.Sc. Thesis, Department of Computer Science, University of Toronto (July 1976).

Shaw, A.C. and Weiderman, N.H. A multiprogramming system for education and research. Proc. IFIP Congress 1971, 1505-1509.

Wirth, N. MODULA: a language for modular multiprogramming. Software - Practice and Experience, Vol. 7,1 (January-February 1977), 3-35.

CHAPTER 4 EXERCISES

1. Suppose the EMPTY built-in function were not present. How would you simulate its operation using other CSP/k features?

2. Many data structures were mentioned in the Chapter 3 Exercises -- FIFO queue, priority queue, stack, and dequeue. What is an appropriate data structure for the CSP/k ready list? For the model of the CSP/k BUSY list?

3. What are the possible different outputs of the following program? Explain your answer without running the program.

```
CROSSTALK:PROCEDURE OPTIONS(CONCURRENT);
   DECLARE(LINE,LIMIT)FIXED;

   INCREMENT:PROCEDURE(COUNTER);
      DECLARE(COUNTER)FIXED;
      /* ADD 1 SLOWLY */
      COUNTER=COUNTER+1+0+0+0+0+0+0+0+0+0+0+0+0+0+0+0
            +0+0+0+0+0+0+0+0+0+0+0+0+0+0+0+0+0+0+0
                  (the same for several lines)
            +0+0+0+0+0+0+0+0+0+0+0+0+0+0+0+0+0+0+0;
      END;

   SETUP:MONITOR;
        DO;
           LINE=0;
           GET LIST(LIMIT);
           END;

   TWEEDLE_DEE:PROCESS;
      DO WHILE(LINE<=LIMIT);
         CALL INCREMENT(LINE);
         PUT SKIP EDIT(LINE,' A PENNY SAVED IS ')(F(2),A);
         PUT EDIT('A PENNY EARNED')(A);
         END;
   TWEEDLE_DUM:PROCESS;
      DO WHILE(LINE<=LIMIT);
         CALL INCREMENT(LINE);
         PUT SKIP EDIT(LINE,' A THING OF BEAUTY IS ')(F(2),A);
         PUT EDIT('A JOY FOREVER')(A);
         END;

   END;
```

Questions 4-8 refer to the single resource monitor example.

4. Implement and run the single resource monitor named RESOURCE in CSP/k with three processes (using the BUSY statement) and include output statements to show the progress of the processes and the states of the resources.

5. In the ACQUIRE entry of the RESOURCE monitor, why does a process not retest to see if IN_USE has become false when the process resumes execution following its WAIT? What would happen if lines 13 and 14 in the RELEASE entry were interchanged?

6. FIFO was described as a fair scheduling policy for resuming a process waiting on a non-priority condition, in that it did not allow a waiting process to be postponed indefinitely. Are the following scheduling policies fair?

   a) LIFO (last-in first-out)
   b) LRR (least-recently-run)
   c) MRR (most-recently-run)
   d) LFR (least-frequently-run)
   e) MFR (most-frequently-run)

7. The monitor concept is at least as powerful as the semaphore concept because it can be used to implement semaphores; this is what the single resource monitor showed. Show the converse: the semaphore concept is at least as powerful as the monitor concept because a monitor can be simulated using semaphores and their associated operations. You should ensure the mutual exclusion present in the execution of monitor entries. The equivalent of the SIGNAL operation should allow some waiting process (if there is one) to execute in the monitor.

8. Suppose the RESOURCE monitor were to enforce an upper bound of N (>1) processes accessing the resource, instead of just 1. Exclusive access is not required now, but an upper limit on the number of active processes accessing the resource must be imposed. How would the monitor be changed?

Questions 9-10 refer to the circular buffer management example.

9. In the SP/k queue example in Chapter 3, an initially empty queue was represented by HEAD=1 and TAIL=0. Why does the CSP/k example for circular buffer management represent an initially empty queue by HEAD=1 and TAIL=1?

10. What would happen if the CONSUMER or the PRODUCER process of the MESSAGE_QUEUE program was omitted?

CHAPTER 5

EXAMPLES OF CONCURRENT PROGRAMS

This chapter presents solutions in CSP/k to concurrent programming problems of a more substantial nature than those encountered earlier in this book. The purpose is to teach more about both concurrency and CSP/k, through examples. The concurrency issues discussed include synchronization, mutual exclusion, deadlock, and indefinite postponement. The CSP/k language features used include the EMPTY built-in function, arrays of condition variables, and priority conditions.

Four problems are stated and their solutions are given in CSP/k. Because the solutions are subtle in many places, we explain in detail how the programs work.

An understanding of this material is essential before going on to the next two chapters, where we discuss the design and implementation of an operating system.

DINING PHILOSOPHERS

Suppose several processes are continually acquiring, using, and releasing a set of shared resources. We want to be sure that a process cannot be deadlocked (blocked so that it can never be signaled) or indefinitely postponed (continually denied a request).

A colorful version of this problem can be stated in terms of a group of philosophers eating spaghetti. It goes like this:

There are N philosophers who spend their lives either eating or thinking. Each philosopher has his own place at a circular table, in the center of which is a large bowl of spaghetti. To eat spaghetti requires two forks, but only N forks are provided, one between each pair of philosophers. The only forks a philosopher can pick up are those on his immediate right and left. Each philosopher is identical in structure, alternately eating then thinking. The problem is to simulate the behavior of the philosophers while avoiding deadlock (the request by a philosopher for a fork can never be granted) and indefinite postponement (the request by a philosopher for a fork is continually denied).

We will concentrate on the case of five philosophers. Here is a picture of a table setting with five plates and forks.

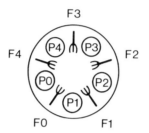

Several points should be clear from the problem description. Adjacent philosophers can never be eating at the same time. Also, with five forks and the need for two forks to eat, at most two philosophers can be eating at any one time. Any solution we develop should allow maximum parallelism.

Consider the following proposed solution. A philosopher acquires his forks one at a time, left then right, by calling a monitor entry PICKUP, giving as a parameter the appropriate fork number. Similarly, a philosopher returns his forks one at a time, left then right, by calling a monitor entry PUTDOWN. The philosopher's activity is represented by a process that repeatedly executes the statements

    CALL PICKUP(left);
    CALL PICKUP(right);
    Busy eating;
    CALL PUTDOWN(left);
    CALL PUTDOWN(right);
    Busy thinking;

The entries are part of a monitor that controls access to the forks. The data of the monitor includes the one-dimensional

Boolean array FORK_FREE, where FORK_FREE(I) gives the availability of the Ith fork. Only when a philosopher acquires his two forks does he begin eating. Periods of eating and thinking by a philosopher can be represented by BUSY statements of appropriate duration.

Unfortunately, this simple solution suffers from a serious defect, namely deadlock. Consider a sequence of process executions in which the philosophers each acquire a left fork, then each attempt to pick up a right fork. Each philosopher will be blocked in the PICKUP entry on a condition that can never be signaled; the request for a right fork can never be granted. Deadlock occurs in this situation because processes hold certain resources while requesting others. Clearly, we need a solution that prevents deadlock.

We now discuss a solution that prevents deadlock. Each philosopher is represented by a process that repeatedly executes the statements

```
CALL PICKUP(I);
Busy eating;
CALL PUTDOWN(I);
Busy thinking;
```

where I is the number of the philosopher. Picking up the forks is now represented as a single monitor entry call.

We will develop a monitor named FORKS with two entries, PICKUP and PUTDOWN, which acquire and release the forks. The structure of these entries differs from that of the previous entries. The monitor must have variables that keep track of the availability of the five forks. This could be done by having an array of five elements; this is the earlier FORK_FREE method. We will use a different approach. There is still an array of five elements, but the elements will correspond to the five philosophers. The array will be called #_FORKS, where #_FORKS(I) is the number of forks available to philosopher I: either 0, 1, or 2. In the PICKUP entry, philosopher I is allowed to pick up his forks only when #_FORKS(I)=2. Otherwise, he waits on the condition variable READY(I); each philosopher thus has his own condition for which he waits. When he succeeds in picking up his forks, he must decrease the fork counts of his neighbor philosophers. He then leaves the monitor and commences eating.

The neighbors of philosopher I are numbered LEFT(I) and RIGHT(I). Based on our earlier diagram, LEFT(3) is 2 and RIGHT(3) is 4. It is important to note that RIGHT(4) is 0 and LEFT(0) is 4. LEFT and RIGHT could be implemented as vectors initialized to the appropriate values or as functions using the MOD built-in function to calculate the proper neighbor number.

```
1 SPAGHETTI:PROCEDURE OPTIONS(CONCURRENT);
2    DECLARE(TRUE,FALSE)BIT;
3    FORKS:MONITOR;
4         DECLARE(#_FORKS(0:4))FIXED,
5             (READY(0:4))CONDITION,
6             (J,#_PHILOS)FIXED;
          ... (define LEFT and RIGHT) ...
7         DO;
8             #_PHILOS=5;
9             DO J=0 TO #_PHILOS-1;
10                #_FORKS(J)=2;
11                END;
12            TRUE='1'B;
13            FALSE='0'B;
14            END;

15       PICKUP:ENTRY(ME);
16          DECLARE(ME)FIXED;
17          IF #_FORKS(ME)¬=2 THEN
18             WAIT(READY(ME));
19          #_FORKS(RIGHT(ME))=#_FORKS(RIGHT(ME))-1;
20          #_FORKS(LEFT(ME))=#_FORKS(LEFT(ME))-1;
21          END;

22       PUTDOWN:ENTRY(ME);
23          DECLARE(ME)FIXED;
24          #_FORKS(RIGHT(ME))=#_FORKS(RIGHT(ME))+1;
25          #_FORKS(LEFT(ME))=#_FORKS(LEFT(ME))+1;
26          IF #_FORKS(RIGHT(ME))=2 THEN
27             SIGNAL(READY(RIGHT(ME)));
28          IF #_FORKS(LEFT(ME))=2 THEN
29             SIGNAL(READY(LEFT(ME)));
30          END;
31       END /* OF FORKS MONITOR */;

32    COMMON_PHILOSOPHER:PROCEDURE(I);
33       DECLARE(I)FIXED;
34       DO WHILE(TRUE);
35          CALL PICKUP(I);
36          Busy eating;
37          CALL PUTDOWN(I);
38          Busy thinking;
39          END;
40       END;

41     PHILOSOPHER_0:PROCESS;
42        CALL COMMON_PHILOSOPHER(0);
43        END;
44     PHILOSOPHER_1:PROCESS;
45        CALL COMMON_PHILOSOPHER(1);
46        END;

       ... (other philosophers) ...

47     END /* OF SPAGHETTI */;
```

When a philosopher returns his forks in the PUTDOWN entry, he should increase the fork counts of his neighbors. If the philosopher then finds that either (or both) of his neighbors has two forks available, he should signal the appropriate neighbor. The philosophers therefore pass the ability to access the forks among themselves using SIGNAL statements.

In our CSP/k solution to the dining philosophers problem, each philosopher process calls a common procedure, supplying his number as the argument. This CSP/k program illustrates several language features, among them an array of condition variables (READY).

We now examine the solution for deadlock and indefinite postponement. Deadlock would occur if a philosopher became blocked and could not continue executing regardless of the future of the system. Let us look at the program to see where this might occur. A philosopher cannot become blocked forever when eating or thinking (lines 36 and 38). Therefore, we look at execution in the two monitor entries to see if deadlock can occur there. The PICKUP entry shows that a requesting philosopher suspends his execution when his two forks are not available. The philosopher does not pick up one fork and wait for the other. This means that the system can never get into the state where each philosopher holds one fork (his left one, say) and is waiting for the other -- this is deadlock, brought about by holding resources while requesting others. The rest of the PICKUP entry shows that the fork counts are correctly decreased. The PUTDOWN entry increases the fork counts and correctly signals other waiting philosophers.

The above discussion shows informally that deadlock cannot occur in our solution. Indefinite postponement is a different matter.

Indefinite postponement occurs if a philosopher becomes blocked and there exists a future execution sequence in which he will remain forever blocked. Consider the following situation for philosophers 1, 2, and 3 in which philosopher 2 is indefinitely postponed.

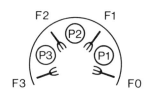

Suppose philosopher 1 picks up his two forks (forks 0 and 1). Next, philosopher 3 picks up his two forks (forks 2 and 3). Next, philosopher 2 enters PICKUP and finds that his required forks are being used, so he waits. Next, the following unfortunate sequence occurs repeatedly. Philosopher 1 puts down his forks, thinks, and then picks them up again; then, philosopher 3 puts down his forks, thinks, and picks them up again, and so on. During this repeated sequence, at least one of the forks of philosopher 2 is always being used. Given that it is possible for this sequence to repeat indefinitely, we see that philosopher 2 can suffer indefinite postponement. We have not solved the problem!

There are several ways to overcome this defect. The most obvious one keeps track of the "age" of requests for forks, and when one request gets too old, other requests are held up until the oldest request can be satisfied. This could be done, for example, by counting the number of meals enjoyed by a philosopher's two neighbors while he is waiting for his forks. If he is bypassed more than, say, 10 times, his neighbors are blocked until he gets a chance to pick up his forks. (Does this solution allow maximum parallelism?) We leave this extension to the reader (see the Exercises at the end of this chapter).

This concludes our discussion of the dining philosophers problem. We saw that deadlock was avoided, but our simple solution unfortunately did not rule out indefinite postponement.

READERS AND WRITERS

We will now consider the problem of several processes concurrently reading and writing the same file. Any number of reader processes (processes accessing but not altering information) may access the file simultaneously. However, any writer process updating the file must have exclusive access to the file; otherwise, inconsistent data may result.

This problem arises in an airline reservations system, for example. Several ground personnel, each using a computer terminal, are issuing boarding passes for a flight. Reservations for the flight have been stored in a file. Reading the file allows an attendant to verify a passenger's reservation. Writing the file allows an attendant to add a new passenger to the flight when a customer arrives at the counter without a prior booking.

The problem, as stated so far, is a slight extension of the mutual exclusion example (COUNTING) given in Chapter 3. There still must be mutually exclusive access to the reservations file, but the new feature is that any number of reader processes may be accessing the file simultaneously. Writers still need exclusive access, however. The enqueue/dequeue feature discussed in Chapter 2 can solve the problem as stated.

A simple solution to this problem using monitors might be developed as follows. A reader wishing to access the file calls a monitor entry START_READ. If there is no active writer (there may be several active readers), the number of active readers is increased by 1 and the new reader accesses the file. If there is an active writer, the reader waits. A reader resumed after a WAIT in START_READ signals other waiting readers that they also may access the file. A reader finishing accessing the file calls a monitor entry END_READ. It decreases the number of active readers by 1, and if this number reaches zero, it signals a writer that the file is available. (There can be no readers waiting.) A writer wishing to access the file calls a monitor entry START_WRITE. If there is an active writer or at least one active reader, the writer waits. A writer finishing accessing the file calls a monitor entry END_WRITE, and signals waiting readers or writers that the file is now available for accessing.

The simple solution unfortunately has an important defect. Once one reader begins accessing the file, the writers may be indefinitely postponed by a heavy stream of other reader processes accessing the file. Some additional restriction on the problem must be made to remove the possibility of indefinite postponement.

We will impose the following requirements on the order of accessing the file. (They make the example more realistic and indefinite postponement is avoided.) We require that a new reader not be permitted to start if there is a writer waiting for the currently active readers to finish. Similarly, we require that all readers waiting at the end of a writer execution be given priority over the next writer. This latter restriction avoids the danger of the indefinite postponement of readers because of many active writers.

We now discuss a solution to the readers and writers problem with these restrictions. We will use a monitor with four entries (the names of these entries are the same as those above, but their structure is different): a reader process calls START_READ before reading and END_READ after reading; a writer process calls START_WRITE before writing and END_WRITE after writing. The following decision rules for the entries satisfy our ordering requirements. These rules will be compared with the rules for the monitor entries of the simpler problem.

START_READ   - If there is an active writer or a waiting writer, the reader waits. Once activated, it signals other readers to become active.

END_READ   - If the finishing reader finds that it is the last active reader, it signals a waiting writer.

START_WRITE - If there are active readers or if there is an active writer, the new writer waits.

END_WRITE   - If there are readers waiting, the finishing writer
               signals a reader. Otherwise, it signals another
               writer.

We will now consider the decision rules for these entries in
more detail.   In START_READ, a reader waits if either of two
situations exists: there is an active writer (obviously) or
there is a waiting writer. If the file is not available, a
writer registers its wish to access the file by executing a WAIT
statement on a condition variable. Because a reader in
START_READ needs to distinguish between readers and writers in
the list of processes waiting to access the file, there should be
separate condition variables on which the readers (OK_TO_READ)
and writers (OK_TO_WRITE) wait.   The EMPTY built-in function can
be used to test whether there are processes waiting on these
conditions.   Once a waiting reader in START_READ is resumed, it
increases the number of active readers (#_READING) by 1.   This
reader knows that the file is now available for reading, so it
signals another reader that was waiting for access to the file.
A resumed reader in START_READ thus contributes to a cascade of
signaling readers which were waiting.   No other process (such as
an arriving reader or writer) can enter the monitor while this
cascade is in progress.   In time, all readers that were waiting
for access after a writer are signaled.   The logic of this entry
differs from that of the previous START_READ entry because here a
reader waits if there is a waiting writer. This is one of the
new restrictions on the problem.

In END_READ, a reader decreases the number of active readers
by 1.   If it finds that it is the last reader accessing the file,
it signals a waiting writer.   The logic of this entry is
therefore identical to that of the previous END_READ entry.

In START_WRITE, a writer waits if either of two situations
exists: there is at least one active reader (obviously) or there
is an active writer (obviously).   The Boolean variable
WRITER_ACTIVE records whether writing is taking place.   The logic
of this entry is therefore identical to that of the previous
START_WRITE entry.

In END_WRITE, a writer first checks if there are readers
waiting to access the file.   If there are, the writer signals a
waiting reader.   If there are not, the writer signals a waiting
writer.   This again illustrates the need for separate condition
variables for readers and writers.   The logic of this entry
differs from that of the previous END_WRITE entry because here a
writer tries to signal a reader before it signals a writer.   This
is another of the new restrictions on the problem.

A solution to the readers and writers problem in CSP/k is
given on the next page.   The solution should be studied to see
how the decision rules of the monitor entries have been
translated into CSP/k statements.

```
1  READERS_AND_WRITERS:PROCEDURE OPTIONS(CONCURRENT);
2     DECLARE(TRUE,FALSE)BIT;
3     FILE_ACCESS:MONITOR;
4           DECLARE(#_READING)FIXED,
5             (ACTIVE_WRITER)BIT,
6             (OK_TO_READ,OK_TO_WRITE)CONDITION;
7           DO;
8               TRUE='1'B;
9               FALSE='0'B;
10              #_READING=0;
11              ACTIVE_WRITER=FALSE;
12              END;

13        START_READ:ENTRY;
14           IF ACTIVE_WRITER|¬EMPTY(OK_TO_WRITE) THEN
15              WAIT(OK_TO_READ);
16           #_READING=#_READING+1;
17           SIGNAL(OK_TO_READ) /* ALLOW OTHER READERS IN */;
18           END;
19        END_READ:ENTRY;
20           #_READING=#_READING-1;
21           IF #_READING=0 THEN
22              SIGNAL(OK_TO_WRITE);
23           END;

24        START_WRITE:ENTRY;
25           IF #_READING¬=0|ACTIVE_WRITER THEN
26              WAIT(OK_TO_WRITE);
27           ACTIVE_WRITER=TRUE;
28           END;
29        END_WRITE:ENTRY;
30           ACTIVE_WRITER=FALSE;
31           IF ¬EMPTY(OK_TO_READ) THEN
32              SIGNAL(OK_TO_READ);
33           ELSE
34              SIGNAL(OK_TO_WRITE);
35           END;
36        END /* OF INFORMATION */;

37     READER:PROCESS;
38        DO WHILE(TRUE);
39           CALL START_READ;
40           Busy reading;
41           CALL END_READ;
42           END;
43        END;
44     WRITER:PROCESS;
45        DO WHILE(TRUE);
46           CALL START_WRITE;
47           Busy writing;
48           CALL END_WRITE;
49           END;
50        END;

51     END /* OF READERS_AND_WRITERS */;
```

The restrictions imposed on the readers and writers problem require that: 1) waiting readers are given priority over waiting writers after a writer finishes, and 2) a waiting writer is given priority over waiting readers after all readers finish. It is interesting to note that this form of "precedence" scheduling using SIGNAL statements is accomplished <u>without</u> priority condition variables. Simple tests on a counting variable (line 21) and on the waiting list of a condition (line 31) suffice to achieve the desired order of accessing the file.

Finally, we discuss the SIGNAL statement on line 17. A reader executing it suspends execution and allows a waiting reader to enter the monitor; this creates the cascade of resuming waiting readers. When the last waiting reader is resumed, it will signal on an empty condition variable. The semantics of the SIGNAL statement in this situation are that the signaling process continues execution, possibly after other monitor entries are entered. The correctness of our solution is not affected, however. No writer can intervene during any of the suspended reader executions because the writer first checks on #_READING in line 25 of the STARTWRITE entry. In these cases, #_READING is greater than 0, thanks to the increment in line 16 being in front of line 17.

A reader attempting to enter the monitor by a CALL statement during the cascade of resuming readers will be blocked until the monitor becomes free. At that point, if the reader finds that there is a waiting writer, it will wait; if there is not a waiting writer, it will proceed.

This concludes our discussion of the readers and writers problem. We saw that some complex scheduling decisions could be made without the need for priority condition variables. The next example shows that priority condition variables are sometimes convenient.

SCHEDULING DISKS

Good scheduling algorithms can greatly improve the performance of operating systems. For example, the average turnaround time for jobs can be minimized by running short jobs before long jobs.

In this section, we want to minimize the time that processes wait for disk input and output. Before discussing disk scheduling algorithms, we need to know how disks access their data. A disk consists of a collection of platters, each with a top and bottom surface, attached to a central spindle and rotating at constant speed. There is usually a single arm, with a set of read/write heads, one per surface; the arm moves in or out, across the disk surfaces. This type of disk is called a movable head disk. When the arm is at a given position, the data passing under all read/write heads on all platters constitutes a cylinder. At a given cylinder position, the data passing under a particular read/write head constitutes a track.

Files of data are stored on a disk. A file consists of records; a record consists of fields of data. Some disks allow many records on a track. On other disks, a record must correspond exactly to a track. A program requests a data transfer to or from a disk by giving the cylinder number, track number, and record number.

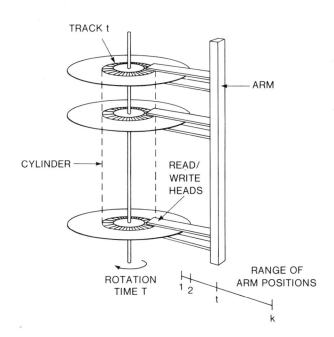

There are various delay factors associated with accessing data on a movable head disk. Seek time is the time needed to position the arm at the required cylinder. Rotational delay is the time needed for the disk to rotate so that the desired record is under the read/write head. Transmission time is the time needed to transfer data between the disk and main memory.

Seek time increases with the number of cylinders that the arm is moved. Rotational delay can vary from zero to the time needed to complete one revolution; on the average, it is one-half the rotation time, a hardware characteristic. Transmission time is dependent on the rotation time and recording density, and these factors vary from disk to disk. The following table shows that the seek time delay is the dominant factor in a typical transfer of a 1000-character record on a movable head disk.

Factor	Length of Time
Seek time	30.0 ms (milliseconds)
Rotational delay	8.3 ms
Transmission time	1.2 ms

Generally, a simple scheduling algorithm can do nothing to decrease rotational delay or transmission time. But ordering of disk read/write requests can decrease the average seek time. This can be accomplished by favoring those requests that do not require much arm motion.

Perhaps the simplest scheduling algorithm to implement is the FIFO algorithm; it moves the disk arm to the cylinder with the oldest pending request. With light disk traffic, the FIFO algorithm does a good job. But when the queue of disk requests starts building up, the simple nature of FIFO results in unnecessary arm motion. For example, suppose a sequence of disk requests arrives to read cylinders 12, 82, 12, 82, 12, and 82, in that order. (Such a sequence can easily occur if several jobs are using a file on cylinder 12 while others are using a file on cylinder 82.) The FIFO algorithm will unfortunately cause the disk to seek back and forth from cylinder 12 to 82 several times. A clever scheduling algorithm could minimize arm motion by servicing all the requests for cylinder 12 and then all the requests for cylinder 82. We will discuss two scheduling algorithms that are more sophisticated than FIFO.

One such algorithm is the shortest seek time first (SSTF) algorithm. It operates as follows: the request chosen to be serviced next is the one that will move the disk arm the shortest distance from its current cylinder. The SSTF algorithm thus attempts to reduce disk arm motion. However, it can exhibit unwanted behavior; requests for certain cylinder regions on the disk may be indefinitely overtaken by requests for other cylinder regions closer to the current disk arm position. This results in certain disk requests not being serviced at all.

The SCAN algorithm is another scheduling algorithm that achieves short waiting times but prevents indefinite postponement. It attempts to reduce excessive disk arm motion and average waiting time by minimizing the frequency of change of direction of the disk arm. The SCAN algorithm operates as follows: while there remain requests in the current direction, the disk arm continues to move in that direction, servicing the request(s) at the nearest cylinder; if there are no pending requests in that direction (possibly because an edge of the disk surface has been encountered), the arm direction changes, and the disk arm begins its sweep across the surfaces in the opposite direction. This algorithm has also been called the elevator algorithm because of the analogy to the operation of an elevator, that runs up and down, receiving and discharging passengers.

A DISK ARM SCHEDULER

We will now give an implementation of the SCAN disk scheduling algorithm. SCAN gives good performance and illustrates the use of priority conditions. We will assume that there is a single disk and access to it is controlled by a monitor. (If there are several disks, each would have its own monitor.) The monitor has two entries:

ACQUIRE(DEST_CYL) - called by a process prior to transferring data to or from cylinder DEST_CYL.

RELEASE - called by a process after it has completed data transfer on the current cylinder.

The monitor must guarantee that only one process at a time uses the disk. The local data of the monitor keeps track of the current state of the disk. There must be a current disk arm position, ARM_POSITION (which can vary from 1 to the maximum cylinder number, MAX_CYL_#), the current direction of the arm sweep, DIRECTION (with character values 'UP' and 'DOWN'), and a Boolean variable indicating whether the disk is currently busy, IN_USE. The UP direction corresponds to increasing cylinder numbers, the DOWN direction to decreasing cylinder numbers.

A solution to the SCAN disk scheduling problem is given on the next page. A process using the disk would execute

CALL ACQUIRE(destination cylinder);
Read from or write to disk;
CALL RELEASE;

```
1     SCAN:MONITOR;
2         DECLARE(ARM_POSITION,MAX_CYL_#)FIXED,
3             (TRUE,FALSE,IN_USE)BIT,
4             (DIRECTION)CHARACTER(4)VARYING,
5             (DOWNSWEEP,UPSWEEP)CONDITION PRIORITY;
6         DO;
7             TRUE='1'B;
8             FALSE='0'B;
9             ARM_POSITION=1;
10            DIRECTION='UP';
11            IN_USE=FALSE;
12            MAX_CYL_#=400;
13            END;

14     ACQUIRE:ENTRY(DEST_CYL);
15         DECLARE(DEST_CYL)FIXED;
16         IF IN_USE THEN
17             IF ARM_POSITION<DEST_CYL|
                   (ARM_POSITION=DEST_CYL&DIRECTION='DOWN') THEN
18                 WAIT(UPSWEEP,DEST_CYL);
19             ELSE
20                 WAIT(DOWNSWEEP,MAX_CYL_#-DEST_CYL);
21         IN_USE=TRUE;
22         ARM_POSITION=DEST_CYL; /* RECORD THE ARM POSITION */
23         END;

24     RELEASE:ENTRY;
25         IN_USE=FALSE;
26         IF DIRECTION='UP' THEN
27             IF EMPTY(UPSWEEP) THEN
28                 DO;
29                     DIRECTION='DOWN';
30                     SIGNAL(DOWNSWEEP);
31                     END;
32             ELSE
33                 SIGNAL(UPSWEEP);
34         ELSE
35             IF EMPTY(DOWNSWEEP) THEN
36                 DO;
37                     DIRECTION='UP';
38                     SIGNAL(UPSWEEP);
39                     END;
40             ELSE
41                 SIGNAL(DOWNSWEEP);
42         END;

43     END /* OF SCAN */;
```

It is particularly enlightening to discuss the SCAN solution in detail. In the ACQUIRE entry, if the disk is free the arm is moved to the desired cylinder and the process leaves the monitor. Otherwise, the process waits. It is not sufficient to use a single condition variable for waiting. (Why?) What we need is a set of condition variables that relate the priority of a waiting request to the distance the requested cylinder is from the current cylinder. We could use an array of condition variables, one for each cylinder. Then, when a process releases the disk, it would determine the "closest" non-empty condition waiting list in the current arm direction and signal that condition variable. This approach is clumsy and we will use priority conditions instead.

There are two priority conditions, each corresponding to a given arm direction (UPSWEEP or DOWNSWEEP). In the ACQUIRE entry, a process waits on UPSWEEP if its destination cylinder has a larger number than the current cylinder. A process waits on DOWNSWEEP if its destination cylinder has a lower number than the current cylinder. Two questions arise: What happens if the destination cylinder equals the current cylinder? What priorities are specified in all of these waits?

We answer the priority question first. The priorities must indicate the distance the destination cylinder is from one end of the disk. For example, suppose the current arm position is at cylinder 25 and the direction is UP. What happens with processes that request cylinders 100 and 200? Both requests are ahead of the disk arm and therefore will wait on UPSWEEP. The request for cylinder 100 is closer than the request for cylinder 200, so cylinder 100 has priority over cylinder 200 (and therefore has a lower priority number). In our example, the request for cylinder 100 has a priority value of 100, while the one for cylinder 200 has a priority value of 200. Cylinder 100 will therefore be serviced before cylinder 200 on the upsweep.

Consider another example. Suppose the current cylinder 250, the maximum cylinder number is 400, and the direction is UP. What happens with processes that request cylinders 150 and 50? Both requests are behind the disk arm and therefore will wait on DOWNSWEEP. When the disk arm begins its sweep in the down direction, cylinder 150 is closer to it than cylinder 50. Cylinder 150 has priority over cylinder 50 (and should have a lower priority number). This can be accomplished by subtracting the destination cylinder from the maximum cylinder number to produce the priority value; the result will always be in the range from zero to MAX_CYL_# and will indicate the relative distance of arm motion. Cylinder 150 will have a priority value of 250 and cylinder 50 will have a priority value of 350. Cylinder 150 will therefore be serviced before cylinder 50 on the downsweep.

In our example, the priority values are specified in the WAIT statements in lines 18 and 20. We have been careful in our discussion here to be explicit about the arm direction, because the correct condition variable to wait on and the correct priority depend on that direction. But the arm direction is only tested (in line 17) when the destination cylinder equals the current cylinder.

The answer to this apparent mystery is that the arm direction generally does not matter. If the arm position is less than the destination cylinder, the process should wait on UPSWEEP regardless of the arm direction. If the arm position is greater than the destination cylinder, the process should wait on DOWNSWEEP regardless of the arm direction. Only when the arm position equals the destination cylinder does the arm direction matter. We are back to the first question we asked, so it is appropriate to answer it now.

To see what happens if the destination cylinder equals the current cylinder, we will discuss an alternative to line 17, showing that it can lead to indefinite postponement. (Questions 10 and 11 in the Exercises mention other alternatives.) These alternatives make the reasoning behind line 17 clearer.

Consider the following alternative to line 17.

```
IF ARM_POSITION<DEST_CYL THEN
```

A process with a destination cylinder equal to the current cylinder will wait on DOWNSWEEP in line 20. Suppose the current direction of the disk is down. A process releasing the disk will signal DOWNSWEEP in line 41 because there is a process waiting on it. If there is a stream of processes similar to the first one in this example, all with requests for the current cylinder, the disk arm will remain at the current cylinder servicing all these requests. Indefinite postponement results because requests for other cylinders are being continually denied.

The alternatives here and in the Exercises show that implementing the SCAN algorithm is a tricky matter. How does the current line 17 preclude indefinite postponement?

```
IF ARM_POSITION<DEST_CYL |
   (ARM_POSITION=DEST_CYL&DIRECTION='DOWN') THEN
```

A process with a destination cylinder equal to the current cylinder will wait on UPSWEEP when the direction is down. When the direction is up, such a process will wait on DOWNSWEEP. Thus, in the original line 17, a process with a destination cylinder equal to the current cylinder waits on the condition variable associated with the opposite of the current arm direction. Such a request does not cause the disk arm to remain at the current cylinder because it does not wait on the condition associated with that direction. The request will not be serviced on the current sweep, but on the next sweep in the opposite direction. Indefinite postponement is precluded in this way.

There is another benefit in the way we organized our solution. All requests waiting for a cylinder before the arm gets to that cylinder will be served on the same sweep. This benefit comes from the priority values. All requests for the same cylinder have the same priority value. When the destination cylinder equals the current cylinder, the priority value associated with the destination cylinder is the smallest priority value in the current arm direction. Thus, the signals in lines 33 and 41 will resume all processes that requested the current cylinder and were waiting before the arm got to that cylinder, before going on to another cylinder in the same direction or changing directions. This improves performance because it reduces waiting time.

In the RELEASE entry, control of the disk is returned and the process to be serviced next is signaled. If there is a waiting request in the current direction, it is signaled (lines 33 and 41). If there is no waiting request in the current direction, the arm direction is changed (lines 29 and 37) and a waiting request in the new direction is signaled (lines 30 and 38). In all cases, the process to be serviced next is the one that has the closest request in the current arm direction.

We have devoted much space to considerations of indefinite postponement. Deadlock is a simpler matter.

Deadlock cannot occur in our solution. Processes are never blocked in their process code. In the monitor code, only a single resource (the disk) is being used; processes can never hold some resource units while requesting others. Finally, processes wait on the correct conditions and specify the correct priority values.

This concludes our discussion of the SCAN disk scheduling algorithm. Priority condition variables were used to advantage for scheduling. We showed that indefinite postponement was prevented in our solution.

BUFFER ALLOCATION FOR LARGE MESSAGES

In this section we discuss an example that builds upon the circular buffer manager of Chapter 4. In that example, a producer wishing to add information to the queue called the monitor entry SPOOL. The buffers were represented by an array, and the information to be added was stored in an array element. A consumer wishing to remove information from the queue of buffers called the monitor entry UNSPOOL.

That example was suitable for the case of low-volume information (e.g., message queues), where the copying of information into and out of the buffers did not seriously degrade process performance. Such a design is not suitable for the transmission of high-volume information (e.g., files of records) because of the large amount of data movement. For the situation of large messages, we can use the circular buffer manager to store the <u>locations</u> of the buffers of information, rather than the actual information. Data movement will be reduced because only locations will be added to or removed from the queue.

We now describe the large message or "pipeline" environment in more detail. There are several pairs of producers and consumers, each producer generating data for its consumer through a queue unique to the pair. Shared among all the producer/consumer pairs is a pool of free buffers. (The shared pool allows more efficient use of buffers.) A producer repeatedly acquires a free buffer (and notes its buffer location), fills the buffer, and adds the buffer location to the queue shared with its consumer. A consumer repeatedly removes a buffer from the queue, empties the buffer, and releases the buffer (by returning its buffer location to the pool of free buffer locations).

A producer and consumer need mutually exclusive access to their common queue, so accesses to the queue will go through a monitor. We can use the CIRCULAR_BUFFER monitor from Chapter 4; each producer/consumer pair will have its own CIRCULAR_BUFFER monitor, with entries SPOOL and UNSPOOL. Producers and consumers must go through a monitor (named BUFFERS) to ACQUIRE and RELEASE buffer locations.

The code for the producer and consumer processes appears below. SPOOL and UNSPOOL are entries of a CIRCULAR_BUFFER monitor local to a producer/consumer pair. ACQUIRE and RELEASE are entries of the BUFFERS monitor common to all processes. The BUFFERS monitor allocates buffer locations from the pool and returns them to the pool.

```
PRODUCER:PROCESS;
   DECLARE(BUFFER_#)FIXED;
   DO WHILE (TRUE);
      CALL ACQUIRE(BUFFER_#);
      Fill buffer BUFFER_#;
      CALL SPOOL(BUFFER_#);
      END;
   END;

CONSUMER:PROCESS;
   DECLARE(BUFFER_#)FIXED;
   DO WHILE(TRUE);
      CALL UNSPOOL(BUFFER_#);
      Empty buffer BUFFER_#;
      CALL RELEASE(BUFFER_#);
      END;
   END;
```

The BUFFERS monitor follows next. It contains the ACQUIRE and RELEASE entries which the PRODUCER and CONSUMER processes, given above, call. The list of buffer locations is kept in an array named POOL. This array is managed as a stack, which uses TOP to point to the next free buffer location. When a producer finds that TOP=0, the free list has been exhausted and the producer must wait (on the condition variable BUFFER_FREE). Note the way in which the buffer pool is initialized.

```
1  BUFFERS:MONITOR;
2        DECLARE(POOL(100))FIXED,
3            (CAPACITY,TOP,I)FIXED,
4            (BUFFER_FREE)CONDITION;

5        DO;
6            CAPACITY=100;
7            TOP=CAPACITY;
8            DO I=1 TO CAPACITY;
9                POOL(I)=I;
10               END;
11           END;

12     ACQUIRE:ENTRY(BUFF_LOC);
13         DECLARE(BUFF_LOC)FIXED;
14         IF TOP=0 THEN
15             WAIT(BUFFER_FREE);
16         BUFF_LOC=POOL(TOP);
17         TOP=TOP-1;
18         END;

19     RELEASE:ENTRY(BUFF_LOC);
20         DECLARE(BUFF_LOC)FIXED;
21         TOP=TOP+1;
22         POOL(TOP)=BUFF_LOC;
23         SIGNAL(BUFFER_FREE);
24         END;

25     END;
```

If the pool of free buffers is empty and several producer/consumer pairs are operating at widely different speeds, the scheduling policy in BUFFERS can degrade the performance of the process pairs. The first-in-first-out policy of CSP/k conditions will allocate alternate buffers to two competing producers; this seems reasonable at first glance. But if two competing consumers are a 2000 line/minute line printer and a 15 line/minute console typewriter, all buffers will eventually be allocated to the pair having the slower consumer (the console). The pair having the faster consumer will be reduced to the speed of the slower pair. (We do not consider pairs in which the consumer is always faster than the producer, because such pairs will only have a small number of buffers allocated to them.)

Under heavy load conditions, the pool of free buffers should be shared among the producer/consumer pairs in a reasonable manner. One scheduling policy that achieves a compromise between fast and slow pairs of processes is to allocate a free buffer location to the producer whose pair currently has the smallest number of buffers allocated to it. This method tries to keep a balanced system of competing pairs, operating as far away from the undesirable situation of too many buffers committed to slow consumers.

This scheduling policy can be implemented using priority condition variables. Two additional items are needed in the BUFFERS monitor: an entry parameter, PAIR, giving the pair number of the requesting process and a tally of the number of the buffers currently allocated to a pair, COUNT(PAIR). COUNT(PAIR) is increased by one in the ACQUIRE entry and is decreased by one in the RELEASE entry. The priority wait appears in lines 14 and 15 as

```
IF TOP=0 THEN
    WAIT(BUFFER_FREE,COUNT(PAIR));
```

The SIGNAL statement in the RELEASE entry will activate the process having the smallest priority value; this allocates a free buffer to the pair currently having the smallest number of buffers allocated to it.

This completes our discussion of the buffer allocator for large messages. This allocator uses the circular buffer monitor of Chapter 4 to transmit large amounts of information; it avoids the overhead of copying by passing locations of data rather than the data itself.

This also concludes our presentation of some larger CSP/k examples. These examples provided a better setting to illustrate CSP/k language features than the simple examples of the previous chapter. Perhaps the best test for a concurrent language comes in the design and implementation of an operating system. This is the subject of the next two chapters.

CHAPTER 5 SUMMARY

In this chapter we stated four problems in concurrent programming and gave solutions to them in CSP/k.

The dining philosophers problem involved the concurrent accessing of a set of common resources. A naive solution of picking up one fork and then the other fork can lead to deadlock. A solution of picking up both forks at once cannot lead to deadlock. Our solution avoided deadlock but did not avoid indefinite postponement. We showed an execution sequence in which a philosopher could be indefinitely overtaken by his neighbors.

The readers and writers problem involved the concurrent reading and writing of a file. Without putting additional restrictions on the simple problem, the indefinite postponement of writers was a possibility. We imposed restrictions that specified the desired order of accessing the file. Deadlock and indefinite postponement were not possible in our solution. The complex scheduling rules followed after a SIGNAL statement were implemented using two condition variables, one for readers and one for writers.

The disk scheduling problem involved the priority ordering of accesses to a movable head disk. Following a discussion of disks and disk scheduling, we developed a SCAN algorithm. We showed how priority conditions were used to service the next closest request in the current arm direction. We also showed that several ways of ordering pending requests lead to indefinite postponement. Our solution avoided indefinite postponement and deadlock, and gives good performance to batches of requests for the same cylinder.

The large message problem involved the transmission of high-volume information without the overhead of data movement. We used a circular buffer manager to store the locations of the buffers of information, rather than the actual information. The locations were acquired from and released to a pool of free buffer locations, controlled by a monitor. When pairs of producers and consumers operate at widely different speeds, our initial solution could produce undesirable performance. We amended the solution by introducing priority waits to achieve reasonable resource allocation.

CHAPTER 5 BIBLIOGRAPHY

Our version of the dining philosophers problem and solution is based on material from Brinch Hansen [1973] and Kaubisch et al. [1976]. The readers and writers problem and the disk arm scheduler come from Hoare [1974]. An early version of the readers and writers problem was given by Courtois et al. [1971]. Material on numerical and simulation studies of disk scheduling can be found in Teorey and Pinkerton [1972]. The large message problem was first studied by Dijkstra [1972]. Further comments on it were made by Brinch Hansen [1973] and Hoare [1974]. Dijkstra's article [1968] remains a good treatment of concurrency issues, although monitors are not used.

Brinch Hansen, P. Operating Systems Principles. Prentice-Hall (1973).

Brinch Hansen, P. Concurrent programming concepts. Computing Surveys 5,4 (December 1973), 223-245.

Courtois, P.J., Heymans, F., and Parnas, D.L. Concurrent control with readers and writers. Comm. ACM 14,10 (October 1971), 667-668.

Dijkstra, E.W. Cooperating sequential processes. In Programming Languages (F. Genuys, editor), Academic Press (1968).

Dijkstra, E.W. Information streams sharing a finite buffer. Information Processing Letters 1,5 (October 1972), 179-180.

Hoare, C.A.R. Monitors: an operating system structuring concept. Comm. ACM 17,10 (October 1974), 549-557.

Kaubisch, W.H., Perrott, R.H., and Hoare, C.A.R. Quasiparallel programming. Software - Practice and Experience, Vol. 6 (1976), 341-356.

Teorey, T.J. and Pinkerton, T.B. A comparative analysis of disk scheduling policies. Comm. ACM 15,3 (March 1972), 177-184.

CHAPTER 5 EXERCISES

1. Implement and run all examples given in this chapter in CSP/k. Insert output statements at appropriate places in the examples to show the progress of the processes and the states of the resources.

Questions 2-6 refer to the dining philosophers problem.

2. Discuss the effects of changing the PUTDOWN entry to have the following form: increase left count, if left philosopher has two forks then signal him, increase right count, if right philosopher has two forks then signal him.

3. Discuss the following proposed solution: a hungry philosopher first attempts to pick up his left fork through an entry call; he then attempts to pick up his right fork through another entry call; holding both forks, he begins eating.

4. Discuss the following proposed solution: a hungry philosopher first attempts to pick up his left fork through an entry call; he then attempts to pick up his right fork through another entry call; if the right fork is available, he picks it up and begins eating; otherwise, he puts down his left fork and repeats his cycle.

5. Discuss the following proposed solution: all philosophers are initially thinking; each philosopher waits until both his neighbors are thinking; he then stops thinking, picks up both his forks, and starts eating; when finished eating, he puts down the forks and starts thinking.

6. Discuss the following proposed solution:

```
IF right fork is taken THEN
    DO;
        WAIT for right fork;
        IF left fork is taken THEN
            WAIT for left fork;
        END;
ELSE
    DO;
        IF left fork is taken THEN
            WAIT for left fork;
        IF right fork is taken THEN
            WAIT for right fork;
        END;
```

7. Develop a solution to the dining philosophers problem which precludes indefinite postponement.

Questions 8-9 refer to the readers and writers problem.

8. Discuss the solution proposed by Kaubisch et al. [1976]. In particular, compare their STARTREAD entry with our STARTREAD entry and their use of a counting variable for the number of writers with our use of a Boolean variable.

9. Courtois et al. [1971] considered two variants of the simple readers and writers problem. These variants differed from our version in the restrictions they imposed on the order of accessing the file.

   a) No reader should be kept waiting unless a writer has already obtained permission to use the file. That is, no reader should wait simply because a writer is waiting for other readers to finish.

   b) Once a writer is ready to write, it performs its write as soon as possible. That is, no writer should wait simply because there is a stream of reader requests waiting after an active writer.

Why is a solution to problem b) not a solution to problem a)? Show that it is possible for a writer to be indefinitely postponed in problem a). Show that it is possible for a reader to be indefinitely postponed in problem b). Develop solutions to these variants in CSP/k and compare them to the solution given in this chapter.

Questions 10-14 refer to the disk arm scheduling problem.

10. Show that the following alternative to line 18 in the SCAN monitor allows indefinite postponement.

```
IF ARM_POSITION<=DEST_CYL THEN
```

11. Show that the following alternative to line 18 in the SCAN monitor allows indefinite postponement.

```
IF ARM_POSITION<DEST_CYL |
   (ARM_POSITION=DEST_CYL&DIRECTION='UP') THEN
```

12. Implement the FIFO disk scheduling algorithm in CSP/k and test it using a sequence of disk requests.

13. Implement the SSTF disk scheduling algorithm in CSP/k and test it using a sequence of disk requests.

14. A disk can be simulated by a process that executes the following statements.

```
DO forever;
   CALL get_cyl_to_seek(dest_cyl);
   IF dest_cyl>current_cyl THEN
      distance=dest_cyl-current_cyl;
   ELSE
      distance=current_cyl-dest_cyl;
   BUSY(distance);
   END;
```

Compare the average waiting time for disk I/O using the SCAN, SSTF, and FIFO algorithms. Note: the simulation (BUSY) feature of CSP/k provides utilization statistics automatically.

Questions 15-16 refer to the buffer allocator for large messages.

15. In the large message problem, what steps can be taken to overcome the difficulties caused by a consumer stopping altogether.

16. Discuss methods different from that in the text for achieving reasonable resource allocation in a heavy-load condition.

Questions 17-19 are new problems.

17. Develop a simulation of the sleeping barber problem [Dijkstra 1968] in CSP/k: There is a barbershop with two rooms, one with the barber's chair, the other a waiting room. Customers enter from the outside into the waiting room one at a time; from the waiting room, they can proceed into the barber's room. The entrances to the two rooms are side-by-side and share a sliding door (which always closes one of them). When the barber finishes, the customer leaves by a separate exit and the barber inspects the waiting room by opening the door to it. If the

waiting room is not empty, he invites the next customer in; otherwise, he goes to sleep in one of the waiting room chairs. When an entering customer finds a sleeping barber, he wakes up the barber; otherwise, he waits his turn.

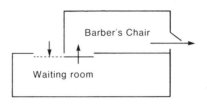

18. Develop a solution to the alarm clock problem in CSP/k and discuss its overhead: A program wishes to delay itself a specified number of time units, or "clock ticks". Assume that a hardware clock can update a simulated software clock which is available for program inspection. The hardware clock can be simulated by a process that executes the following:

```
DO forever;
   CALL tick;
   BUSY(1);
   END;
```

19. Develop a solution to the four-of-a-kind problem in CSP/k: There is a deck of twenty-four cards, split into six different kinds, four cards of each kind. There are four players; each player can hold four cards. Between each pair of players there is a (possibly empty) pile of cards. Each player behaves according to the following program.

```
DO WHILE((hand does not contain four of a kind)&
         (no one has won));
   Discard a card into the left-hand pile;
   Pick up a card from the right-hand pile;
   END;
IF hand contains four of a kind THEN claim victory;
```

There are no ties; when a player has claimed victory, all other players stop. The game begins by dealing four cards to each player and putting two cards on the pile between each pair of players.

CHAPTER 6

DESIGN OF AN OPERATING SYSTEM:

INPUT AND OUTPUT SPOOLERS

Many of the issues involved in the handling of concurrent processes first arose in the design of operating systems. The concept of a process appears naturally at several levels in such a system: the asynchronous hardware processes, the software processes that impose discipline on them, and the user processes (jobs). The design of an operating system is thus a logical extension of the simpler examples in the previous chapter, providing a convincing demonstration of the structuring and expressive abilities of the programming language.

In this chapter and the one that follows, we present the design of a multiprogramming, virtual memory, spooling, batch operating system. The design will be expressed in the CSP/k language. The operating system will manage the Z7 machine, a simulated computer consisting of a card reader, a line printer, a drum, a console and a CPU, all of which are represented as CSP/k processes. The design and implementation of this system has been used for a number of years as the major project in an operating systems course at the University of Toronto. The project is nicely situated on the continuum from real to toy: real in the sense that many important operating systems concepts are explored at a concrete level; toy in the sense that this is accomplished without a huge investment in programming time and without concern for the irrelevant details that absorb the energies of those writing production operating systems.

After discussing the operating system in general terms, this chapter describes the hardware devices and the monitors that interface with them, and specifies the design of the input and output spoolers, which read and print user jobs. In Chapter 7, we introduce the CPU and specify the design of the executive, which manages the actual execution of user jobs.

AN OVERVIEW OF THE OPERATING SYSTEM

The hardware of our simulated computer system consists of a CPU, user memory, control memory for the operating system, a card reader, a line printer, a drum, and a console.

Through microprogramming, the CPU supports two different languages, a user language and a system language. The latter (conveniently) is the CSP/k language; WAIT and SIGNAL are thus system primitives. The CPU provides user jobs with dynamic address translation. The Z7 machine comes with a small amount of support software: each input/output device is equipped with a very simple synchronous monitor interface.

This chapter and the next present a general design for an operating system for this machine. You may wish to implement the system in CSP/k. The operating system includes the following facilities:

Spooling: The system reads user jobs and their associated data, and places this information on the drum. In this way, the CPU seldom has to wait for the relatively slow card reader; instead, necessary information is available on the considerably faster drum. In a similar manner, the system stores each job's output on the drum, sending it to the relatively slow line printer when that device is free.

Multiple buffering: Whenever information is to be transferred between two devices, more than one buffer is used. This technique compensates for variations in the speed of the devices, allowing each to proceed more or less independently of the other.

Multiprogramming: Although there is only a single CPU, more than one user job can be available for execution in user memory. Multiprogramming improves utilization of the CPU, since while one user job is blocked awaiting service from an input/output device, another can be executing.

Virtual memory: The dynamic address translation facility is used to allow each user job to execute in a virtual address space and to improve memory utilization. (This will be discussed in more detail in Chapter 7.)

CSP/k programs have been written to simulate each of the hardware components we have described. The CPU is simulated by an interpreter for the user language (a simple machine language, avoiding the expense of a compiler). The hardware devices access user memory, simulated by an array of numeric values. Control memory is not explicitly represented; it consists of the variables used by operating system programs but not by the simulated hardware devices. The following figure illustrates the interconnections of the Z7 hardware devices.

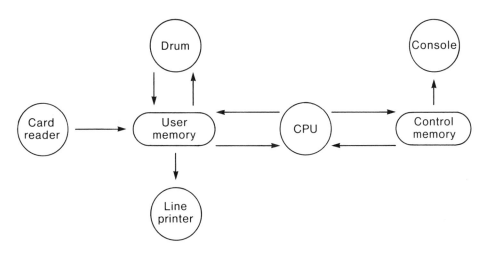

The Z7 machine

All of this is not to imply that we are dealing in pure fiction. The machine that we have described could readily be implemented. A small kernel supporting processes and the WAIT and SIGNAL primitives could be constructed in software on a suitable CPU. Interface routines for the input/output devices could be written and a compiler constructed, resulting in a virtual machine identical to the one that we have described. In Chapter 8 we discuss the implementation of such a kernel.

THE HARDWARE

The operating system divides naturally into three major components: an <u>input</u> <u>spooler</u> (which reads user jobs and places them on the drum), an <u>executive</u>, which manages the actual execution of user jobs, and an <u>output</u> <u>spooler</u> (which takes jobs that have been executed from the drum and prints them).

These three components can be designed independently of one another once their interfaces are specified. We will take advantage of this good fortune by postponing consideration of the executive for the time being. This approach has a number of attractive properties. The input spooler and output spooler, once designed and implemented, can be tested independently of the executive. Additionally, the details of the user language and of CPU interfacing and internals can be ignored for the present. But before we can design the input and output spoolers we must describe memory and the input/output devices.

CSP/k programs that simulate each of the input/output devices appear in Appendix 6. The paragraphs that follow are intended to specify their interfaces in an informal way.

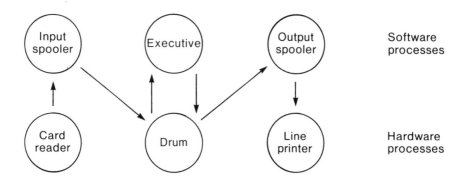

Structure of the operating system

THE USER MEMORY

User memory is simulated by the numeric array MEMORY of MEMORY_SIZE words. The distinction between user and control memory is not an obvious one. The CPU and all input/output devices (except the console) deal with user memory addresses, and any information that is referenced directly by these devices must reside there. In addition to active user jobs and their data, this information typically includes input and output spooling buffers and the various tables used by the dynamic address translation unit.

Since CSP/k does not allow characters to be stored in numeric variables, user memory may not contain characters. Thus the Z7 I/O devices can neither write characters to, nor read characters from, user memory. Control memory locations are used instead. In the world of hardware, idiosyncracies are the rule rather than the exception, and we follow the normal course by providing clean software interfaces for each device.

MANAGING THE CARD READER

To simplify the management of the hardware card reader, a synchronous interface monitor, called DO_READER_IO, is provided. By synchronous, we mean that the monitor runs in lock-step with the I/O device, and will not allow a process that has called it to continue until the I/O has been performed. A separate interface monitor is provided for each I/O device.

The input stream of user jobs will consist of control cards (which begin with character strings) and numeric programs with their input data. Each call to DO_READER_IO causes the card reader to operate until either its buffer is full or a control card is encountered, at which point the monitor will return. The interface is called as follows:

```
CALL DO_READER_IO(BUFFER_ADDR,BUFFER_LENGTH,
    REMAINING_LENGTH,TEXT);
```

where the meanings of the parameters are:

BUFFER_ADDR: The user memory address of the start of the buffer.
BUFFER_LENGTH: The number of words in the buffer.
REMAINING_LENGTH: A numeric parameter that will be set to the number of buffer words left unfilled.
TEXT: A character parameter (maximum length 80) that will be used should a control card be encountered.

If a control card is encountered, the value of REMAINING_LENGTH will be non-zero. The character string that begins the control card will have been placed in TEXT, and can be used to identify the control card. Note that any numeric information on the control card will not have been read, but will be read by the next call to DO_READER_IO. (Control card formats will be described subsequently.)

MANAGING THE LINE PRINTER

The monitor that interfaces with the line printer has two entries, one to print textual information (such as job headings and accounting information) and one to print numeric information. The former prints data that resides in control memory; the latter deals with user memory buffers. The entries are called as follows:

```
CALL DO_TEXT_PRINTER_IO(TEXT);
```

where TEXT is a character string (maximum length 120); and

```
CALL DO_NUMERIC_PRINTER_IO(BUFFER_ADDR,BUFFER_LENGTH);
```

where the meanings of the parameters are:

BUFFER_ADDR: The user memory address of the start of the buffer to be printed.
BUFFER_LENGTH: The number of words in that buffer.

When the text printer interface monitor is called, the line printer first skips to a new line, then prints the string, and finally skips to another new line. When the numeric printer interface monitor is called, it prints the words in the buffer, ten per line, beginning at the current carriage position.

In some instances (e.g., accounting information) it may be desirable to print numeric information along with text. If so, the number must be converted to a character string.

MANAGING THE DRUM

The drum is organized as DRUM_PAGES pages of PAGE_SIZE words each. An entire drum page is read or written each time the interface monitor is called:

        CALL DO_DRUM_IO(OP_TYPE,DRUM_PAGE,MEMORY_ADDR);

where the meanings of the parameters are:

    OP_TYPE: Indicates whether the desired operation is a write to drum (0) or a read from drum (1).
    DRUM_PAGE: The number of the drum page (0 to DRUM_PAGES-1) involved in the transfer.
    MEMORY_ADDR: The user memory address of the start of the page involved in the transfer.

MANAGING THE CONSOLE

The console should be used by the various operating system processes to report on the status of user jobs. It is called as follows:

        CALL DO_CONSOLE_IO(TEXT);

where TEXT is a character string (maximum length 120).

Since the console is logically separate from the line printer, it does not affect the carriage position used by the numeric printer interface monitor.

THE INPUT AND OUTPUT SPOOLERS

A user job in the system can be regarded as a process. Each user job has a job descriptor, which contains its various attributes. The job descriptor could be a single entity, or it could (and will, in our design) be distributed. We will refer to the set of job descriptors as the job table, and will view the job table as a matrix with one row corresponding to each user job currently in the system and one column corresponding to each attribute.

The input spooler's task is to prepare user jobs for the executive. When a new user job is encountered, a job descriptor must be obtained. The job's object code and data must be placed on the drum, and their locations must be entered in the job's descriptor (along with other information which we will discuss shortly). The executive must then be informed that the job is ready for execution.

It is natural to control the allocation of job descriptors by means of a monitor. There must be some limit to the size of the job table, and it is by no means assured that a descriptor will be available when the input spooler encounters a new user job. Allocating job descriptors by means of a monitor ensures that operation of the input spooler will be suspended should such a shortage occur.

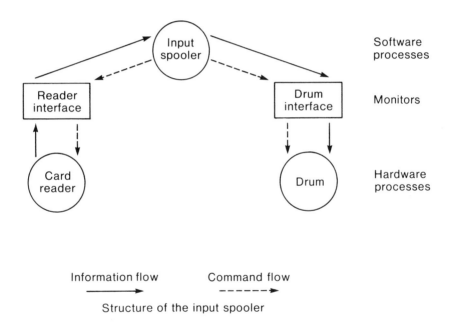

Structure of the input spooler

The input spooler is basically simple. It first calls the card reader interface and writes any input to drum. If a control card is encountered, the spooler makes any necessary additions to the job table. Finally, it calls the card reader interface once again.

USER JOB INPUT FORMAT

The user language consists of a sequence of numbers that
represent a machine language program. Each instruction is one to
three words long. Valid operation codes are in the range 0 to
15. The user language is a stack language, and the maximum size
of the stack must be provided with each job. To simplify the
operating system design we assume that the input is free of
errors. Each user job has the following format:

    #JOB
        .
        .   object code
        .
    #DATA   (used only if data follows)
        .
        .   data (optional)
        .

The job card will contain #JOB in columns 1-4, followed by a job
name and four numeric parameters:

    - A limit on CPU instructions to be executed.
    - A limit on output operations.
    - An external priority, from 0 (lowest) to 4 (highest).
    - A limit on stack size.

The end of the entire input batch of user jobs will be signified
by a #END card. (See Appendix 8 for example user jobs.)

DESIGN OF THE INPUT SPOOLER

We will use a buffer of PAGE_SIZE words for the card reader.
(This is the unit of drum transfer.) The diagram on the
following page gives the state transitions for the input spooler;
it describes the action that should be taken upon encountering
each type of input, depending upon the input previously read.

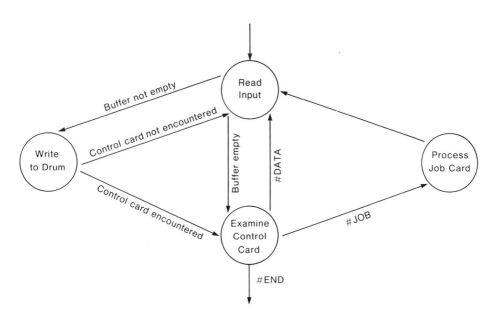

State transition diagram for the input spooler

The following actions should be taken upon entering each state:

Read Input: Call DO_READER_IO. Examine REMAINING_LENGTH. If it does not equal PAGE_SIZE, then input was placed in the buffer and must be written to drum. If it equals PAGE_SIZE, a control card was the first item encountered and the buffer is empty.

Write to Drum: Obtain a drum page. Call DO_DRUM_IO with the contents of the buffer. Re-examine REMAINING_LENGTH. If it is zero, the card reader can be started once again. Otherwise, a control card was encountered and must be processed.

Examine Control Card: A control card was encountered. Examine TEXT to determine its nature and take the appropriate exit.

Process Job Card: A job card was encountered (TEXT was set to '#JOB', plus the name of the job). Obtain an unassigned job descriptor. Call DO_READER_IO to obtain the parameters from the job card (4 values). Enter this information into the descriptor.

The input spooler and drum have a producer/consumer relationship. The card reader produces card images which, after a slight transformation, are consumed by the drum. It would be inefficient to run the two hardware devices in lock-step, because one device would often be required to be idle, waiting for the other. It is necessary to provide some elasticity between the card reader and the drum, and we must do so without sacrificing the simplicity of our device interfaces.

Our solution is to split the input spooler into two processes, one to communicate with the card reader and one to communicate with the drum. These processes will synchronize with one another by means of a set of user memory buffers managed by a buffer monitor similar to the one described in the previous chapter. We will discuss this more fully in the next chapter.

INPUT SPOOLER DETAILS

We will use two processes, the reader manager and the input drum manager. They communicate with each other through a monitor called the input buffer manager. It has four entry points, since the reader manager and the input drum manager each require entries for requesting and releasing buffers. We will continue to assume that buffers are of PAGE_SIZE words.

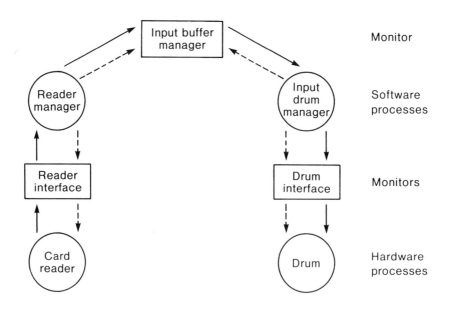

Expanded structure of the input spooler

The input drum manager is passed two pieces of information with each buffer: the type of data contained in the buffer, and the number of words left unfilled. The type of data in the buffer will be one of the following:

- The start of a new user job. The buffer will contain the four numeric parameters from the job card.
- Object code. The buffer may or may not be full.
- Data. The buffer may or may not be full.
- End of batch. The buffer will be empty.

We distinguish between object code and data because they are stored as separate files on the drum. Each file consists of a linked list of drum pages. For each list, the job descriptor can contain the location of the first page, a page count, and the number of items in the last page. Control memory can contain an array with one entry corresponding to each drum page, in which the linked lists are maintained. The logic of the input drum manager follows:

```
/* Code skeleton for the input drum manager */
DO until end-of-batch;
    Obtain a buffer from the reader manager;
    IF it marks the end of a user job THEN
        Terminate the linked list of drum pages for that job
            (either object code or data, whichever is current)
            and indicate that the job is ready to run;
    IF it marks the start of a user job THEN
        Request a job descriptor and enter the job card
            parameters;
    IF it contains object code THEN
        Call DO_DRUM_IO, either beginning or updating
            the linked list of drum pages;
    IF it contains data THEN
        IF it is the first data buffer for this user THEN
            Terminate the linked list of object code drum
                pages and call DO_DRUM_IO, beginning the
                linked list of data;
        ELSE
            Call DO_DRUM_IO and update the linked list;
    IF it marks the end of the input job stream THEN
        Set the end-of-batch flag;
    Release the buffer;
    END;
```

We have not specified how to allocate drum pages; a simple monitor must be constructed for this purpose. In designing the executive it will become obvious that deadlock considerations affect drum page allocation. It may prove wise to pre-allocate pages for output (a maximum claim system for deadlock avoidance). Operation of the input spooler may sometimes have to be suspended because of a shortage of drum pages. (This will be handled as a matter of course by the monitor responsible for drum page allocation.)

The reader manager is responsible for preparing buffers in the manner specified by the design of the input drum manager. Its design is nicely reflected by the previous state transition diagram. When reading input, a buffer must be obtained prior to calling DO_READER_IO. When writing to drum, the call to DO_DRUM_IO is equivalent to releasing the buffer with a length and type specification. When processing the job card, another buffer must be obtained to hold the job card parameters. Finally, the reading of a #END card must be signaled by releasing an empty buffer with the end-of-batch type indicated.

This completes the design of one component of the operating system, the input spooler. The next section describes an analogous component, the output spooler.

THE OUTPUT SPOOLER

The output spooler prints each job's object code and output, along with job statistics obtained from the job descriptor. Like the input spooler, the output spooler is split into two processes to provide elasticity between drum and line printer.

The output drum manager, like its counterpart in the input spooler, will view the drum as a dedicated virtual device (virtual in the sense that the transfer may not take place immediately and the process may be blocked for an arbitrary period of time). DO_DRUM_IO, the simple monitor entry that interfaces with the drum hardware, now has two request streams to choose from; when the executive is added, there will be three. DO_DRUM_IO is free to schedule the various requests as it sees fit. A basic first-in-first-out interface is provided, but you might consider modifying it to give priority to certain sources of requests. Any such modification would be transparent to the processes using the drum, although they might find themselves blocked for longer or shorter periods of time. The concept of virtual I/O devices allows us to achieve simplicity and clarity at no expense in efficiency.

The other component of the output spooler, the printer manager, will contain most of the intelligence. The output drum manager is simply handed a list of drum pages to read, and the amount of control information that must accompany each buffer is minimized. Because the output spooler resembles the input spooler so closely, the creation of a code skeleton is left as an exercise.

CHAPTER 6 SUMMARY

In this chapter we have described the simulated hardware devices of the Z7 computer, and have given the structure of two of the main components of our operating system for this machine:

the input spooler and the output spooler. In the next chapter we will describe the virtual memory hardware of the Z7 and will design the third major component of the operating system, the executive. We will also describe the interfaces between the executive and the two spoolers.

A number of interesting concurrent programming issues have been raised in this chapter. Foremost among these is the hierarchy of processes that arises in the design of the input spooler: two levels of processes (the reader manager and the input drum manager at one level, the card reader and the drum at another) synchronizing by means of two levels of monitors (the input buffer manager at one level, the reader and drum interface monitors at another.)

Also, note the manner in which the drum, a shared device, is viewed as a dedicated virtual device by each process that uses it. This approach achieves simplicity and clarity at no expense in efficiency, and allows the drum scheduling policy to be altered without affecting the processes that use the device. We shall have more to say about this topic in the next chapter.

Should you choose to implement the operating system in CSP/k, the input and output spoolers described in this chapter can be completed and tested independently of the material to be presented in the next chapter.

CHAPTER 6 EXERCISES

1. Write a code skeleton for the output spooler. You may find the input spooler code skeleton in this chapter useful as a model.

2. Implement both the input spooler and the output spooler in CSP/k. Appendix 9 contains an extremely simple operating system for the Z7; you may find it useful as a guide to the use of the I/O devices.

3. Using the programs from Appendix 6, test your input and output spoolers on the example user jobs from Appendix 8. Use a dummy job processor (executive) that does not invoke the CPU.

4. Describe in detail the possible sources of drum deadlock in the operating system. What are the disadvantages to the maximum claim scheme for deadlock avoidance? What are some possible alternative approaches, and their relative advantages and disadvantages?

5. The input spooler was split into two processes in order to provide elasticity between the card reader and the drum. This split was made at an arbitrary point. Propose another functional split, and write a code skeleton for it.

6. Some batch processing systems do not use spooling. Under what circumstances would spooling not be worthwhile?

CHAPTER 7

DESIGN OF AN OPERATING SYSTEM:

THE EXECUTIVE

In this chapter we continue the design of our operating system for the Z7 computer. In the previous chapter, the hardware devices of the Z7 were introduced, and the design of the input and output spoolers was presented. Here, we will discuss the design of the executive, which is responsible for managing the execution of user jobs by the CPU.

First, we will design long term and short term schedulers for the system. The former is responsible for deciding which user job will next be allowed to execute; the latter is responsible for the allocation of the CPU. Each of these schedulers will be implemented by means of a monitor; the ease with which this can be done will demonstrate that monitors are a natural and flexible mechanism for controlling the process interactions that arise in an operating system.

We will describe the Z7 CPU, along with its virtual memory hardware. The architecture is typical of many commercially available virtual memory systems, and in mastering it you will attain a working knowledge of this important concept. Finally, we will fill in the details of the design of the executive.

AN OVERVIEW OF THE EXECUTIVE

In Chapter 1, we described the states that a user job passes through in being handled by an operating system. In this section we will precisely identify these states for the Z7 operating system. The first two have already been discussed:

(1) In the input spooler
(2) Awaiting execution (input spooling complete)

At any one time there may be several jobs awaiting execution. From these, the executive must select a small number that it will consider to be

(3) Active

or eligible to compete for the CPU and executive services. The choice of active jobs is not an arbitrary one; a large number of criteria may be taken into account. The selection function is referred to as <u>long term scheduling</u>.

The final two states that a user job may assume have already been identified. They are:

(4) Execution complete (awaiting output spooling)
(5) In the output spooler

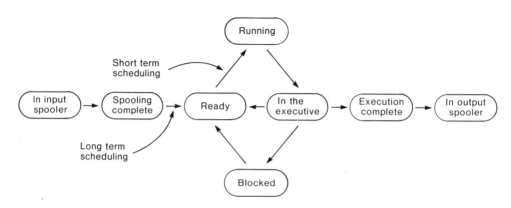

The states of a user job

We must refine the notion of active, for there are a number of distinguishable sub-states. It is possible, of course, that an active job is actually using the CPU. In this case it is referred to as

(3.1) Running

A running job may require the services of the executive from time to time, and will indicate this by relinquishing the CPU with a return code known as a <u>trap</u>. Traps come in two flavors. The first, which we call a <u>minor trap</u>, requires minimal intervention by the executive. An example would be a request to perform an input/output operation. Since (as we shall see) the executive buffers input/output operations for user jobs, actual I/O is performed infrequently and the user job is immediately ready to proceed. While the executive is actively serving a user, that job is said to be

(3.2) In the executive

When the service is complete the job becomes

(3.3) Ready to run

The second type of trap, called a <u>major</u> <u>trap</u>, requires more substantial intervention. The best example is a page fault. Thus far we have avoided discussing the virtual memory and paging aspects of the system. For the time being, suffice it to say that in such an environment a job may be active without being entirely resident in user memory. When a job references a non-resident portion of its address space a <u>page</u> <u>fault</u> occurs, and the page containing that address must be retrieved from drum. Until this transfer is complete the user job is unable to proceed and is referred to as

(3.4) Blocked

When the transfer is complete, the job becomes ready to run.

All user jobs that are ready to run (state 3.3) are eligible to enter state 3.1 (running). The selection of a particular job is referred to as <u>short</u> <u>term</u> <u>scheduling</u> and, just as long term scheduling, is far from arbitrary.

THE EXECUTIVE AS A SET OF ENVELOPE PROCESSES

When a user job is active, it will undergo state transitions frequently. We could design a monolithic executive that would explicitly keep track of the state transitions of each user job. A far more reasonable approach, though, is to design the executive as a process itself. More properly, the executive will be a set of identical processes, one of which will completely encapsulate each active user job. Because of this encapsulation, these processes are referred to as <u>envelopes</u>. The mechanics of state switching will be performed implicitly by the CSP/k kernel of the system, rather than explicitly by the executive, and the state of a user job will be indicated by the state of its envelope process.

Each envelope process will interface with three principal monitors: the long term scheduler entry GET_JOB, which furnishes a job to activate; the short term scheduler entry REQUEST_TO_RUN, which allows the envelope process to place its user job in the running state; and the terminator, which takes the job from the envelope process once the job has finished executing. A second entry to the short term scheduler, DONE_RUNNING, allows the envelope process to inform the short term scheduler that the user job is no longer in the running state. Here is a high-level view of an envelope process:

```
/* Code skeleton for an envelope process */
DO forever;
   Call GET_JOB to obtain a user job;
   Perform some initialization;
   DO until the job completes execution;
      Call REQUEST_TO_RUN;
      DO until a major trap occurs;
         Hand job to CPU to execute until a trap occurs;
         IF the trap is minor THEN
            Service the trap;
         END;
      Call DONE_RUNNING;
      Service the major trap;
      END;
   Call TERMINATOR to transfer job to output spooler;
   END;
```

The next two sections will discuss long term and short term scheduling, in other words, the details of GET_JOB and REQUEST_TO_RUN.

LONG TERM SCHEDULING

The long term scheduler must determine which and how many (up to some predetermined maximum) user jobs should be active at any particular time. It considers at least these four criteria:

Throughput: Throughput is typically measured in jobs completed per unit time. The obvious way to enhance throughput is to activate first the jobs that are the shortest and smallest.

Thrashing: In a virtual memory system, the length of time that an individual job will run before page faulting is determined by the amount of user memory available to it. If page faults occur too frequently, system performance will be degraded, because the CPU will often be forced to wait for drum transfers. This condition is known as thrashing. It is good practice in a paging system to monitor the level of drum activity, and to ensure that each user job has enough memory to enable it to run efficiently.

User-specified priorities: Presumably the user who bribes the system by paying for higher priority should receive better service.

Indefinite postponement: The previous three criteria indicate that we should bias our long term scheduling in favor of short, small, high priority jobs. This means that a job possessing none of these characteristics might be discriminated against so heavily that it would never become active. The problem of indefinite postponement is a common one; it can occur, among other places, in the problem of the dining philosophers.

The elegance of envelope processes is especially striking with regard to long term scheduling, for the multiprogramming level (the number of active jobs) is so easily regulated. Whenever an envelope process finishes with a user job, it calls the long term scheduler. Should system resources be over-committed at the moment, GET_JOB can simply block the envelope process until the congestion is relieved.

We leave the design of an intelligent long term scheduler as an exercise. The basic framework involves the entry GET_JOB, described above, and the entry INSPOOLING_COMPLETE. This last entry is called by the input drum manager when the final page of a user job has been written to drum. The index of the job's descriptor is passed as a parameter. INSPOOLING_COMPLETE places the job on a queue from which it will be taken by GET_JOB.

When an envelope process requests a job, GET_JOB may use whatever criteria it likes in deciding whether a job should be activated, and if so, which one. In a simple implementation, the multiprogramming level can be fixed by defining a specific number of envelope processes, and jobs can be activated in first-in-first-out order.

SHORT TERM SCHEDULING

The CSP/k kernel of our operating system shares the CPU among the various processes of the operating system. Although it chooses more or less arbitrarily among the processes that are ready to run (i.e., those that are not blocked by a WAIT), any scheduling discipline could be employed. Also, the kernel could easily control a multiple-CPU environment.

The assignment of the CPU to user jobs is logically a separate function. When an envelope process is ready to run its user job, it informs the short term scheduler by calling the entry REQUEST_TO_RUN. The short term scheduler may choose to block the envelope process, in which case the kernel will allocate the CPU to another operating system process, possibly another envelope.

The short term scheduler has two mechanisms that it can use to control the progress of user jobs. The first is deciding which job to run. The second is restricting the time interval for which a user job can control the CPU. This time interval is called a quantum or slice. Its value is computed by the short term scheduler, passed to the envelope process by means of a parameter, and then passed on to the CPU when the user job starts running. If the quantum expires, a major trap is returned, and the envelope will call DONE_RUNNING. The call to REQUEST_TO_RUN is:

CALL REQUEST_TO_RUN(IDENTIFIER,QUANTUM);

We will leave the design of an intelligent short term scheduler as an exercise. For now, the quantum can be considered a constant and user jobs can be run in first-in-first-out order. The design of the short term scheduler is independent of the scheduling and quantum selection mechanisms that are employed. The number of envelope processes provides an upper bound on the level of multiprogramming. When an envelope process calls REQUEST_TO_RUN, its identity, as indicated by the index it passes as a parameter, is placed on an internal queue. We define an array of condition variables of a size equal to the number of envelope processes. REQUEST_TO_RUN causes the envelope process to issue a WAIT on the condition variable corresponding to it.

When an envelope process calls DONE_RUNNING, control of the CPU can be given to another envelope. The short term scheduler scans the queue, selecting an envelope from those available. The quantum is calculated, the envelope's identifier is removed from the queue, and a SIGNAL is issued on the corresponding condition variable. If no envelope processes are waiting, the CPU is left idle.

The rest of the executive design must be deferred until we have discussed the details of the CPU.

THE CPU

The Z7 CPU includes a dynamic address translation facility. Each user job references a simple virtual address space. These references are translated by hardware into physical memory references, based on address mapping tables maintained by the envelope processes.

Each job's virtual address space consists of two variable-length segments. At the highest level, a virtual address reference by a job consists of two parts, a segment number and an offset within that segment. In the Z7 CPU the segment number is implicit: all program references (e.g., instruction fetches and branches) are to segment zero (the program segment) and all data references (e.g., variables and stack references) are to segment one (the data segment). The program segment is provided with execute-only protection, facilitating the sharing of programs. The data segment allows both read and write access.

Each segment is further subdivided into a number of pages, which are fixed-length, contiguous blocks of words. As a result, addresses consist of two components, a page number and an offset within that page. A complete virtual address, then, consists of four components: a job number (to identify the virtual address space), an implicit segment number, a page number, and an offset within the page.

The physical memory of the Z7 system is simulated by the array MEMORY of MEMORY_SIZE words. It is subdivided into page frames of PAGE_SIZE words each; words 0 through PAGE_SIZE-1 comprise page frame 0, and so on. These page frames correspond in size to the pages in each user's virtual address space. As we have mentioned previously, a user program that is running will have some (but not necessarily all) of its pages occupying these page frames.

The translation of a virtual address into a physical address involves several steps: identifying the virtual address space, finding the correct page table, locating the correct page frame, and referencing the desired word. Failure of this translation process is called a page fault, and the envelope process must take appropriate action.

The Z7 hardware makes provision for ACTIVE_JOBS number of active address spaces. These active address spaces are numbered 0 through ACTIVE_JOBS-1, and the address space number of the currently running job is passed as a parameter to the CPU.

FINDING THE CORRECT PAGE TABLE

Corresponding to each segment is a page table that maps virtual pages to page frames. Each job's segment table contains entries pointing to its two page tables. The segment table format is:

    word 0: user memory address of the page table for segment 0
    word 1: length of that page table, in words
    word 2: user memory address of the page table for segment 1
    word 3: length of that page table, in words

The segment tables for all active address spaces are concatenated into a contiguous area of user memory, the starting address of which must be placed into the register SEGMENT_TABLE_ADDR. Given a job number and (implicitly) a segment number, the dynamic address translator can locate the correct page table.

The length of each segment must be a multiple of PAGE_SIZE words. If a page table extends over several page frames, these page frames must be contiguous in user memory.

Although it is not necessary that page tables be resident in user memory at all times, the design of the system is simplified considerably if they are.

LOCATING THE CORRECT PAGE FRAME AND WORD

The next step in the address translation process is to find the user memory address of the page that has been referenced. The correct page table is indexed, using as an offset the page number computed from the virtual address. (Should this result in an offset beyond the end of the page table, a trap is returned.) The page table entry contains either the user memory address of the page frame in which the page is located or an invalid address (such as a negative number) indicating that the page resides on the drum. It is the job of the envelope processes to maintain the page tables to the satisfaction of the hardware.

If there is a valid address, the translation process proceeds to the next step. Otherwise a <u>page fault handler</u> (part of the envelope process) must read the page into user memory, possibly displacing another page, and update the status of the page in various tables. The envelope processes must maintain whatever tables are necessary to handle drum I/O for paging.

The correct user memory location (the appropriate offset from the beginning of the page frame) is now referenced. The CPU will, as a side effect, update the <u>core status table</u> entry corresponding to the page frame. The core status table, which like the segment table and each page table must reside in contiguous user memory, is for the use of the envelope processes in servicing page faults. It contains a one-word entry corresponding to each user memory page frame. Whenever a page frame is explicitly referenced, bit 0 (the rightmost bit) of its core status table entry is set to 1. Whenever a page frame is altered, bit 1 is also set to 1. The starting user memory address of the core status table must be placed in the register CORE_STATUS_ADDR.

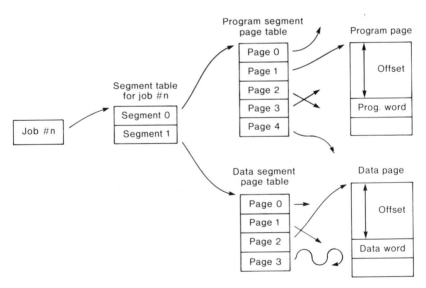

Address mapping by the Z7 CPU

Although there are a few details yet to come, the concept of dynamic address translation should be clear. There is a register containing the address space number of the currently running job. This number is used to locate the correct segment table, which contains a pointer to the page table of each segment in the job's address space. The segment table is indexed by the implicit segment number component of the virtual address, and the correct page table is thereby located. This page table, which is indexed by the page number component of the virtual address, contains an entry corresponding to each page in the segment. The entry indicates whether the page is in user memory (and if so, where) or on secondary storage. If the former, a physical memory reference is made. If the latter, the hardware returns a trap.

DETAILS OF THE CPU

The identification of the address space and the location of the correct page tables are performed only once each time a user job enters the running state, and the results are saved in registers. Additionally, the dynamic address translator has a simulated associative array, which speeds up the rest of the address translation process considerably. There are three entries in this array, containing the virtual address / physical address pair of the most recently referenced pages. If the page being referenced is contained in the associative array, the page table indexing step of the address translation process can be bypassed. The associative array is automatically cleared each time a different user job is run.

Once REQUEST_TO_RUN has allowed an envelope process to proceed, the CPU is turned over to the user job as follows:

    TRAP = CPU (ADDRESS_SPACE_NUMBER,INSTRUCTION_ADDR,TRAP_ADDR,
        IO_ADDR,STACK_MAX,STACK_PTR,OP_CODE,TIMER);

In a sense, the parameters are the state variables of a user job. Some of the parameters (ADDRESS_SPACE_NUMBER, IO_ADDR, STACK_MAX and STACK_PTR) will never be examined by the executive; they will simply be initialized for each user job (or set upon request) and passed to the CPU each time it is called. The remaining parameters (INSTRUCTION_ADDR, TRAP_ADDR, OP_CODE and TIMER) will be examined by the executive in handling various traps. The meanings of the parameters are:

    ADDRESS_SPACE_NUMBER: The number of the address space
        corresponding to the user job.
    INSTRUCTION_ADDR: The location of the current instruction,
        expressed as an offset from the start of the program
        segment. This parameter must be initialized to the
        fourth from the last location of the job the first time
        the job is allowed to run. (This is the entry point
        address for the test jobs that we have provided. The
        input spooler must determine the length of the object

code for each job.) This parameter will be used by the
executive in printing error messages.

TRAP_ADDR: The displacement within its segment of the
reference that caused a trap. (Needed for servicing
page fault traps.)

IO_ADDR: Used for handling user job input/output requests,
as will be described subsequently.

STACK_MAX: Recall that the user language is a stack
language. STACK_MAX must be set to the maximum size of
its stack. This value can be determined from the job
card parameters.

STACK_PTR: Must be set to 0 the first time a particular job
is allowed to run.

OP_CODE: A single instruction can contain multiple memory
references, any of which can cause a page fault. The
CPU must be able to suspend and later resume operation
in the middle of an instruction. The accuracy of
INSTRUCTION_ADDR depends upon the phase of instruction
execution as indicated by OP_CODE: if OP_CODE is a
valid operation code (0-15), INSTRUCTION_ADDR has been
incremented by one, to point to the word following the
start of the current instruction. OP_CODE must be set
to -1 the first time a particular job is allowed to run.

TIMER: The number of instructions that the CPU will execute
before returning a timer trap. Each time an instruction
is executed, TIMER is decremented.

The CPU will execute instructions until a trap occurs, at
which point it will return with an appropriate code. The trap
codes are:

1	GET instruction encountered
2	PUT instruction encountered
3	STOP instruction encountered (normal exit)
11	Timer trap
12	Zero divide
13	Illegal operation code
21	Page fault in program segment
22	Page fault in data segment during attempted fetch
23	Page fault in data segment during attempted store
31	Invalid segment table address
32	Invalid core status table address
33	Invalid address space number
34	Invalid program segment page table address
35	Invalid data segment page table address
41	Attempt to execute nonexistent part of program segment
42	Attempt to read nonexistent part of data segment
43	Attempt to write nonexistent part of data segment

To complete the design of the envelope processes, we must
specify how the various traps are handled and what initialization
is required when an envelope process receives a new user job from
the long term scheduler.

Few of the traps require more than a small amount of intervention, since most are indicative of an error in either the user job or the operating system. The two major exceptions are page faults and user I/O requests; these are discussed in the next two sections.

HANDLING PAGE FAULTS

Paging is a form of memory management. The overall objective of a memory management policy is to keep resident in user memory those pages that have the highest probability of being referenced in the near future and thus are of the greatest value to active programs.

The servicing of a page fault has two aspects: locating the page that is required, and selecting a page frame into which it can be placed. This latter aspect will involve page replacement if all page frames have already been allocated. The page replacement policy is critical to the performance of a paging system, since the pages that are least likely to be needed in the near future must be removed from memory to make room for pages that are in demand. We leave the choice of a page replacement policy open; in the exercises we describe one that can be implemented easily.

When seeking a page frame, it is clear that the first choice should be one that is not currently assigned to any job. The address space number of the job (if any) to which a page frame is assigned can be saved in the core status table (or in a control memory table corresponding to it), so free page frames can be identified easily.

If no free page frames exist, the referenced and altered bits in the core status table can assist the executive in making a wise page replacement choice. These bits are automatically set by the hardware, but can be modified by the executive so that they provide more information. For instance, by periodically probing the core status table and saving the value of the referenced bit, either the least recently used or the least frequently used replacement policies can be approximated. The altered bit, if zero, indicates that the information in the page frame has not been changed and a current copy already exists on drum, so no write operation is necessary if the corresponding page frame is selected.

If a page frame is stolen from an active job, that job's page table must be updated to reflect the fact that the page is no longer resident. This means that in addition to the address space number of the job that owns the page frame, we need the segment number and the page number, or else the user memory address of the page table entry. This information can be kept in the core status table. Note that certain page frames (e.g., those containing the core status table, the segment tables, and the page tables) should never be used by user jobs. A bit in the core status table entry can be used to indicate those page frames that cannot be touched.

Finally, if the page has been altered it must be written to drum before the page frame can be re-used. The drum address of each page in user memory can be kept in the core status table, or the list of drum pages for the job to which the frame belongs can be scanned.

Now, consider the problem of locating the required page. From the trap number, the envelope process knows the segment in which the page fault occurred. The page number within that segment can be obtained by taking the integer part of TRAP_ADDR divided by PAGE_SIZE. To find the drum address of the required page, we could follow the linked list of drum pages for the segment. Since this is a slow operation, it makes sense to convert this linked list into an array at the time the job becomes active. This array may be kept in control memory, or it may be stored in the page table as negative values, given that provision is made to store elsewhere (the core status table is a logical choice) the drum addresses of pages that are actually occupying user memory page frames.

Page fault servicing is particularly susceptible to subtle concurrency-related errors. Mutual exclusion must be provided for the core status table (and for the page tables as well, when they are being modified). This includes guarding against the possibility that another user job will become active and cause the CPU hardware to update the table. Since the Z7 system has a single CPU, certain errors can be prevented by accessing the tables prior to releasing the CPU by a call to DONE_RUNNING. (DONE_RUNNING must be called before initiating the page transfer, so that the CPU will be available to other users.)

Other errors are possible, though. Consider the following: Job 1 causes a page fault. The page frame selected for replacement is currently assigned to job 2. This page has been altered, so must be written to drum. Job 1's envelope updates job 2's page table, calls DONE_RUNNING, and initiates a virtual drum operation. The CPU is next given to job 2, which immediately references the page in question, causing a page fault. Since drum operations are not necessarily scheduled FIFO, the processing of this page fault by job 2's envelope might result in an out-of-date copy of the page being retrieved.

The solution to this problem involves the addition of a state to page table entries: if a page fault occurs on a page that is "in transit to drum", the page frame is reclaimed. An envelope process attempting to steal a page frame checks at the conclusion of the drum write operation to be certain that the page frame has not been reclaimed. Mutual exclusion must be provided for access to the state variable.

HANDLING USER I/O

A job's data segment must contain three distinct items. The first is the stack. The user language is stack-oriented, and the maximum stack size is provided as a parameter on the job card. The stack must begin at offset zero of the data segment. A user job may not explicitly reference beyond the end of the stack; traps 42 or 43 will result.

At offsets in the data segment beyond the end of the stack, space must be reserved for the other two items in the segment: user input and output areas. When the CPU returns a GET trap (1), it is requesting that the data segment displacement of the next word of input data be placed in IO_ADDR by the executive. Similarly, when a PUT trap (2) is returned, the CPU is requesting that the data segment displacement of the next space for user output be placed in IO_ADDR. The envelope processes must handle these requests as part of buffering user input/output operations. Either the virtual I/O approach or the moving window approach can be used.

In the virtual I/O approach, all of the job's input data, as well as sufficient pages to accommodate its anticipated output, are included in the data segment when the page table is constructed. The envelope process simply maintains running pointers into each of these areas, and allows its page fault handler to take care of fetching and removal transparently. This approach is quite elegant, but the data segment page table, which must be resident in user memory, can sometimes be quite large.

An alternative approach is to have single-page input and output buffers in the data segment that act as moving windows onto data areas on drum. When a buffer has been exhausted, the envelope process resets its buffer pointer (by subtracting PAGE_SIZE) and adjusts the information in the page table so that a page fault bringing in the next page will occur when the CPU attempts to reference the address in IO_ADDR as part of the next GET or PUT operation.

INITIALIZATION FOR USER JOBS

When an envelope process receives a new user job from the long term scheduler, it must construct a page table for each segment. Constructing the program segment page table is straightforward, since all of the drum pages containing object code are in a linked list that can be translated easily into a table. Constructing the data segment page table is a bit more complex, because it must be assembled from the stack and the input and output areas. The job's two page tables can be concatenated, and enough contiguous user memory page frames must be found to accommodate them. Finally, the two segment table entries must be set.

Initially, both the stack and the output area will be composed of scratch pages (pages on which no information resides). It is unnecessary to perform a drum read the first time each of these pages is referenced. The page frame that is allocated will presumably contain data belonging to some other user, though, and privacy considerations dictate that it should be cleared prior to re-use.

CHAPTER 7 SUMMARY

In many ways, the design of an operating system is the ultimate test of a concurrent programming language. In this and the previous chapter, Concurrent SP/k has been used to design a multiprogramming, virtual memory, spooling, batch operating system for a simulated computer.

From the standpoint of concurrent programming, four aspects of the design are particularly noteworthy. First is the hierarchy of processes that arise in the design of the input spooler process, described in the previous chapter.

The envelope process approach to executive design is also interesting. Although the philosophy is not new, it is often subverted by the design of do-nothing envelopes that must frequently pass state information to various operating system programs.

We should also recall the manner in which the drum, a shared device, is viewed as a dedicated virtual device by the input spooler, each envelope process, and the output spooler.

Finally, the way in which monitors provided a natural solution to the various scheduling and synchronization problems we encountered demonstrates both their versatility and their appropriateness.

A number of rather sophisticated operating systems concepts were introduced in this chapter. The virtual memory hardware of the Z7 machine closely resembles that of several commercially available computers, and in mastering it you will have achieved a practical understanding of this important aspect of modern computers.

Throughout this chapter, we have maintained the distinction between mechanisms and policies. (A mechanism is a means by which a policy can be achieved.) We have discussed the design of the system in terms of mechanisms, and have reserved the implementation of specific policies (long term scheduling, short term scheduling, and page replacement) as exercises. Our design demonstrates that monitors, properly used, constitute a flexible mechanism that can accomodate a wide range of policy alternatives.

Completing the design of this operating system will be a valuable exercise. Implementing it in CSP/k will be even more valuable; a successful project demonstrates a significant understanding both of operating systems and of concurrent programming.

CHAPTER 7 BIBLIOGRAPHY

Like so much of what we have discussed, the term "envelope" can be traced to Hoare [1974]. The hardware design of the Z7 computer has evolved over a number of years through the efforts of many people in the University of Toronto's Computer Systems Research Group. The technical report by Czarnik et al. [1973] describes an earlier version. Shaw and Weiderman [1971] discuss a similar system.

Czarnik, B. (editor), Tsichritzis, D., Ballard, A., Dryer, M., Holt, R.C., and Weissman, L. A student project for an operating system course. CSRG-29, Computer Systems Research Group, University of Toronto (1973).

Hoare, C.A.R. Monitors: an operating system structuring concept. Comm. ACM 17, 10 (October 1974), 549-557.

Shaw, A.C., and Weiderman, N.H. A multiprogramming system for education and research. Proc. IFIP Congress 1971, 1505-1509.

CHAPTER 7 EXERCISES

1. Complete the design of the executive by writing code skeletons for the various programs and fully specifying the interfaces to the input and output spoolers.

2. Program the executive in CSP/k. Using your input and output spoolers from Chapter 6, as well as the simulated hardware that we provide, test your complete operating system by processing the example user jobs from Appendix 8. The simple Z7 operating system in Appendix 9 may prove useful as a model.

3. Implement an intelligent long term scheduling policy. The policy should be biased in favor of short, small, high priority jobs. Since indefinite postponement must be precluded, the amount of time that a job has been waiting must also be taken into account. One approach is to compute an internal priority based upon the first three factors. The job with the highest internal priority will always be selected for activation, and each time a job is activated, the internal priority of all other jobs in the queue is increased by a fixed amount. The multiprogramming level should be regulated so that thrashing does not occur. The easiest way to detect thrashing is to monitor the level of drum activity.

4. Implement the following variant of <u>foreground-background</u> short term scheduling. Jobs that are ready to run are organized into two queues, a high priority queue (foreground) and a low priority queue (background). A newly activated job joins the foreground queue, which is managed first-in-first-out. After receiving a quantum of service in the foreground queue, a job may be re-assigned to the foreground queue or, if it has received more than a specified amount of foreground service, it may be relegated to the background queue. The background queue is also managed first-in-first-out, but is served only if the foreground queue is empty. When a job on the background queue is allowed to run, it is placed on the foreground queue until its quantum is exhausted, then returned to the background queue.

To define this algorithm completely, we need to specify three parameters: the basic quantum length for a job in the foreground queue, the basic quantum length for a job in the background queue, and the threshold of attained service beyond which a job is relegated to the background queue. The actual quantum that a job receives should be the basic quantum for its queue, times a factor related to external priority (as specified on the job card).

5. Implement the following variant of the <u>second chance</u> page replacement policy. Use a pointer that cycles through the core status table examining the allocated page frames. (Any free page frames are used prior to invoking this algorithm.) If a frame has the referenced bit on, turn it off and record the altered bit in a test bit elsewhere in the core status table entry. Then proceed to the next entry. If a frame has the referenced bit off, examine the test bit. If it is on, turn it off and proceed to the next entry. If it is off, select that page frame for replacement.

6. In the system design that we have described, a user job causing a page fault may have to create a free page frame by writing the contents of some page frame to drum. This delay can be eliminated if an additional system process is introduced, which concurrently writes to drum those pages that have been altered, creating a pool of available page frames. Modify the design that we have presented to include such a process.

CHAPTER 8

IMPLEMENTING A KERNEL

In previous chapters we have used processes and monitors without worrying about their implementation. We were content to treat them as well-defined abstractions, supported by the operating system, the language processor, or perhaps by some special machine (a virtual machine). This idea of an abstraction implemented by underlying software and hardware is one of the most powerful program structuring tools available, and is used constantly in software engineering. This concept has allowed us to concentrate on concurrency algorithms and operating system structures without the confusion of low-level, machine-dependent mechanisms such as interrupts.

But now we will confront the implementation problem, and take a close look at the "next lower level". Exactly how do we implement processes and concurrency constructs? The module (software or microprogram or hardware) that supports processes is called a kernel, and this chapter explains how to build a kernel. We give the design of a kernel for single CPU systems and show how this design can be implemented using production hardware (a PDP-11). We also give the design of a kernel for multiple CPU systems.

STRUCTURE OF A KERNEL

The main purpose of a kernel is to share CPU time among processes, so that each process has its own "virtual CPU". The kernel must also provide the process/process interface (to support interprocess communication) and the process/device interface (to support device management).

As the following diagram shows, the kernel receives traps from processes, dispatches processes (gives them the CPU), receives interrupts from devices, and issues Start I/O commands to devices. The kernel also receives interrupts from a clock.

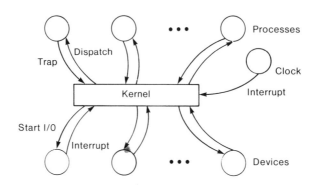

The kernel is the only module in the system that is aware of interrupts. All software activity outside the kernel is performed by processes, whose virtual CPUs are slowed down but otherwise unaffected by interrupts. In place of interrupts, the kernel provides special mechanisms (primitives) that device manager processes use for controlling devices.

The kernel uses process descriptors, one per process, to keep track of the status of the processes and to allocate CPU time among them. When a process has not been allocated a CPU, its descriptor contains all the information needed to restart it. Typically, the descriptor will have fields for the process's instruction counter, general registers, floating point registers, addressing registers, and so on. The kernel dispatches a process (gives the process a CPU) by loading the CPU's registers from the process's descriptor. The loading of the CPU's instruction counter causes transfer of control to the process and the process resumes execution.

The kernel maintains a ready queue by linking together the descriptors of those processes that would be executing, except that a CPU is not available. The kernel also keeps track of blocked processes; to support monitors, it maintains a queue of process descriptors for each condition. A kernel might support any of the concurrency schemes described in Chapter 2, but in this chapter we will concentrate on the support of monitor features such as those in CSP/k.

PROCESS/DEVICE COMMUNICATION

The process/device communication that must be supported by the kernel can be either synchronous or asynchronous. The synchronous method is conceptually simpler and is based on the DO_IO operation. A device manager directs its device to perform a particular operation by executing

DO_IO(DEVICE#,COMMAND,STATUS);

The STATUS parameter is optional and can be used to indicate whether the operation was successful. The process executing DO_IO is blocked until the requested I/O is complete.

DO_IO can be implemented as an entry point in the kernel, invoked by a supervisor call (a trap). After the kernel starts up the device, using the given COMMAND, the kernel can allocate the CPU to another process. When the device completes the operation, it notifies the kernel (by an interrupt) and the kernel can again dispatch the device manager.

The DO_IO operation is conceptually simple because it makes the device manager process synchronous with its device. Because of its simplicity, we used it in the Z7 operating system in Chapters 6 and 7. The device is active only when the manager is blocked waiting for the DO_IO operation. The problem with DO_IO is that the manager may need to continue execution while the I/O is in progress. For example, the manager may need to accept further user I/O requests and sort these requests before the I/O completes. This problem can always be solved by splitting the manager into two processes, as was done in the Z7 operating system. The first uses DO_IO to control the device and the second receives users' requests and transfers them to the second. This is a good solution, but if processes and interprocess communication are costly, an alternative to DO_IO may be required.

The alternative method allows the device and its manager process to be asynchronous. It uses the following commands.

SIGNALDEVICE(DEVICE#,COMMAND);
WAITDEVICE(DEVICE#,STATUS);

Executed one immediately after the other, these two commands are equivalent to DO_IO. When executed separately, they allow the manager process to continue execution during the I/O. A variation of WAITDEVICE could allow the manager to test the device to see if the operation is completed, without being forced to wait for the completion. SIGNAL/WAITDEVICE is somewhat more costly than DO_IO to implement, because the kernel is forced to maintain a descriptor to record the status of each device. With DO_IO, these descriptors can be avoided because the status of a completing device can be immediately transferred to the device's

waiting   manager.   In   this   chapter   we   will   ignore
WAIT/SIGNALDEVICE in favor of the simpler DO_IO.

QUEUE MANAGEMENT

The kernel manages several queues of process descriptors,
including the ready queue. To support monitors, there must also
be a queue for each of the conditions. We will use the following
notation for queue removal and insertion operations:

    Remove ITEM from QUEUE;
    Insert ITEM into QUEUE;

For process queues, each ITEM can be represented by a pointer to
its process descriptor. The queues in the kernel are typically
ordered by priority or by FIFO (first-in-first-out). Either
method of ordering can be accomplished by very simple programs,
which we will now develop. Persons who have had a great deal of
experience with queueing algorithms may choose to skip the rest
of this section.

FIFO queues can be represented by FIRST and LAST pointers and
NEXT fields in each item, as shown here.

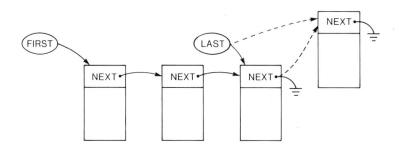

The dotted arrows show how a new item is inserted at the end of
the queue. When the FIFO queue is empty, it has this form:

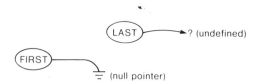

The test to see if the queue is empty is accomplished by
comparing FIRST to the null pointer. Here are the programs for
removing and inserting items in FIFO queues:

```
Remove ITEM from QUEUE:
   ITEM=FIRST;
   FIRST=NEXT(FIRST);

Insert ITEM into QUEUE:
   IF FIRST=NULL THEN /* EMPTY QUEUE? */
      FIRST=ITEM;
   ELSE
      NEXT(LAST)=ITEM;
   NEXT(ITEM)=NULL;
   LAST=ITEM;
```

The operations for priority queues are only slightly more complicated, and we will now develop them.

Priority queues can be represented by a FIRST pointer together with NEXT and PRIORITY fields in each item, as shown here:

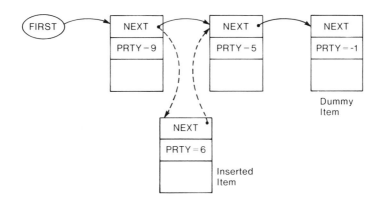

We are assuming that high-numbered priorities come first in the queue. The dotted arrows show how a new item with priority 6 would be inserted between items with priorities 9 and 5. The dummy item has a priority that is smaller than any real item; its purpose is to simplify insertion, so there is no special case for inserting at the tail (just before the dummy). The test to see if the queue is empty is accomplished by comparing FIRST to the pointer to the dummy item. Here are the programs for removing and inserting items.

```
Remove ITEM from QUEUE:
   ITEM=FIRST;
   FIRST=NEXT(FIRST);

Insert ITEM into QUEUE:
   IF PRIORITY(ITEM)>PRIORITY(FIRST) THEN
      DO;  /* INSERT ITEM FIRST */
         NEXT(ITEM)=FIRST;
```

```
            FIRST=ITEM;
            END;
      ELSE  /* FIND PLACE TO INSERT ITEM */
         DO;
            PREV=FIRST;
            LINK=NEXT(FIRST);
            DO WHILE(PRIORITY(ITEM)<=PRIORITY(LINK));
               PREV=LINK;
               LINK=NEXT(LINK);
               END;
            NEXT(PREV)=ITEM;
            NEXT(ITEM)=LINK;
            END;
```

In a following section we describe how a kernel can use queues to support monitors.

ENTRIES INTO THE KERNEL

The kernel can be entered due to action on the part of a process, a device or a clock, as was shown in the diagram of the kernel's structure. These are the types of entries:

Traps - calls from processes, requesting operations such as DO_IO or WAIT.

Device interrupts - signal that requested operations are complete.

Clock interrupts - signal the end of a process's time slice.

To implement a kernel, we will need a program for each of these entries. Given that the kernel supports monitors, the trap entries should include the following:

ENTERMONITOR(M): The process is entering monitor M and mutual exclusion must be guaranteed.

EXITMONITOR(M): The process is leaving monitor M, and another process may be allowed to enter M.

SIGNAL(C): The process is inside a monitor and signals condition C; if a process is waiting for C, it must be awakened.

WAIT(C): the process is inside a monitor and waits for condition C; this releases the CPU so it can be allocated to another process.

DO_IO(DEVICE#,COMMAND,STATUS): the command is to be passed to the specified device, and the executing process is to be blocked until the device completes its operation; this releases the CPU so it can be re-allocated.

If monitors are embedded in a high-level language, it is the responsibility of the compiler to generate code for the traps. If the programmer is using a language that does not support monitors, for example, assembly language, he can still use monitors by using macros or procedures that invoke appropriate traps.

Before giving programs to implement these entries, we will discuss some conditions that can make implementation of monitors easier.

SIMPLIFYING CONDITIONS

A kernel can be small and fast, or large and inefficient, depending on the hardware's interrupt structure and addressing mechanisms, and on the operating system's memory allocation, accounting and protection policies. The complexity of the kernel also depends on details of process/process and process/device communication; for example, message passing is inherently more complex than semaphores.

In this chapter we will largely ignore the problems of memory allocation, accounting and protection. Since those problems are handled simply in many minicomputer operating systems, the kernel designs we will give are directly applicable to such systems. Simple solutions to these problems are also typically used in the inner layers of large operating systems; in these our designs are of immediate use to support activities such as device management. The implementation of users' processes in, say, a paging system is more difficult, though it can still be based on the model we will give.

The architecture that the hardware provides for controlling devices can make or break an operating system. If these mechanisms, primarily the Start I/O instruction and device interrupts, are unstructured and imply extensive interactions among channels and devices, no reasonable structure may be possible. In such a case it will be hopeless to try to impose the elegance of a mechanism such as DO_IO. We will assume for our kernel implementation that the architecture is relatively clean.

A KERNEL FOR SINGLE CPU SYSTEMS

A kernel that supports multiple processes, monitor entry and exit, and signal/wait can be quite small. For example, the kernel developed in a following section for a PDP-11 consists of less than 50 machine instructions. In the present section we will give a detailed design for a kernel that could be implemented on typical production computer systems. We will assume that there is only one CPU because this makes the design simpler, but in a later section we will show how to handle multiple CPUs.

The reason a single CPU system is particularly easy to handle is that mutual exclusion can be guaranteed simply by disabling interrupts. Taking this idea to extremes leads to the monolithic monitor, as discussed in Chapter 1, in which all operating system activities are performed with interrupts disabled. By contrast, our design will disable interrupts only while the kernel or a monitor is active. Our structure implies that at most one monitor can be active at any given time.

The following diagram illustrates the queues of process descriptors that the kernel manages. The diagram shows one running process, three ready processes, two processes waiting for condition COND1, none for COND2, one for COND3, none for DEVICE1, and one for DEVICE2.

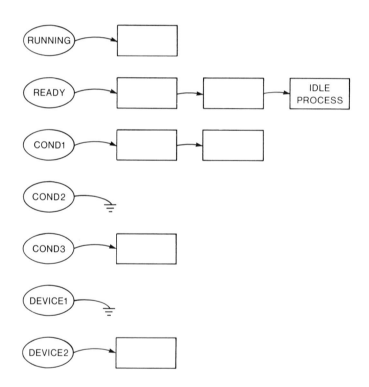

Each rectangle in this diagram represents a process descriptor. The links to descriptors can be represented as machine addresses. If priority-ordered queues are used, the null pointer can correspond to the address of the dummy descriptor.

When all processes are blocked, the CPU becomes idle. This special situation can be handled in an elegant way by using an

"idle process", which has a lower priority than any other
process. In the diagram the idle process is shown last on the
ready queue. When all "real" processes become blocked, the idle
process is dispatched (becomes the running process). Any "real"
process that becomes ready will immediately be given the CPU
because its priority is greater than the idle process. With this
arrangement, the kernel needs no special logic to handle the case
of the idle CPU. If desired, the idle process can absorb CPU
time by executing a non-urgent program, such as computing the
digits of the irrational number pi. (Note: the priority of the
idle process must be greater than the priority in the dummy
descriptor, which always marks the end of the ready queue.)

The speed of the kernel depends largely on the time taken to
save and restore process status. Some computers have facilities
that save or restore status in a single instruction; in others,
there may be multiple register sets and the saving or restoring
is accomplished simply by changing the pointer to the register
set. Unfortunately, on some computers, status saving and
restoring is relatively slow. For example, on the System
360/370, the process status consists of over 100 bytes of
information (program status word, float and general registers),
and several instructions must be executed to do the saving.

In many computer systems, the enter and exit monitor
operations, which disable and enable interrupts, can be
implemented by single machine instructions. We will assume that
a special register determines whether interrupts are enabled;
this register is part of a process's status and must be saved in
the process's descriptor.

With these preliminaries out of the way we now give the
program for each of the entries into the kernel. In these
programs, we use a pointer called "running" to locate the process
descriptor of the running process. For example, the line "Remove
running from ready" means to remove a process descriptor from the
ready queue and to place the descriptor's location in the pointer
called "running".

```
Entermonitor: Disable interrupts;

Exitmonitor: Enable interrupts;

WAIT(C): Save status of running;
         Insert running into C;
         Remove running from ready;
         Restore status of running;

SIGNAL(C): IF ¬empty(C) THEN
             DO;  /* Give CPU to waiting process */
               Save status of running;
               Insert running into ready;
               Remove running from C;
               Restore status of running;
               END;
```

```
SLICE:  /* Clock interrupt */
        Save status of running and disable interrupts;
        Insert running into ready;
        Remove running from ready;
        Restore status of running and enable interrupts;
```

The program for WAIT saves the running process's status, puts its descriptor on the queue for condition C, takes another process's descriptor from the running queue, and dispatches that process. The line "Save status of running" uses the pointer called "running" to locate a process descriptor, and saves the current status of the CPU in that descriptor. The line "Insert running into C" places the value of this pointer in the queue for condition C. The line "Remove running from ready" changes the pointer called "running" so it locates another process descriptor. The line "Restore status of running" includes resetting the instruction pointer and thus transferring control to the new process. Since WAIT and SIGNAL can only be executed inside a monitor, we know interrupts have been disabled by entermonitor. This disabling guarantees mutually exclusive access to the queues of processes.

The program for SIGNAL does nothing unless it finds a process waiting for the condition. If one is found, the running process has its status saved and its descriptor placed on the ready queue. Then a waiting process's descriptor is removed from the condition queue and that process is dispatched.

Each time slice allows another process to run. We are assuming that the ready queue is priority-ordered, and that for a given priority, it is FIFO; this corresponds to the implementation of priority queues we have given earlier in this chapter. The program for SLICE saves the status of the running process and puts its descriptor on the ready queue; then it takes a descriptor from the ready queue and dispatches that process. If all processes have the same priority, this results in round-robin scheduling. If the interrupted process has a higher priority than any ready process, the SLICE program causes the interrupted process to be re-dispatched. In this last case, status saving and restoring could be avoided by first comparing the running priority to the first ready priority, and immediately re-dispatching if appropriate. An expanded version of SLICE with this extra test would be more efficient in computers that have slow status saving and restoring.

Our kernel allows a low priority process in the ready queue to be indefinitely overtaken by higher priority processes. If this situation can arise (for other than the idle process) in a particular system, it can be avoided by having the kernel dynamically decrease the priority of processes that use a lot of CPU time.

We have now given all of the kernel except the part that allows processes to control devices.

HANDLING INPUT AND OUTPUT

We can augment our kernel to handle input and output by giving it an entry point called DO_IO and a handler for input/output interrupts. We will assume that processes can call DO_IO only from outside monitors. The implementations are as follows.

```
DO_IO(DEVICE#,COMMAND):
    Save status of running and disable interrupts;
    Insert running into queue(DEVICE#);
    Startio(DEVICE#,COMMAND); /*Hardware instruction */
    Remove running from ready;
    Restore status of running and enable interrupts;

IO_DONE(DEVICE#): /* Handle I/O interrupt */
    Save status of running and disable interrupts;
    Insert running into ready;
    Remove running from queue(DEVICE#);
    Restore status of running and enable interrupts;
```

The DO_IO operation causes the kernel to place the executing process on a queue waiting for the device to finish, start up the device, and then find a new process to dispatch. We will assume that only one process will request I/O for a particular device. That process will be the device's manager and may receive I/O requests from other processes. There are a number of advantages of using a separate manager process, such as providing I/O buffering and protection.

The IO_DONE routine handles I/O interrupts. First it saves the status of the running process and puts its descriptor on the ready queue. Then it removes the waiting process from the device's queue and dispatches that process. The IO_DONE routine could be made a bit more sophisticated by checking to see if the waiting process has a higher priority than the interrupted process. On the other hand, if all device manager processes are relatively simple and fast, IO_DONE as given is probably best because it allows the manager to re-start the device immediately. If there is device status associated with the I/O interrupt, it would be passed by the kernel to the managing process in an extra DO_IO parameter.

Unfortunately, some current computer architectures have a relatively complex I/O structure, with external channels, controllers and devices that must be managed from the CPU. The elegant handling of I/O that we have just developed may not be directly adaptable to those systems, especially if an error on a device can be reported by an interrupt separate from the one for device completion. Since the PDP-11 architecture is clean and widely used, we will show how our kernel design can be translated into its machine language. Persons who are not familiar with machine language may choose to skip the following section.

A KERNEL FOR THE PDP-11

The two preceding sections have given the design of a kernel that supports monitors, time-slicing and process/device communication for a single CPU system. We can implement a kernel for a particular computer by translating this design into machine instructions. For the PDP-11 this translation is particularly simple, and we will now give it.

On the PDP-11, process status consists of a processor status word (PS), a program counter (PC), a stack pointer (SP), and six general purpose registers called R0, R1, up to R5. All these must be saved when the process is interrupted. Each process has a stack (a contiguous allocation of memory) whose currently last active word is pointed to by its SP register.

The PS contains a hardware priority with values from 0 to 7. This priority is not the priority used in ordering the ready queue. Rather, the hardware priority determines the disabling of devices. When the PS priority is 7, no device can interrupt. When it is n, any device with a hardware priority greater than n can interrupt. For our kernel we will use this disabling mechanism in the simplest possible way: we will use only priority 7 (to disable all interrupts) and priority 0 (to enable all interrupts). Whenever an interrupt or trap occurs, the PDP-11 hardware stores the current PS and PC on the current stack and loads a new PS and PC corresponding to the interrupt or trap. The remainder of a process's status (SP and six registers) can then be saved by the kernel.

We will assume that the kernel maintains a descriptor for each process that has the following fields:

```
NEXT    - pointer to next process descriptor
PRTY    - priority for ready queue
SAVER1  - saves status of R1
...
SAVER5  - saves status of R5
SAVESP  - saves status of SP
```

Since the PS and PC are automatically saved on the process's stack, they do not require fields in the process descriptor.

We will assume that whenever a process is running, register R0 is pointing to the process's descriptor. We will use the mnemonic RRUN as a synonymn for R0. Following an interrupt, the following instructions complete the saving of the interrupted process's status:

```
MOV    R1,SAVER1(RRUN);
MOV    R2,SAVER2(RRUN);
...
MOV    R5,SAVER5(RRUN);
MOV    SP,SAVESP(RRUN);
```

When a process is to be dispatched, these registers can be restored by loading R0 (RRUN) with the address of the appropriate descriptor and executing:

```
MOV     SAVER1(RRUN),R1;
MOV     SAVER2(RRUN),R2;
...
MOV     SAVER5(RRUN),R5;
MOV     SAVESP(RRUN),SP;
RTI;
```

The RTI (return from interrupt) instruction restores the PC and PS from the top of the process's stack, and the process resumes execution. Note that the descriptor does not require a field for R0 (RRUN) because the link field pointing to the descriptor will hold R0's value.

The following diagram gives the descriptors of a system having five processes and a single condition queue.

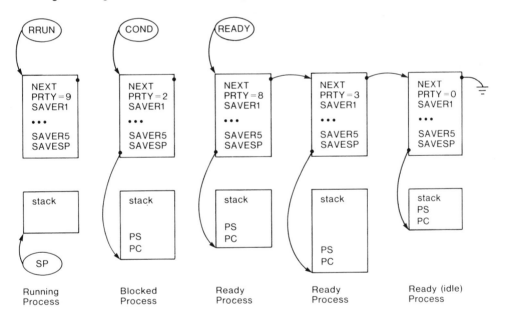

As shown, one process is running and another is waiting for a condition. Three processes, including the idle process, are in the ready queue.

There are two assumptions we will make so our kernel will be more efficient. First, we will assume that when a process executes a trap instruction, it is not currently using registers R1 through R5. This assumption saves time in the kernel by eliminating the saving and restoring of those registers before and after traps. Second, we will assume that each condition will have at most one process waiting for it. This second assumption may be too severe for some systems, but it simplifies our kernel. Besides, it is always possible to program using only single process conditions by using arrays of conditions; this must be done in the language Concurrent Pascal which supports only single process condition queues. If desired, our implementation can easily be expanded to handle the more general case.

With these preliminaries out of the way, we will give the actual code for the PDP-11 kernel. Interrupts can be enabled or disabled by single instructions that set the PS priority to 0 and 7, as follows.

```
Entermonitor: BIC #PBITS,PS; Clear priority bits to zero
Exitmonitor:  BIS #PBITS,PS; Set priority bits to ones
```

The BIC (bit clear) and BIS (bit set) instructions set the three-bit hardware priority field to zeroes (octal zero) or to ones (octal 7). These two instructions should be emitted in-line whenever a monitor is to be entered or exited.

The code to implement wait and signal is a bit longer, so we will factor it out into kernel routines that are called by traps. Each call to the wait routine is done by this in-line code:

```
Call Wait: MOV  COND,RCOND; Put # of condition in a register
           TRAP WAIT;       Trap, passing # of wait routine
```

A similar calling sequence is used for signal. Recall that we are assuming that at the call, registers R1 to R5 (except RCOND) are not in use, so the kernel will not need to save them.

The trap causes the hardware to save the process's PC and PS and to pick up a new PC and PS from a fixed location in low memory. The new PS will be set up to have priority 7, so interrupts will remain disabled. The new PC points to the following segment of code, called ROUTER, that in turn transfers control to the appropriate trap handler.

```
ROUTER: MOV  (SP),RTEMP;      Locate trap instruction
        MOVB -(RTEMP),RTEMP;  Load trap # from instruction
        JMP  @VECTOR(RTEMP);  Jump to correct handler
```

The jump to the correct trap handler is done indirectly using a "transfer vector", which is a sequence of words in memory that holds the addresses of the handlers.

The wait and signal routines, which gain control from ROUTER, are pleasingly small: only 11 instructions for wait and 9 instructions for signal. The signal routine includes a call to an INSERT routine (16 instructions) that inserts a process descriptor into the priority-ordered ready queue. The INSERT routine is also called by the SLICE routine. Here is the code for these routines.

```
WAIT:   MOV  SP,SAVESP(RRUN);      Save status of running
        MOV  RRUN,(RCOND);         Insert running into C
DISPCH: MOV  READY,RRUN;           Remove running
        MOV  NEXT(RRUN),READY;       from ready
        MOV  SAVER1(RRUN),R1;      Restore registers of running
        MOV  SAVER2(RRUN),R2;         "        "       "     "
        MOV  SAVER3(RRUN),R3;         "        "       "     "
        MOV  SAVER4(RRUN),R4;         "        "       "     "
        MOV  SAVER5(RRUN),R5;         "        "       "     "
        MOV  SAVESP(RRUN),SP;         "        "       "     "
        RTI;                       Restore PC and PS

SIGNAL: TST  (RCOND);              If empty(C) THEN
        BNE  SWAP;                    Cause return to signaler
        RTI;                       ELSE
        ;                             DO
SWAP:   MOV  SP,SAVESP(RRUN);         Save status of running
        JSR  PC,INSERT;               Insert running into ready
        MOV  (RCOND),RRUN;            Remove running
        CLR  (RCOND);                    from C
        MOV  SAVESP(RRUN),SP;         restore status of running
        RTI;                          END /* restore PC, PS */

SLICE:  MOV  R1,SAVER1(RRUN);      Save registers of running
        MOV  R2,SAVER2(RRUN);         "        "       "     "
        MOV  R3,SAVER3(RRUN);         "        "       "     "
        MOV  R4,SAVER4(RRUN);         "        "       "     "
        MOV  R5,SAVER5(RRUN);         "        "       "     "
        MOV  SP,SAVESP(RRUN);         "        "       "     "
        JSR  PC,INSERT;            Insert running into ready
        BR   DISPCH;              Remove running from ready and
        ;                             dispatch running

INSERT: MOV  READY,RLINK;           link=ready
        CMP  PRTY(RRUN),PRTY(RLINK); IF prty(running)>prty(link)
        BLE  MERGE;                DO
        MOV  RLINK,NEXT(RRUN);        next(running)=link
        MOV  RRUN,READY;              ready=running
        RTS  PC;                   END
        ;                          ELSE
        ;                             DO
MERGE:  MOV  RLINK,RPREV;             prev=link
        MOV  NEXT(RLINK),RLINK;       link=next(link)
LOOP:   CMP  PRTY(RRUN),PRTY(RLINK);  DO WHILE(prty(run.)
        BGT  HOOKUP;                     <=prty(link))
        MOV  RLINK,RPREV;             prev=link
        MOV  NEXT(RLINK),RLINK;       link=next(link)
        BR   LOOP;                    END
HOOKUP: MOV  RRUN,NEXT(RPREV);        next(prev)=running
        MOV  RLINK,NEXT(RRUN);        next(running)=link
        RTS  PC;                   END
```

We will not give the routines for handling I/O. The DO_IO routine can be modeled after wait and the I/O interrupt handler can be modeled after SLICE. The PDP-11 kernel we have given can

be expanded in many ways; in the exercises we suggest a number of
improvements and expansions.

A KERNEL FOR MULTIPLE CPU SYSTEMS

We have given an efficient kernel that is based on
traditional, interrupt-oriented, single CPU architecture. In
this section we will give the design of a kernel that implements
processes and supports monitors when there are several CPUs. The
implementation will be quite small, but requires some study to be
well understood.

We will present the design in terms of an abstraction (a
virtual machine) which is not directly supported by currently
available hardware. Then we will show how this abstraction can
be implemented by a few machine instructions.

Our abstraction allows the logic of the kernel to be quite
elegant, because it lets us assume that the kernel runs on its
own machine (a virtual processor). Since this processor executes
only the kernel and it does not accept interrupts, mutually
exclusive access to queues of descriptors is guaranteed.
Whenever a process wishes to execute a primitive, such as WAIT,
the process's request is delayed until the kernel is idle; then
the kernel is activated by invoking its appropriate routine, and
is handed a pointer to the calling process's descriptor. It is
assumed that the calling process has stopped running and its
status has been saved. Once activated, the kernel is free to
manipulate whatever queues it maintains.

The kernel's ready queue gains a very special significance.
Whenever a process descriptor is inserted into the ready queue,
the kernel's virtual processor allocates a CPU to the process.
This convenient assumption means the kernel does not need to
worry about the mechanics of dispatching processes or sharing
CPUs. The kernel is concerned only with making processes ready
(by putting them on the ready queue). Later we will show how
these convenient assumptions are supported.

To implement monitors, the kernel has queues for each
condition. It also has an entry queue for each monitor, and
allows more than one monitor to be active at once. Of course, at
any given time it does not allow more than one process to be
active in a particular monitor. Associated with each monitor is
a flag which records whether the monitor is currently busy.

Given these data structures and our delightfully powerful
virtual processor, the kernel can be implemented in the following
few lines.

```
Entermonitor(M):
    If busy(M) THEN
        Insert caller into M;
    ELSE
        DO;
            busy(M)=TRUE;
            Insert caller into ready;
            END;

Exitmonitor(M):
    IF empty(M) THEN
        busy(M)=FALSE;
    ELSE
        DO; /* Transfer process from M's queue to ready queue */
            Remove p from M;
            Insert p into ready;
            END;
    Insert caller into ready;

Wait(c):
    Insert caller into C;

Signal(C):
    IF empty(C) THEN
        Insert caller into ready;
    ELSE
        DO; /* Transfer process from C's queue to ready queue */
            Remove p from C;
            Insert p into ready;
            Insert caller into M;
            END;
```

The entermonitor routine tests to see if the monitor is busy. If
so the calling process, whose descriptor is pointed to by
"caller", is placed on a queue waiting for the monitor to be
free. If not, the busy flag is set to true, and the process is
re-activated by placing its descriptor on the ready queue. The
other routines are straightforward and we will not discuss them.

    The handling of I/O is also straightforward, and can be
implemented as follows:

```
DO_IO(DEVICE#,COMMAND):
    Startio(DEVICE#,COMMAND); /*Actually start the device*/
    Insert caller into queue(DEVICE#);

IO_DONE(DEVICE#): /* I/O interrupt handler */
    Remove p from queue(DEVICE#);
    Insert p into ready;
```

The Start I/O instruction reactivates the device, and the
interrupt signals that the device is again idle. One of the
beauties of this arrangement is that processes and devices are
very similar from the point of view of the kernel. The analog of

the Start I/O for a device is the insertion of a process descriptor into the ready queue. The analog of a device interrupt is a process trap. The interrupt (trap) tells the kernel that the device (process) requires attention. The device (process) remains idle until re-started by the kernel. The device (process) is restarted by a Start I/O instruction (by insertion into the ready queue).

We have now designed the multiple CPU kernel, but we have not yet shown how to support its virtual processor. We might ask a hardware designer or a microprogrammer to implement the special processor. There would be a bonus to such an implementation: it could as well be used to implement other synchronization schemes such as semaphores or message passing. So, the virtual processor would be useful on its own right, independent of monitors. If special hardware or microprogramming are not available, we can still easily and efficiently implement the kernel's processor, as we will now show.

We will make the following assumptions about the system's architecture. There are n identical CPUs, and each CPU has its own interrupting clock. We will use n idle processes to sop up idle CPU time. All the CPUs can address the same memory, so each CPU can run any process and each CPU can access the kernel's data structures. Each device can interrupt any CPU, and arbitrarily picks one of the CPUs to interrupt, with the following constraint. If a CPU is currently running an idle process, it will be favored for the I/O interrupt. We will not dedicate a CPU to the kernel (that would be an awful waste). Instead, we give the kernel the appearance of having a dedicated CPU by temporarily borrowing whatever CPU received the interrupt (or trap).

The following three code segments implement the special virtual processor. They share the n CPUs among the processes that have been put on the ready queue, and they make sure that only one CPU at a time enters the kernel. These code segments use routines called enterkernel and exitkernel to save process status, gain mutual exclusion and dispatch processes. These two routines will be shown later.

```
TRAP(TRAP#): /* Process invokes the kernel */
    Enterkernel; /* Save status and gain mutual exclusion */
    CALL kernel(TRAP#); /* Handle trap and return here */
    Remove running from ready;
    Exitkernel; /* Release mutual exclusion and dispatch */

SLICE: /* The CPU's clock interrupts the CPU */
    Enterkernel; /* Save status and gain mutual exclusion */
    Insert running into ready;
    Remove running from ready;
    Exitkernel; /* Release mutual exclusion and dispatch */
```

```
IO_INTERRUPT(DEVICE#): /* Device interrupts CPU */
   Enterkernel; /* Save status and gain mutual exclusion */
   CALL IO_DONE(DEVICE#);
   Exitkernel; /* Release mutual exclusion and dispatch */
```

For these routines, each CPU must have private variables (these could be registers) called TRAP#, running, and DEVICE#.

On a single CPU system, we can implement enterkernel (exitkernel) by simply saving (restoring) registers and disabling (enabling) interrupts. With these implementations, the kernel we have just given can be used on a single CPU system. This single CPU kernel has the advantage that it allows more than one monitor to be active at once (this is not possible with the previous single CPU kernel). The disadvantage of this new single CPU kernel is that it is considerably slower than our previous design.

In a multiple CPU system we must guarantee that only one of the several CPUs is allowed into the kernel at a given time. This can be done by a test-and-set loop as described in Chapter 2. For the multiple CPU system, the following instruction sequences implement enter/exitkernel.

```
   Enterkernel:
      Save status of running and disable interrupts;
      TESTANDSET(kernelbusy);
      DO WHILE(kernelwasbusy); /* Test previous value of flag */
         TESTANDSET(kernelbusy);
         END;

   Exitkernel:
      kernelbusy=FALSE;
      Restore status of running and enable interrupts;
```

We have now given code segments that implement the virtual processor required by the kernel, and we have given the code segments that comprise the kernel. Together these support monitors for a multiple CPU computer system. Such a system has obvious advantages in terms of reliability and expandability. Reliability is improved because any failing CPU can simply be retired with its current process transferred to the ready queue. (Hopefully, the failing CPU does not destroy any critical data such as the kernel's queues.) Since all CPUs are the same, loss of any particular CPU only slows down the system without causing a disaster. Expandability is improved because when the system needs more computing power, another CPU can be added without affecting any software - not even the kernel! Adding or removing a CPU changes system throughput, but does not affect the system's correctness.

The first chapter of this book described the techniques of basing an operating system on a kernel. The main responsibilities of the kernel were defined as the support of processes along with process/process and process/device communication. From Chapter 1 until the present chapter, we used processes without being concerned about how they were supported. In this chapter we have returned to the subject of kernels, and have shown how the concurrent algorithms presented throughout this book can be supported by a kernel on traditional computer hardware.

CHAPTER 8 SUMMARY

In this chapter we have seen that a kernel is entered when the following occur:

- Trap - a process requests a service. When the service has been provided, the process can be dispatched (given a CPU).
- I/O interrupt - a device completes an operation. When the device is to be restarted, a Start I/O instruction is executed.
- Clock interrupt - may signal the end of a process's time slice.

The traps are used to invoke primitive operations; to support monitors, the kernel may have entries for traps corresponding to:

-Entering a monitor.
-Exiting a monitor.
-Signaling a condition.
-Waiting for a conditon.

In addition, traps may be used to support synchronous I/O (DO_IO) or asynchronous I/O.

We developed an efficient kernel to support monitors on single CPU systems. The simplicity of this kernel is largely due to the technique of disabling interrupts to enforce mutual exclusion inside monitors. This technique implies that at most one monitor at a time can be active.

We also developed a multiple CPU kernel that allows more than one monitor to be active at once. This kernel is based on a virtual processor that prevents multiple simultaneous activations of the kernel.

CHAPTER 8 BIBLIOGRAPHY

The single CPU kernel presented in this chapter was developed from work on the SUE/11 operating system [Greenblatt and Holt] and from an unpublished design by C.A.R. Hoare. The multiple CPU kernel was developed from work on the SUE/360 operating system. Wirth describes another kernel for the PDP-11 that supports monitors and processes, without time slicing. Wirth's kernel supports Modula, a concurrent dialect of Pascal.

Greenblatt, I.E. and Holt, R.C. The SUE/11 operating system. INFOR, Canadian Journal of Operational Research and Information Processing 14,3 (October 1976), 227-232.

Wirth, N. Modula: a language for modular programming (and two other articles by Wirth in the same issue). Software Practice and Experience Vol. 7,1 (January-February 1977), 3-35.

CHAPTER 8 EXERCISES

1. The kernel designs presented in this chapter have no provision for error checking. For example, if a process passes the number of a nonexistent condition to the wait routine, the kernel may crash. What error checking is appropriate for a kernel? Estimate the increase in CPU time required in primitives (e.g., in wait) if error checking is incorporated. What error checking can be done at compile time to avoid run time checking by the kernel?

2. It has been suggested that the signal operation should imply an immediate return of the signaling process from the monitor. This is the case in the Concurrent Pascal language. Modify the single and multiple CPU designs for kernels to support this interpretation of signals. What effect does this have on monitor entries that return values (i.e., entries that behave like function procedures).

3. Augment the PDP-11 kernel given in this chapter to support multiple process priority conditions.

4. Implement a kernel for the System/360 (or some other computer) by translating the design of the single CPU kernel to 360 assembly language.

5. Use a PDP-11 processor handbook and determine the time to execute wait and signal as implemented for the PDP-11 in this chapter. You will need to make certain assumptions, e.g., model of PDP-11 and average number of executions of the INSERT loop.

6. C.A.R. Hoare suggests that when a process wakes up another process using signal, the signaler should be placed on a special "urgent" queue, waiting to get back into the monitor. Each time a process exits the monitor, the urgent queue is checked and, if non-empty, a waiting signaler is given control of the monitor. The implementation of monitors given in this chapter does not use an urgent queue. Instead, the signaler is put on the ready queue. Give the design of a kernel that uses an urgent queue. What logical difference (if any) does the urgent queue make to processes? What difference is there in the kernel's size and

speed? What difference is there in terms of the performance of
processes?

7. Throughout this chapter, we have made no mention of changing
the priorities of processes (used in ordering the ready queue).
In many single systems, fixed priorities may be sufficient,
because the relative importance to performance of each process
may be known at system construction time. However, changing the
priorities dynamically can be important. Specify a primitive
that allows a process to change its priority. The kernel can
improve performance by giving priority to I/O bound jobs. This
is equivalent to decreasing the priority of processes that use a
lot of CPU time. Since the kernel can observe which jobs use
most of the CPU time, it can decrease their priorities. Give a
very simple change to the single CPU kernel's design that
automatically adjusts priorities, so I/O bound jobs are favored.

8. In the design of the multiple CPU kernel it was assumed that
I/O interrupts favor those CPUs that are running idle processes.
Why was this assumption made and what would happen if it were not
true? Redesign the kernel so it does not depend on this
assumption.

9. What would be the result of using the following versions of
enter and exit kernel:

```
Enterkernel:
    Save status of running;
    TESTANDSET(kernelbusy);
    DO WHILE(kernelwasbusy);
        TESTANDSET(kernelbusy);
        END;
    Disable interrupts;

Exitkernel:
    Enable interrupts;
    kernelbusy=FALSE;
    Restore status of running;
```

10. The first kernel design (for single CPU systems) allows only
one monitor to be active at a given time. The second kernel
design allows multiple monitors to be active concurrently. What
are the implications for operating system organization of the
restriction of a single active monitor at a time?

11. The design of the single CPU kernel implements mutual
exclusion in monitors by disabling and enabling interrupts. What
implication does this implementation technique have for the use
of monitors in organizing operating systems? (We assume that it
is obvious that only one monitor at a time can be active.)

12. A virtual processor was defined for use by the multiple CPU
system. That processor gives the kernel mechanisms that are
similar to the mechanisms provided by a monitor, namely, mutual
exclusion and the ability to block/wakeup calling processes.

Specify as a language feature a modified version of a monitor that is like this virtual processor. Give the implementation of these modified monitors in terms of the kernel's virtual processor. Note that this is equivalent to the (recursive) implementation of virtual processors in terms of a virtual processor.

13. Use the virtual processor defined for the multiple CPU system to implement semaphores.

14. Suppose your operating system supports semaphores. Show how these semaphores can be used to support monitors, without the need of a kernel (other than the one that supports semaphores).

15. Specify the functional characteristics for a multiple CPU system that supports (in the hardware) the virtual processor needed for the multiple CPU kernel.

16. Implement SIGNAL/WAITDEVICE for the PDP-11 (or other computer).

17. Implement a kernel for a single CPU PDP-11 system that is based on the multiple CPU kernel given in this chapter. Your kernel will allow several monitors to be active at once. Compare the speed of your kernel with the single CPU kernel given in this chapter.

18. The single CPU kernel for the PDP-11 that was given in this chapter was made smaller and faster by the following assumption. When a process executes a trap instruction it is not currently using registers R1 to R5. Consequently, some saving and restoring of registers was avoided. What are the security implications of sometimes avoiding this saving and restoring? If your process works for (or against) the KGB and another process works against (or for) the KGB, how might your process try to spy on the other process, given the knowledge that saving/restoring registers is sometimes avoided?

APPENDIX 1

SPECIFICATIONS FOR THE SP/k LANGUAGE

SP/k is a sequence of subsets of the PL/I language that has been developed for the purpose of teaching computer programming. SP/k was designed at the University of Toronto, and this appendix is an adaptation of a technical report by Richard C. Holt and David B. Wortman.

Since SP/k is a compatible subset of PL/I, SP/k programs can be run under a variety of compilers, including the University of Toronto's SP/k compiler and Cornell University's PL/C compiler. Details about running SP/k programs under the CSP/k compiler are given in Appendix 5.

In the interest of making PL/I more suitable for pedagogic purposes, SP/k restricts or eliminates many PL/I features. In SP/k every variable must be declared. Declarations are not allowed to specify number bases (binary versus decimal) or precisions; this avoids problems arising from the precision rules of full PL/I. Implicit conversions are not allowed among numeric, logical and character types, thereby eliminating conversion anomalies.

Features implied by the following keywords are not in SP/k: binary, complex, initial, external, pointer, goto, on, and begin. The following PL/I features are eliminated: fixed-length character strings, label variables, operations on entire arrays, pseudo variables, data-directed input/output, static allocation, controlled allocation, based allocation, multitasking, and compile-time processing.

Instead of giving a complete list of the omitted PL/I features, we will specify SP/k by giving a list of included features. Language features introduced by subsets SP/1 to SP/7 are summarized in the following table.

```
Subset    Features Introduced

SP/1      Characters:  letters, digits and special characters
          Constants:  fixed, float and character string
          Expressions:  +, -, *, /, fixed to float conversion
          Simple output:  put list
          Mathematical built-in functions:  mod, sin, cos, atan,
                     log, exp, sqrt.

SP/2      Identifiers and variables
          Declarations:  fixed and float
          Assignment statements (with float to fixed conversion)
          Simple input:  get list

SP/3      Comparisons: <, >, =, <=, >=, ¬=
          Logical expressions:  &, |, and ¬
          Selection:  if-then-else and non-iterative do group
          Repetition:  do while loop and indexed do loop
          Paragraphing
          Logical constants:  '0'B (false) and '1'B (true)
          Logical variables:  the bit attribute

SP/4      Character string expressions: concatenation
          Character string variables (varying length only)
          Character string comparison and blank padding
          Character string built-in functions:  length and substr

SP/5      Arrays (including multiple dimensions)

SP/6      Procedures:  subroutines and functions
          Calling and returning
          Arguments and parameters
          Side effects and dummy arguments
          Arrays and character strings as arguments

SP/7      Detailed control of input and output: get and put edit
```

The following sections give detailed specifications for each subset. In describing the subsets, we will use this notation:

> [item] means the item is optional
> |item| means the item can appear zero or more times

When presenting the syntax of language constructs, items written in upper case letters, for example,

    PROCEDURE

denote keywords; these items must appear in SP/k jobs exactly as presented. Items written in lower case letters, for example,

    statement

denote one of a class of constructs; each such item is defined below as it is introduced.

SP/1: INTRODUCTION OF EXPRESSIONS AND OUTPUT

We now begin the specification of the first subset.

A <u>character</u> is a letter or a digit or a special character.

A <u>letter</u> is one of the following:

   A B C D E F G H I J K L M N O P Q R S T U V W X Y Z $ # ∂

A <u>digit</u> is one of the following:

   0 1 2 3 4 5 6 7 8 9

A <u>special</u> <u>character</u> is one of the following:

   + - * / ( ) = < > . : ; ? % & | ¬
   b (blank)
   ' (apostrophe or single quote)
   _ (break character or underscore)

A <u>fixed</u> <u>constant</u> is one or more digits (without embedded blanks), for example:

   4   19   243   92153

A <u>float</u> <u>constant</u> consists of a mantissa followed by an exponent (without embedded blanks). The <u>mantissa</u> must be one or more digits with an optional decimal point. The <u>exponent</u> must be the letter E, followed by an optional plus or minus sign followed by one or more digits. The following are examples of float constants.

   5.16E+00   50E0   .9418E24   1.E-2

Note that a fixed constant may <u>not</u> contain a decimal point. Note also that a float constant need not contain a decimal point, but <u>must</u> contain an exponent.

There is a maximum allowed number of digits in a fixed constant. There is a maximum allowed number of digits in the mantissa of a float constant and a maximum allowed magnitude of exponent. (These maximum values will vary from compiler to compiler; see Appendix 5.)

A <u>literal</u> (or <u>character</u> <u>string</u> <u>constant</u>) is a single quote (an apostrophe), followed by zero or more occurrences of non-single-quote characters or twice repeated single quotes, followed by a single quote. The following are examples of literals:

   'FRED'   'X=24'   'MR. O''REILLY'

There is a maximum length of character strings (see Appendix 5).

Each constant must appear entirely on one card, i.e., constants must not cross card boundaries.

In SP/1, an <u>expression</u> is one of the following:

        fixed constant
        float constant
        literal
        +expression
        -expression
        expression + expression
        expression - expression
        expression * expression
        expression / expression
        (expression)
        built-in function

Float and fixed values may be combined in expressions. When a fixed value is combined with a float value, the result is a float value.

Evaluation of expressions proceeds from left to right, with the exceptions that multiplications and divisions have higher precedence than (i.e., are evaluated before) additions and subtractions and that parenthesized sub-expressions are evaluated before being used in arithmetic operations. Unary operations (+ and -) are evaluated before binary operations. Division (/) can be used only when one or both of the operands are float values. Division of a fixed value by a fixed value is not allowed (but many compilers will accept it, see Appendix 5). The following are examples of legal expressions.

        -4+20   2*8.5E+00   (4.0E+01-12.0E+01)/-2

The values of these three expressions are, respectively, 16, 17.0E+00, and 4.0E+01.

Character strings cannot be used in arithmetic operations. In SP/k there are no implicit conversions from numeric values to character string values or vice versa.

An SP/1 built-in function call is one of the following:

        MOD(expression , expression)
        SIN(expression)
        COS(expression)
        ATAN(expression)
        LOG(expression)
        EXP(expression)
        SQRT(expression)

The MOD function accepts two fixed expressions as arguments and produces a fixed result. The SIN, COS, ATAN, LOG, EXP, and SQRT mathematical functions accept a single fixed or float expression as an argument and produce a float result. Appendix 4 gives a more detailed description of CSP/k built-in functions.

An SP/1 _statement_ is one of the following:

```
PUT [SKIP] LIST(expression |,expression| );
PUT PAGE LIST(expression |,expression| );
```

An SP/1 _program_ is:

```
T:PROCEDURE OPTIONS(MAIN);
   |statement|
   END;
```

Remember that the notation |statement| means zero or more statements. The following is an example of an SP/1 program:

```
T:PROCEDURE OPTIONS(MAIN);
   PUT SKIP LIST(2, 'PLUS', 3, 'MAKES', 2+3);
   END;
```

The output from this example is: 2   PLUS   3   MAKES   5

Output produced by the PUT LIST statement is placed in successive "fields" across the print line. All fields have the same width. A new print line is started when all fields on the preceding line have been used, or when SKIP (or PAGE) is used in the PUT LIST statement. (See Appendix 5 for the number of and size of these fields.)

When a literal is printed by a PUT LIST statement, its enclosing single quotes are removed. In addition, twice repeated single quotes in a literal are printed as one single quote. A long string may use several fields. If the printed string exactly fills all the columns of a field, then the next field is skipped.

SP/2: INTRODUCTION TO VARIABLES, INPUT AND ASSIGNMENT

We now begin the specifications of the second subset, SP/2.

An _identifier_ is a letter followed by zero or more letters, digits, or break characters (underscores). An identifier cannot contain embedded blanks. Most compilers allow identifiers to be at least 31 characters long. Some compilers limit the identifier which names a program to 7 characters.

An SP/2 _program_ is:

```
identifier:PROCEDURE OPTIONS(MAIN);
   |declaration|
   |statement|
   END;
```

A <u>declaration</u> is:

    DECLARE(variable |,variable|)attribute
     |,(variable |,variable|)attribute|;

An <u>attribute</u> is one of the following:

    FIXED
    FLOAT

A <u>statement</u> is one of the following:

    PUT [SKIP] LIST(expression |,expression|);
    PUT PAGE LIST(expression |,expression|);
    variable = expression;
    GET [SKIP] LIST(variable |,variable|);

In SP/2, each <u>variable</u> is simply an identifier. (There are no arrays in SP/2.)

In SP/k all variables must be declared.

In SP/2 an expression may be a variable.

Float values may be assigned to fixed variables. Any non-integer part of such a float value is truncated (towards zero) before the assignment without a warning message. Fixed values may be assigned to float variables with automatic conversion.

The items in the data (the input stream) read by GET LIST statements must be separated by one or more blanks. When a GET LIST statement is executed, one data item is read for each variable in the statement.

Each item in the input stream must be a literal, a float constant, a fixed constant or a non-integer fixed constant. A <u>non-integer fixed constant</u> is one or more digits <u>with a decimal point</u>. The following are examples of non-integer fixed constants:

    3.14159   243.12

Non-integer fixed constants should not appear in programs, but can appear in data.

Any numeric constant (float, fixed or non-integer fixed) can be read (and will be automatically converted if necessary) into a float variable. Similarly, any numeric constant can be read (and will be automatically truncated if necessary) into a fixed variable. There are no automatic conversions from character string values to numeric values or vice versa.

A <u>keyword</u> is any of the special identifiers, e.g., PROCEDURE, GET, and LIST, that are part of the SP/k syntax. A variable must not be given the same name as a keyword.

Any number of blanks (or card boundaries) can appear between symbols, e.g., between constants, keywords, identifiers, operators +, -, *, / and the parentheses (and). When constants, keywords or identifiers are adjacent, for example, the adjacent keywords PUT and LIST, they must be separated by at least one blank.

A <u>comment</u> consists of the characters /* followed by any characters except the combination */ followed by the characters */. A blank cannot appear between the / and * or between the * and /. Comments can appear wherever blanks can appear. A comment must not cross a card boundary. Hence, any comment which would cross a card boundary should be closed by */ at the end of one card and continued by /* on the next card. In general, it is good practice for comments to appear on separate lines or at the ends of lines. Some compilers do not allow the initial /* of a comment to start in card column 1. Comments cannot appear in the data.

SP/3: INTRODUCTION OF LOGICAL EXPRESSIONS, SELECTION AND REPETITION

A <u>logical</u> <u>condition</u> is one of the following:

```
'0'B
'1'B
¬logical condition
logical condition & logical condition
logical condition | logical condition
comparison
(logical condition)
logical variable
```

A logical condition is sometimes called a <u>logical</u> <u>expression</u>. The constant '0'B means "false" and '1'B means "true".

A <u>comparison</u> is one of the following:

```
expression < expression
expression > expression
expression = expression
expression <= expression
expression >= expression
expression ¬= expression
```

An <u>attribute</u> is one of the following:

```
FIXED
FLOAT
BIT
```

Variables declared to have the BIT attribute are called logical variables. Logical variables can be operands in the logical operations of and (&), or (|) and not (¬). Float and fixed values cannot be operands in logical operations.

(Some compilers, namely, PL/C and PL/I Level F, do not allow logical variables to be declared as simply BIT. For these compilers, the attribute BIT(1) must be used instead.)

The and operator (&) has higher priority than the or operator (|). Logical variables can be compared, assigned, read, and printed. Logical variables can be compared only for equality or inequality.

There is no implicit conversion between numeric values (fixed and float) and logical values. Logical values cannot participate in arithmetic operations.

An SP/3 statement is one of the following:

```
PUT [SKIP] LIST(expression |,expression| );
PUT PAGE LIST(expression |,expression| );
variable = expression;
GET [SKIP] LIST(variable |,variable| );
IF logical condition THEN
   statement
[ELSE
   statement]
DO WHILE(logical condition);
   |statement|
   END;
DO identifier = expression TO expression [BY expression];
   |statement|
   END;
DO;
   |statement|
   END;
```

In the indexed DO group (second DO group above), the index variable (identifier) must have been declared to be a fixed variable. (Even after arrays are introduced, the index must still be simple, i.e., not an array element.) Each of the expressions is evaluated once at the beginning of the execution of the loop. The BY clause specifies a step size. If the BY clause is omitted, a step size of 1 is assumed.

When the third expression (step size) is positive, the indexed DO group is equivalent to the following:

```
        start = first expression;
        limit = second expression;
        step = third expression (or 1 if no by clause);
        identifier = start;
        DO WHILE(identifier <= limit);
            |statement|
            identifier = identifier + step;
            END;
```

If the third expression is negative, the comparison in the above
DO WHILE group becomes >=.

The following is an example of an SP/3 program.

```
        SP3:PROCEDURE OPTIONS(MAIN);
            DECLARE(N,X,TOTAL)FIXED;
            TOTAL=0;
            GET LIST(N);
            DO WHILE(N>0);
                GET LIST(X);
                TOTAL=TOTAL+X;
                N=N-1;
                END;
            PUT LIST('TOTAL IS',TOTAL);
            END;
```

Paragraphing rules are standard conventions for indenting
program lines. Some compilers provide automatic paragraphing of
programs. If this feature is available, it should be used.

A set of paragraphing rules can be inferred from the method
used to present SP/k constructs. For example, the DO WHILE group
was presented in the following form:

```
        DO WHILE(condition);
            |statement|
            END;
```

This form means that the statements enclosed in a DO WHILE group
should be indented beyond the level of the opening "DO WHILE"
line. The construct "END;" which closes the group should be
indented to the same level as the enclosed statements.

Comments should be indented to the same level as their
corresponding program lines. The continuation(s) of a long
program line should be indented beyond the line's original
indentation. If the level of indentation becomes too deep, it
may be necessary to abandon indentation rules temporarily,
maintaining a vertical positioning of lines.

SP/4: INTRODUCTION OF CHARACTER STRING VARIABLES AND EXPRESSIONS

An <u>attribute</u> is one of the following:

```
FIXED
FLOAT
CHARACTER(maximum length)VARYING
BIT
```

Variables declared to have the attribute CHARACTER(maximum length)VARYING are called <u>character</u> <u>string</u> <u>variables</u>. In the declaration of character string variables, <u>maximum</u> <u>length</u> must be a fixed constant. The concatenation operator (||) can be used to join two strings together. Both of its operands must be character strings.

There are two built-in functions, SUBSTR and LENGTH, which operate on character string values. The SUBSTR built-in function can accept two or three arguments. (SUBSTR cannot be used as a PL/I pseudo variable.) See Appendix 4 for a detailed description of SUBSTR.

The LENGTH built-in function has one argument which must be a character string expression. Character strings can be compared, assigned, read and printed. When character strings of different lengths are compared, the shorter string is automatically extended (on the right) with blanks to the length of the longer string.

In general, a character string variable assumes the length of the string which is assigned to it (or read into it via a get list statement). However, if the maximum length of the variable being assigned to is less than the length of the string being assigned, then before assignment the assigned value is automatically truncated (on the right) to this maximum length.

There is no implicit conversion between character string values and numeric or logical values.

SP/5: INTRODUCTION OF ARRAYS

The form of declaration remains as it was:

A <u>declaration</u> is:

```
DECLARE(variable |,variable| )attribute
       |,(variable |,variable| )attribute|;
```

However, the form of <u>variable</u> is now allowed to specify array bounds. In a declaration, a variable is now:

```
identifier [(range |,range| )]
```

A range is one of the following:

        fixed constant
        [-] fixed constant : [-] fixed constant

The first form of range assumes the lower bound is 1, and specifies the upper bound. The second form specifies both the lower and upper bounds.

In an expression, or in a GET LIST statement, a variable has the form:

        identifier [(expression |,expression|)]

Each array index expression must have a numeric value. A float value used as an array index will be truncated to a fixed value.

Array elements may be compared, assigned, read, and printed on an element by element basis, in the same way as scalar variables with similar attributes.

SP/6: INTRODUCTION OF PROCEDURES

In SP/6 the form of program is extended to allow the definition of (internal) procedures.

An SP/6 program is:

        identifier:PROCEDURE OPTIONS(MAIN);
            |declaration|
            |definition|
            |statement|
            END;

A definition is:

        identifier:PROCEDURE [(identifier |,identifier|)]
            [RETURNS(attribute)];
            |declaration|
            |definition|
            |statement|
            END;

Two new statements are added:

        CALL procedure name [(expression |,expression|)];
        RETURN [(expression)];

All parameters to a procedure must be declared. Parameters are passed to procedures "by reference"; this means that when a procedure assigns a value to a parameter, the corresponding

argument in the call to the procedure actually receives the
value. If an array is a parameter, then the ranges for each
array index must be declared by an asterisk (*) in the procedure.
If a character string is a parameter, then the maximum length of
the character string must be declared by an asterisk (*) in the
procedure. This example illustrates these requirements:

```
SUPERSTR:PROCEDURE(S,I);
    DECLARE(S)CHARACTER(*)VARYING;
    DECLARE(I(*,*))FIXED;
    ...
    END;
```

A <u>subroutine</u> is a procedure which does not have the RETURNS
clause in its definition. A subroutine can be invoked only by
the CALL statement. Return from a subroutine must be (a) via a
RETURN statement without the optional RETURN expression or (b)
via the last statement of the subroutine (when the last statement
is not a RETURN statement).

A <u>function</u> is a procedure which has the RETURNS clause in its
definition. A function can be invoked only by using its name
(with arguments if required) in an expression. Return from a
function must be via a RETURN statement having an expression
whose attribute matches the attribute given in the RETURNS
clause. (It is legal to have a fixed value as the RETURN
expression in a float function and vice versa; automatic
conversion of returned values will take place for these cases.)

SP/7: INTRODUCTION OF EDIT DIRECTED INPUT AND OUTPUT

Statements giving explicit control of the format of input and
output data are introduced.

A <u>statement</u> is one of the following:

```
PUT SKIP [(lines to skip)];
PUT [SKIP[(lines to skip)]] LIST (expression
    |,expression|);
PUT PAGE LIST (expression |,expression|);
PUT [SKIP[(lines to skip)]] EDIT (expression
    |,expression|)(format item |,format item|);
PUT PAGE EDIT (expression |,expression|)
    (format item |,format item|);
PUT PAGE;
variable = expression;
GET SKIP [(cards to skip)];
GET [SKIP[(cards to skip)]] LIST (variable
    |,variable|);
GET [SKIP[(cards to skip)]] EDIT (variable
    |,variable|)(format item |,format item|);
```

```
IF logical condition THEN
   statement
[ELSE
   statement]
DO WHILE (logical condition);
   |statement|
   END;
DO identifier=expression TO expression
   [BY expression];
   |statement|
   END;
DO;
   |statement|
   END;
CALL procedure name [(expression |,expression|)];
RETURN [(expression)];
```

PUT EDIT statements allow the specification of a particular number of columns to be printed. When successive items are printed via a PUT EDIT statement, each item is printed immediately next to the preceding item. This is in contrast to PUT LIST statements, which cause items to be printed in equal fields across the page. GET EDIT statements are analogous and allow the specification of particular card columns to be read. This means that EDIT data items need not be separated by blanks or commas.

It is possible to use both LIST directed input-output and EDIT directed input-output in the same program. To avoid confusion, LIST and EDIT directed input-output should not be mixed in printing a particular line, or in reading a particular card. Those who insist upon mixing the two for printing a single line should understand the following details. LIST output always proceeds to the next standard output field, while EDIT output always starts at the current position. LIST output actually prints a blank after each item; hence, when an EDIT item follows a LIST item on a print line, the two will be separated by a blank. Those who insist upon mixing LIST and EDIT directed input when reading a single card should understand the following details. Each LIST data item must be followed immediately by a comma or blank. If the next read is via a GET EDIT statement, the current position is taken to be that just beyond this blank or comma. Following the reading of a data item via GET EDIT, scanning for a LIST data item begins just beyond the EDIT item.

In the PUT SKIP forms, lines to skip can be any numeric expression; if the value is float, it is truncated to fixed. If the lines to skip clause is omitted from the SKIP clause, then the remainder of the current line is left blank and output continues on the next line.

If the value of lines to skip, call it x, is positive, then the printer will return to column 1 while performing x line ejects. Putting this another way, the remaining columns (if any) of the current line will be left blank, and x-1 blank lines will then be printed. If x is zero (or negative), the effect is a return to column 1 of the current line (with no line eject). Note: when x is equal to 1, it is equivalent to omitting the lines to skip clause.

In the GET SKIP forms, if the cards to skip clause is omitted from the SKIP clause, the remainder of the current card is ignored, and input continues from the next card.

In the GET SKIP forms, cards to skip can be an expression. If it is a float value, it is truncated to a fixed value. This fixed value, call it x, must be at least 1. The next x cards (where the remainder of the current card counts as one card) will be ignored. Note: SKIP(1) is equivalent to SKIP with cards to skip omitted.

If a SKIP clause is specified and the current card or line is positioned after the last valid data column, then one card or line is counted as having been skipped by moving to the next card or line even though there were no available data columns to be skipped.

A format item is one of the following:

X(width)	(to skip columns)
COLUMN(position)	(to skip columns)
F(width [,fractional digits])	(for numeric values)
E(width, fractional digits)	(for numeric values)
A[(width)]	(for character strings)
B(width)	(for logical values)
P picture specification	(to print dollars)

The X and COLUMN format items are used only for control of the format (skipping columns). The other format items, F, E, A, B, and P, are data transferring items. In the EDIT forms there must be the same number of data transferring format items as there are data items to be transferred. The last format item of a list must be a data transferring item and can not be X or COLUMN.

The terms position, width, or fractional digits must be arithmetic expressions; usually these are fixed constants. If the value is float, it is truncated to a fixed value.

The format item X(width) causes width columns to be skipped on input, or width blanks to be printed on output. If width is negative it is treated as zero. (Note: punch cards have 80 columns. Lines have 120 columns on many printers; however, other printers may provide, for example, 72, 80 or 132 columns.)

The COLUMN format item causes skipping of columns until the column numbered position is reached. If position is zero or negative, or if position is greater than the size of the card or line, it is replaced by one. If the current card or line is already positioned after column <u>position</u>, a skip to the next card or line is performed, followed by skipping columns until the column numbered <u>position</u> is reached.

The F and E format items are used to read and write both FIXED and FLOAT variables.

For E and F format items on output, fractions are rounded and not truncated when insufficient space is allocated for the fractional digits. The values printed under control of E and F format items are right-justified and padded on the left with blanks.

On input, the F format item causes the next <u>width</u> columns to be read as a fixed number. If <u>fractional digits</u> is given in the format item, it must be at least one and it specifies the insertion of a decimal point the given number of places from the right of the number, producing a non-integer fixed constant; the effect is that if the decimal point is omitted from the data, scaling occurs. If <u>fractional digits</u> is omitted, the data is assumed to be an integer fixed constant. If a decimal point appears in the input data, then the actual value of the data is used, ignoring the specified <u>fractional digits</u>. The number being read may be preceded or followed by blanks. A completely blank field is read as zero. (Note: when a non-integer fixed constant is read into a FIXED variable, the value is truncated to an integer.) On output, if <u>fractional digits</u> is not specified, an integer is printed with no decimal point, but if it is specified, a non-integer fixed constant is printed with the designated precision of fraction. In no case does the F format item cause scaling on output.

The E format item on input causes the reading of a field of size <u>width</u> containing a float constant. If a decimal point is present in the float constant, the specification of <u>fractional digits</u> is ignored. Otherwise, a decimal point is inserted <u>fractional digits</u> from the right of the mantissa (the effect is that if the decimal point is omitted in the data, scaling occurs). If the field is completely blank, this is an error. The exponent can be omitted from values read under control of the E format item. On output, the number is printed as a float constant. (Note: the <u>fractional digits</u> field must be specified in the E format item.)

When using an E format item on output, the field width must be at least large enough to print the float value. In particular, the number of columns specified by <u>width</u> should be at least seven plus <u>fractional digits</u>. (The float value is printed in the form mD.|f|Esdd where m is a possible leading minus sign, D is a non-zero digit (unless the float value is zero), |f| is the string of fractional digits, s is a plus or minus sign, and dd is the exponent magnitude.)

The A format item is used for the transfer of character data. The specified number of characters are transferred. On input, quotes are not required around the data item. On output, if the field is wider than the data item, the item is left-justified and padded with blanks on the right; if the field is not as wide as the data item, the item is truncated on the right. On output width can be omitted and then the current length of the data item is used. (The width field must be specified for input.)

The B format item is used for transfer of logical (declared BIT) data items. On input, the value can be preceded or followed by blanks. On output, the value is printed left-justified and padded on the right with blanks. Logical data values are 0 or 1 (not '0'B or '1'B as they are within a program and for LIST input-output).

For format items F, E, A, and B, width must be greater than zero.

The P format item is used for writing numbers, usually as dollar values. Numbers cannot be read using the P format item. Only FIXED values can be written using this format item. Each P format item consists of the letter P followed by a sequence of picture elements in quotes. For example, P'$ZZ,ZZ9.99DB' is a P format item whose sequence of picture elements is $ZZ,ZZ9.99DB. The following picture elements can be used.

element	use
.	period insertion
,	comma insertion
$	floating dollar sign
Z	digit position, suppress zero
9	digit position
CR	negative indicator
DB	negative indicator

These elements must appear in a picture specification in this order. First, zero or more dollar signs with optional periods and commas. Next, zero or more Zs with optional periods and commas. Next, one or more 9s with optional periods and commas. Finally, an optional CR or DB; this is printed for negative numbers.

The period is printed where specified if a digit is to be printed to its immediate left, otherwise a blank is printed.

(Note: since FIXED variables must have integer values in SP/k, dollar values should be represented internally as cents. When printing such a value, the decimal point for dollars can be inserted using a period in a picture specification.)

Similarly, a comma is printed where specified if a digit is to be printed to its immediate left, otherwise a blank is printed.

The dollar sign indicates that a digit may be printed, unless the digit is a leading zero in which case blank is printed, except for the rightmost of a series of such dollar sign positions, and here a dollar sign is printed. The dollar sign will also "float" across commas and periods that are embedded in a series of dollar signs.

The Z signifies printing of a digit unless it would be a leading zero, in which case a blank is printed.

The nine signifies that a digit (0 to 9) is to be printed.

The credit symbol (CR) or debit symbol (DB) is printed only if the number is negative. If a negative number is to be printed, then DB or CR must be present.

The following is an example of the use of a picture format item:

```
PUT EDIT(21612)(P'$ZZ,ZZ9.99DB');
```

This statement will print $bbb216.12bb (the letter b is used here to represent a blank). Now consider this statement:

```
PUT EDIT(PROFIT)(P'$$,$$9.99DB');
```

This table gives the output for selected values of PROFIT:

PROFIT	output
259271	$2,592.71
39100	$391.00
2516	$25.16
5	$0.05
-481	$4.81DB

APPENDIX 2

SPECIFICATION OF CSP/k EXTENSIONS TO SP/k

The Concurrent SP/k (CSP/k) language is an extension to the SP/k language (SP/7 subset), designed to allow concurrent programming with monitors. SP/k is a compatible subset of the PL/I language, but CSP/k is not, because monitors are not a feature of PL/I. The CSP/k extensions were designed in Spring 1976 at the University of Toronto by Richard C. Holt and Reinhard Menzel.

The concurrency features of CSP/k will be presented in the following order:

(1) Processes, reentrant procedures.
(2) Monitors, entries.
(3) Condition variables, signaling and waiting.
(4) The busy statement, simulation.

The reader is assumed to be familiar with the specifications of SP/k as given in Appendix 1. See Appendix 3 for the syntax of SP/k and CSP/k.

PROCESSES

CSP/k extends the syntax of SP/k by allowing CONCURRENT as an alternative to the keyword MAIN. When MAIN is specified, the program is exactly an SP/k program. When CONCURRENT is specified, the program can include processes and monitors.

A <u>program</u> is one of the following:

```
identifier:PROCEDURE OPTIONS(MAIN);
   |declaration|
   |definition|
   |statement|
   END;
```

```
identifier:PROCEDURE OPTIONS(CONCURRENT);
   |declaration|
   |block|
   |process|
   END;
```

Each of the declarations immediately following the OPTIONS(CONCURRENT) line are for <u>global variables</u>, which are accessible by all statements in the CSP/k program. (These declarations have the same syntax and meaning as SP/k declarations; other terms such as "statement" will not be explained here because they keep their meaning from SP/k, although extended in some cases as explained below).

Each <u>block</u> can be a definition of a procedure or a monitor. (Monitors will be explained in the next section.) Each of these procedures is called a <u>global procedure</u>. A global procedure can be called from any monitor or global procedure that follows it in the source program, and from any process. Each global procedure is reentrant, meaning that it can be executed simultaneously by more than one process. Each time a global procedure is called, space for its local variables is (re)allocated and when the procedure returns these variables lose their values.

A <u>process</u> is:

```
identifier:PROCESS [(memory requirement) ];
   |declaration|
   |definition|
   |statement|
   END;
```

Each process is like an SP/k main program. These processes execute concurrently. A process terminates by executing its last statement (or by executing a RETURN statement). The identifier preceding the keyword PROCESS is for program documentation; a process cannot be called; it begins executing automatically.

The processes can communicate with each other by changing and inspecting global variables, although this can easily lead to errors. Generally, processes communicate by means of monitors.

Each process requires a certain amount of memory space for its variables. When the process calls a procedure, the requirement increases, to provide space for the procedure's local variables. When the procedure returns, the requirement decreases to its former amount. The CSP/k processor estimates these requirements and allocates space for each process at compile time. For small programs that do not use recursion, these estimates are sufficient. When procedures are called recursively (called by themselves directly or indirectly) the compiler can make no reasonable estimate of required space. The programmer can provide his own estimate of a process's required space as a parenthesized integer following the keyword PROCESS. This estimate is in bytes and can be based on statistics from previous program executions.

MONITORS AND ENTRIES

As was explained in the last section, a block can be the definition of a procedure or can be a monitor. Monitors will now be specified.

A block is one of the following:

```
definition

identifier:MONITOR;
    |declaration|
    |definition|
    DO;
        |statement|
        END;
    |entry|
    END;
```

The identifier preceding the keyword MONITOR is for program documentation; a monitor can only be invoked by calling one of its entries (see below).

The declarations immediately inside a monitor are for variables that can be accessed only from inside the monitor; these variables are permanent in that they retain their values from invocation to invocation of the monitor. It is only in these particular declarations that "condition variables" can be created (see next section).

The procedures that are defined following these declarations can be called only from within the monitor.

The statements inside DO and END comprise the initialization for the monitor. These statements are executed before the processes begin their execution. Given several monitors, their initializations are performed one after the other in the order the monitors appear in the program. The initialization of each monitor must be specified, but can be null as in "DO;END;". Initialization statements in a monitor can be used to initialize global variables.

An <u>entry</u> is:

```
identifier:ENTRY [(identifier |,identifier| )]
   [RETURNS(attribute)];
   |declaration|
   |definition|
   |statement|
   END;
```

Entries are similar to procedures and can be called like subroutines (by the CALL statement) or like functions. Calling and returning from entries is similar to calling and returning from procedures. An entry has access to the variables declared inside its monitor; the only way a process can modify or inspect these variables is by calling an entry. Global procedures can be called from entries and global variables can be accessed from entries.

It is guaranteed that only one process at a time will be executing inside a monitor. As a result, mutually exclusive access to a monitor's variables is implicitly provided. If process P calls an entry of a monitor while another process is executing in the monitor, process P will be blocked and not allowed in the monitor until no other process is executing in the monitor.

Like procedures, entries are reentrant. Space for local variables is allocated at each call and released at each return.

CONDITION VARIABLES

CSP/k introduces the CONDITION attribute with an optional PRIORITY specification.

An <u>attribute</u> is one of the following:

```
FIXED
FLOAT
CHARACTER(maximum length)VARYING
BIT
CONDITION [PRIORITY]
```

The only place the CONDITION attribute can be used is in one of the declarations immediately inside a monitor. The only allowed use of condition variables is in the WAIT and SIGNAL statements and in the EMPTY built-in function; conditon variables cannot be assigned, compared or passed as parameters. Arrays of condition variables are allowed.

Two new statements are introduced:

```
WAIT(condition variable [,priority value] );
SIGNAL(condition variable);
```

The WAIT and SIGNAL statements specify a variable defined as a CONDITION. These statements can appear only in monitors (but not in monitor initialization statements).

When a process executes a WAIT statement for condition C it is blocked and is removed from the monitor. When a process executes a SIGNAL statement for condition C, one of the processes (if there are any) waiting for condition C is unblocked and allowed immediately to continue executing in the monitor. The signaling process is temporarily removed from the monitor and is not allowed to continue execution until no processes are in the monitor. If no processes were waiting for condition C, the only effect of the SIGNAL statement is that the signaling process may temporarily be removed from the monitor. The signaling process cannot in general know whether other processes have entered the monitor before the signaler continues in the monitor.

If the condition variable is declared with the PRIORITY option, the WAIT statement must specify a priority value; otherwise the priority value is not allowed in WAIT. The priority value is an expression that must evaluate to a nonnegative fixed value. The processes waiting for a CONDITION PRIORITY variable are ranked in order of their specified priority values, and the process with the smallest priority value is the first to be unblocked by a SIGNAL statement.

In the case of processes waiting for non-priority condition variables, or waiting with identical priorities for a priority condition variable, the scheduling is "fair", meaning that a particular waiting process will eventually be unblocked given enough signals on the condition. (In the CSP/k implementation, this fairness is accomplished by FIFO ranking of processes.)

A built-in function named EMPTY accepts a condition variable as an argument. It returns true ('1'B) if no processes are waiting for the condition variable, otherwise false ('1'B). Like WAIT and SIGNAL, EMPTY can appear only inside a monitor (but not in initialization statements).

The variables in a monitor represent its state. For example, if a monitor allocates a single resource, only one monitor variable is needed and it can be declared as BIT. When this variable is true ('1'B) it represents the state in which the resource is available, when false it represents the state of being allocated. When a process enters a monitor and finds that it does not have a desired state, the process leaves the monitor and becomes blocked by executing a WAIT statement on a condition variable. The condition variable corresponds to the state that the process is waiting for. Suppose a process enters a monitor and changes its state to a state that may be wanted for by other processes. The process should execute a SIGNAL statement for the condition variable corresponding to the new state. If there are processes waiting for this state transition, then they will be blocked at the condition variable, and one of them will immediately resume execution in the monitor. Because of this immediate resumption, the signaled process knows the monitor is in the desired state, without testing monitor variables. The signaling process is allowed to continue executing only when no other processes are in the monitor. If no processes were waiting at the condition variable, the only effect of the SIGNAL statement is to temporarily remove the signaler from the monitor.

As specified by Hoare, monitors and condition variables are intended to be used in the following manner. The programmer should associate with the monitor's variables a consistency criterion. The consistency criterion is a logical expression that should be true between monitor activations, or whenever a process enters or leaves a monitor. Hence, the programmer should see that it is made true by the monitor's initialization statements and is true before each SIGNAL or WAIT statement in the monitor and before each return from an entry of the monitor. The programmer should also associate a logical expression, call it Ei, with each condition variable Ci. The expression Ei should be true whenever a SIGNAL is executed for condition variable Ci. A process that is unblocked after waiting for a condition variable knows that Ei is true because the signaled process (not the signaling process) executes first. (The consistency criterion and each Ei for a condition variable do not necessarily appear as executable code in the monitor.) In general, when a process changes the monitor's state so that one of the awaited relations Ei becomes true, the corresponding condition variable Ci should be signaled.

THE BUSY STATEMENT

A statement is introduced to allow simulation using timing delays:

    BUSY(time);

The "time" must be an expression that evaluates to a nonnegative fixed value. The BUSY statement can be understood in terms of simulated time recorded by a system clock. This clock is set to zero at the beginning of execution of a program. With the exception of the BUSY statement (or WAIT statements causing an indirect delay for a BUSY statement), statements take negligible simulated time to execute. When the programmer wants to specify that a certain action requires time to complete, the BUSY statement is used. The process that executes a BUSY statement is delayed until the system clock ticks (counts off) the specified number of time units. (In the CSP/k processor, this is implemented by ordering the queue of delayed processes according to their desired wakeup times and running only the process with the earliest wakeup time.) At the completion of a program's execution, the utilization of each process that used the BUSY statement is reported. This utilization is defined as the process's busy time (its time spent waiting for a BUSY statement) divided by a final value of the system clock.

APPENDIX 3

THE STATEMENT SYNTAX OF SP/k AND CSP/k

Notation: [item] means the item is optional.
         |item| means the item is repeated zero or more times.

A <u>program</u> is one of the following:
```
                identifier:PROCEDURE OPTIONS(MAIN);
                    |declaration|
                    |definition|
                    |statement|
                    END;

                identifier:PROCEDURE OPTIONS(CONCURRENT);
                    |declaration|
                    |block|
                    |process|
                    END;
```

A <u>declaration</u> is: DECLARE(variable |,variable|)attribute
```
                    |,(variable |,variable| )attribute|;
```

An <u>attribute</u> is one of the following:
```
                FIXED
                FLOAT
                CHARACTER(maximum length)VARYING
                BIT
                CONDITION [PRIORITY]
```

A <u>definition</u> is: identifier:PROCEDURE[(identifier |,identifier|)]
```
                    [RETURNS(attribute)];
                    |declaration|
                    |definition|
                    |statement|
                    END;
```

A <u>block</u> is one of the following:
                  definition

```
                  identifier:MONITOR;
                     |declaration|
                     |definition|
                     DO;
                        |statement|
                        END;
                     |entry|
                     END;
```

An <u>entry</u> is:
```
                  identifier:ENTRY[(identifier |,identifier|)]
                     [RETURNS(attribute)];
                     |declaration|
                     |definition|
                     |statement|
                     END;
```

A <u>process</u> is:
```
                  identifier:PROCESS[(memory requirement)];
                     |declaration|
                     |definition|
                     |statement|
                     END;
```

A <u>statement</u> is one of the following:
```
                  PUT SKIP [(lines to skip)];
                  PUT [SKIP[(lines to skip)]] LIST (expression
                     |,expression|);
                  PUT PAGE LIST (expression |,expression|);
                  PUT [SKIP[(lines to skip)]] EDIT (expression
                     |,expression|)(format item |,format item|);
                  PUT PAGE EDIT (expression |,expression|)
                     (format item |,format item|);
                  PUT PAGE;
                  variable = expression;
                  GET SKIP [(cards to skip)];
                  GET [SKIP[(cards to skip)]] LIST (variable
                     |,variable|);
                  GET [SKIP[(cards to skip)]] EDIT (variable
                     |,variable|)(format item |,format item|);
                  IF logical condition THEN
                     statement
                  [ELSE
                     statement]
                  DO WHILE(logical condition);
                     |statement|
                     END;
                  DO identifier = expression TO expression
                     [BY expression];
                     |statement|
                     END;
                  DO;
                     |statement|
                     END;
```

```
CALL identifier [(expression [,expression])];
RETURN [(expression)];
WAIT(condition variable[,priority value]);
SIGNAL(condition variable);
BUSY(time);
```

Note: The only place a condition variable can be declared is immediately inside a monitor.

APPENDIX 4

BUILT-IN FUNCTIONS IN SP/k AND CSP/k

a. An arithmetic built-in function.

MOD(i,j) - remainder of i divided by j; i and j must be fixed
    values. The result is fixed.

b. Mathematical built-in functions.

For these functions, the arguments may be float or fixed.
The result is float.

SIN(x) - sine of x radians.
COS(X) - cosine of x radians.
ATAN(x) - arctangent of x in radians.
LOG(x) - natural logarithm of x.
EXP(x) - e to the x power.
SQRT(x) - square root of x.

c. String built-in functions.

LENGTH(s) - number of characters (currently) in string s.
SUBSTR(s,i [,j]) - substring of s from i-th to last character
    [or from i-th character for a length of j characters].

In SUBSTR, s must be a character string; i [and j] must be
fixed or float; the result is a character string. The values of
i and j are truncated to fixed values when given as float. The
substring selected by i [and j] must be contained entirely within
s. This means that i should be at least one, j should be
positive or zero and i plus j minus one should not exceed the
length of string s; otherwise there is an error. Some compilers,
such as PL/C, require that i must be at most equal to the length
of s. Other compilers, such as the CSP/k compiler, allow i to be
one more than the length of s when j is zero or j is omitted.

d. A condition built-in function.

EMPTY(c) - true ('1'B) if no processes are waiting for
    condition c, false ('0'B) otherwise.

APPENDIX 5

THE SP/k AND CSP/k COMPILERS

The CSP/k compiler was constructed by Reinhard Menzel at the University of Toronto as an extension of the existing SP/k compiler. CSP/k includes SP/k as a subset; SP/k is a subset of PL/I. See Appendix 1 for the specifications of the SP/k language and Appendix 2 for CSP/k extensions to SP/k.

As of summer 1977 the SP/k compiler runs on the IBM 360/370 computers, Digital Equipment PDP-11 computers and UNIVAC 9030 computers. The CSP/k compiler runs on the IBM 360/370 computers. Persons interested in obtaining one of these compilers should contact: SP/k Distribution Manager, Computer Systems Research Group, 216C Sandford Fleming Building, University of Toronto, Toronto, Ontario, M5S 1A4, Canada.

CONTROL CARD PARAMETERS

The first card of a CSP/k job is called the job card, for example

    $JOB ID='ADAM HOLT'

The ID parameter as shown in this example job card causes the name ADAM HOLT to be printed in a header box preceding the printing of the CSP/k program. The three characters ID= are optional, so the above job card is equivalent to

    $JOB 'ADAM HOLT'

Other parameters can be given on the job card, as we show in this example:

    $JOB ID='ADAM HOLT',STMTS=10000,LINES=300

The parameter STMTS=10000 specifies that the job is to be allowed to execute 10000 statements before being terminated for excess running time. The parameter LINES=300 specifies that the job is to be allowed to print, via PUT statements, 300 lines before being terminated for excess lines. STMTS can be abbreviated as S and LINES can be abbreviated as L. Individual computer centers may have different job card parameters.

The CSP/k program is terminated by the following card

$DATA

Data cards (if any) for the CSP/k job follow.

HANDLING ERRORS IN CSP/k PROGRAMS

When an error is found in a CSP/k program, the CSP/k compiler generally makes an attempt to repair the error. The programmer is warned that these repairs are not to be taken as intelligent advice for producing a correct program, but instead as a method of allowing processing to continue. This strategy of automatic error repair is intended to minimize programmer frustration and required computer runs.

We will now show how a number of common errors are handled. Since compilers are always being modified, the treatment of these errors by a particular version of the CSP/k compiler may differ slightly from what we present.

Here is the listing of a simple CSP/k program in which the PROCEDURE OPTIONS line has been forgotten.

```
   1
      ?
 ****     SYNTAX ERROR IN PREVIOUS LINE.  LINE IS REPLACED BY:
   1 $NIL:PROCEDURE OPTIONS(MAIN);

   2     PUT LIST('HELLO');
   3     END;
```

As you can see, the missing line is supplied by the compiler and the program is given the name $NIL. The program is executed and prints HELLO. If the programmer forgets a semicolon, the compiler is often able to insert it, as is shown here:

```
   2     PUT LIST('HELLO')
                         ?
 ****     SYNTAX ERROR IN PREVIOUS LINE.  LINE REPLACED BY:
   2     PUT LIST('HELLO');
```

If the programmer forgets the right-hand quote mark from a literal, the compiler inserts a quote mark, although probably not in the desired place. In the following example, the quote mark between the O of HELLO and the right parenthesis has been omitted. The compiler inserts a quote mark after the semicolon. As a result, the line requires a new right parenthesis and semicolon because the original right parenthesis and semicolon were absorbed into the literal. Note that the right quote mark was not present on the card, but was inserted by the compiler.

```
    2    PUT LIST('HELLO); '

 ****    STRING IS ENDED WITH QUOTE(')

 ****    SYNTAX ERROR IN PREVIOUS LINE.  LINE IS REPLACED BY:
    2    PUT LIST('HELLO); ');
```

When this program runs, it will print HELLO); instead of HELLO.

In the next example, a forgotten right parenthesis is inserted by the compiler.

```
    2    PUT LIST('HELLO';
                          ?
 ****    SYNTAX ERROR IN PREVIOUS LINE.  LINE IS REPLACED BY:
    2    PUT LIST('HELLO');
```

In the next example, the keyword PROCEDURE has been misspelled.

```
    1 SAMPLE:PROCDEURE OPTIONS(MAIN);
              ?
 ****    SYNTAX ERROR IN PREVIOUS LINE.  LINE IS REPLACED BY:
    1 SAMPLE:PROCEDURE OPTIONS(MAIN);
```

The following CSP/k program does not make sense because it tries to use the value of the variable named INCHES, but INCHES is never given a value. To allow the program to execute, INCHES is given the value 1.

```
    1 SP2:PROCEDURE OPTIONS(MAIN);
    2    DECLARE(CENTIMETERS,INCHES)FLOAT;
    3    CENTIMETERS=2.54E0*INCHES;
    4    PUT LIST('LENGTH IS',CENTIMETERS);
    5    END;
 ****ERROR IN LINE 5: FLOAT VARIABLE HAS NO VALUE; 1.0E+00 USED
LENGTH IS         2.54000E+00
```

The next program attempts to read data items into two variables: WIDTH and HEIGHT. The data as provided by the programmer contains only one data item, so the program is stopped because it attempts to read beyond the end of the data.

```
    1 SP2:PROCEDURE OPTIONS(MAIN);
    2    DECLARE(WIDTH,HEIGHT)FLOAT;
    3    GET LIST(WIDTH,HEIGHT);
    4    PUT LIST('AREA IS',WIDTH*HEIGHT);
    5    END;
 ****ERROR IN LINE 3: NO MORE INPUT DATA
```

The next program has WEIGHT misspelled as WIEGHT in line 4. The compiler assumes (wrongly) that WEIGHT and WIEGHT are different variables; fortunately, it warns us about its wrong assumption. Note that the value of WEIGHT remains as 7.5E0.

```
1 SP2:PROCEDURE OPTIONS(MAIN);
2     DECLARE(WEIGHT)FLOAT;
3     WEIGHT=7.5E0;
4     WIEGHT=2.2E0*WEIGHT;
5     PUT LIST('WEIGHT IS',WEIGHT);
6     END;
****ERROR IN LINE 4: UNDECLARED VARIABLE ASSUMED FIXED
WEIGHT IS        7.50000E+00
```

In the next program, it was forgotten to read values of NUMBER inside the loop. As the program now stands, there is an infinite loop because NUMBER is not changed inside the loop.

```
1 SP3:PROCEDURE OPTIONS(MAIN);
2     DECLARE(NUMBER,SUM)FIXED;
3     SUM=0;
4     NUMBER=0;
5     DO WHILE(NUMBER¬=-99999);
6         SUM=SUM+NUMBER;
7         END;
8     PUT LIST('SUM IS',SUM);
9     END;
****ERROR IN LINE 6: EXECUTION LIMIT EXCEEDED
```

The next program tries to find the last name of Bill McKeeman, but since the name McKeeman contains 8 letters and not 9 letters, the substring does not lie within the string.

```
1 SP4:PROCEDURE OPTIONS(MAIN);
2     DECLARE(NAME,LAST_NAME)CHARACTER(20)VARYING;
3     NAME='BILL MCKEEMAN';
4     LAST_NAME=SUBSTR(NAME,6,9);
5     PUT LIST('LAST NAME IS',LAST_NAME);
6     END;
****ERROR IN LINE 4: SPECIFIED SUBSTRING NOT WITHIN STRING
LAST NAME IS    ?
```

In the next program the NAME array contains elements NAME(1), NAME(2), NAME(3), and NAME(4). The program is supposed to read four names followed by the dummy name ZZZ. When the program runs, there is an error because an attempt is made to read ZZZ into NAME(5), but NAME(5) does not exist. The error can be corrected by increasing the declared upper bound of NAME to 5.

```
 1 SP5:PROCEDURE OPTIONS(MAIN);
 2    DECLARE(NAME(4))CHARACTER(20)VARYING;
 3    DECLARE(I)FIXED;
 4    I=1;
 5    GET LIST(NAME(I));
 6    DO WHILE(NAME(I)¬='ZZZ');
 7       PUT LIST(NAME(I));
 8       I=I+1;
 9       GET LIST(NAME(I));
10       END;
11    END;
****ERROR IN LINE 9: SUBSCRIPT OUT OF RANGE;   LOWER BOUND USED
```

CHARACTERISTICS OF THE CSP/k COMPILER

In this section we list limits of the CSP/k compiler and those language aspects that it handles in its own particular way.

Error Recovery. A large number of errors in programs will be automatically "repaired".

Card boundaries. Identifiers, keywords, constants and comments cannot cross card boundaries in a program. Constants read by GET LIST cannot cross card boundaries. If a constant uses the last columns of one card and another constant uses the first columns of the next card, the two constants are read separately.

Use of card columns for programs. When a program is presented using punch cards, all 80 columns are used.

Reserving of keywords. Keywords must not be used as the names of variables. Variables must not begin with the characters $JOB or $DATA.

Two character operators. This compiler does not in general enforce the convention that blanks may not be embedded in two character operators such as >=. (In fact, it allows blanks in >=, <= and ¬= but not in ||.)

Length of identifiers. Identifiers can be at most 31 characters long.

Width of print fields. For printers with 120 or 132 columns, there are 5 fields per print line with 24 columns per field. For printers with 72 or 80 columns, there are 5 fields per line with 14 columns per field.

Form of printed numbers. Each fixed or float value printed by a PUT LIST statement is right-justified in the first 12 columns of the next print field. Float values are printed in the form mD.dddddEsdd where m is an optional minus sign, D is a non-zero digit, each d is a digit, and s is a plus or minus sign. (Exception: D is zero when the float value is zero.)

Range of fixed values. Fixed values have a maximum magnitude of 999999999.

Non-integer fixed constants. Non-integer fixed constants, e.g., 214.8, are flagged as errors in programs and are automatically converted to float. Non-integer fixed constants are accepted (without error messages) in data.

Range of float values. Float values have a maximum magnitude of 1E36.

Precision of float arithmetic. Float arithmetic is accurate to approximately 6 significant figures.

Length of character strings. Character strings can be, at most, 127 characters long.

Definition before use. The definition of a procedure or entry must appear before its invocation. (Calling of a following procedure which has the same name and parameter attributes as a global procedure will result in a call to the global procedure instead of a call to the following procedure; no error message will be issued.)

Checks for recursion. Any procedure (except the main procedure) can be called recursively.

Conversion of arguments. Conversion of fixed scalar arguments to float scalar formal parameters (and vice versa) is automatic and creates a dummy argument.

Dummy arguments. Arguments preceded by a unary plus or enclosed in parentheses will have a dummy argument created. Assignment of a value to a parameter having a dummy argument does not change the value of the actual argument.

Division of fixed values. Division of fixed values, for example 7/3, results in an error message, and the truncated (towards zero) value of the quotient is used.

Collating sequence. The version of the CSP/k compiler that runs on the IBM 360/370 has IBM standard (EBCDIC) order of characters for comparisons:

b.<(+|&$*);¬-/,%_>?:#@'=ABCDEFGHIJKLMNOPQRSTUVWXYZ0123456789

Reserved words. The following are keywords in CSP/k and must not be used as names of variables or procedures.

BIT	DO	IF	PROCEDURE	THEN
BUSY	EDIT	LIST	PROCESS	TO
BY	ELSE	MAIN	PUT	VARYING
CALL	END	MONITOR	RETURN	WAIT
CHARACTER	ENTRY	OPTIONS	RETURNS	WHILE
CONCURRENT	FIXED	PAGE	SIGNAL	$DATA
CONDITION	FLOAT	PRIORITY	SKIP	$JOB
DECLARE	GET			

RESTRICTIONS ON CONCURRENCY FEATURES

Initialization of monitors. Monitor initialization code must not contain a RETURN statement and must not cause execution of a BUSY, WAIT or SIGNAL statement or the EMPTY function. Conditions are implicitly initialized to be empty. Monitors are initialized in the order they appear within the CSP/k program.

Calls to entries. A process that has entered a monitor cannot call an entry of a monitor or execute a BUSY statement until returning from the monitor.

Coherence of input and output. The CSP/k processor always completes one input/output operation before starting another. Calls to function entries is illegal in GET and PUT statements.

Randomness of concurrency. Concurrency in processes is provided by "pseudo-random" time slicing, which is unpredictable to the programmer, but reproducible in that identical programs with identical data produce identical output.

SIZE RESTRICTIONS OF THE CSP/k COMPILER

Release 1.0 of the CSP/k compiler has the following size restrictions:

    25K bytes of program
    30K bytes of data
    200 symbol table entries
    128 global data items
    128 global entities (procedures, entries and processes)
    128 data items in any one monitor
    32 monitors
    32 depth of statically nested procedures
    16384 is system clock limit

CSP/k IMPLEMENTATION

The CSP/k processor was built by extending the existing SP/k processor. The CSP/k language was designed to allow easy implementation and efficient execution, while providing essential language features for concurrent programming. The changes to the SP/k processor required about six weeks of programming effort (by Reinhard Menzel); the resulting CSP/k processor was (almost) bug-free from the beginning. The speed of executing statements by the CSP/k processor is less than 0.3% slower per process than the SP/k processor in spite of the fact that the CSP/k processor has the overhead of time slicing to provide concurrency. Runs of Z7 operating system projects with over ten processes and almost one million executed CSP/k statements have required about two minutes of IBM 370/165-II CPU time.

Since the parser (the first pass) of the SP/k processor is table-driven, a new parser for CSP/k was implemented by simply changing tables. The second pass of the SP/k system is called the semantic phase. It is also table-driven, but uses semantic routines that had to be extended.

The semantic phase produces code for a pseudo-machine (an SP/k machine), which is specially designed to allow easy compilation and efficient interpretive execution of SP/k programs. There is a simulator for this pseudo-machine, and it acts as the third pass of the SP/k processor. This simulator actually executes the SP/k program. The simulator, like the other two passes, is written in a high-level language, the SUE System Language.

The pseudo-machine for SP/k is in many respects similar to the hardware of the Burroughs B-5000, which is designed for easy compilation and efficient execution of Algol-60 programs.

TIME SLICING

The SP/k pseudo-machine was modified to support concurrent processes. This was done by providing process descriptors, to hold the registers of each process, and by implementing time slicing. Time slices occur at statement boundaries (by inter-statement interrupts) and within statements (by intra-statement interrupts). These interrupts are provided by the pseudo-machine simulator, <u>not</u> by the underlying real compiler hardware.

There already existed a pseudo-machine "line number" instruction at each statement boundary. This instruction was used to record the number of the statement, for possible use in run-time error messages, and to count the number of executed instructions. This instruction was extended to provide inter-statement interrupts, although not on every execution, as that would be too inefficient.

If interrupts can occur only on statement boundaries, a class
of timing dependent errors that can occur in production computer
systems is not possible. For example, with only inter-statement
interrupts, the statement

    I = I+1;

always increments I by 1. This is not true when interrupts can
occur within statements. Interrupts within statements were
implemented to allow such realistic race conditions to occur.

Intra-statements interrupts could have been provided by
having the simulator occasionally cause an interrupt between
pseudo-machine instructions. This possibility was rejected
because it involved extra execution by the simulator for every
instruction; this was deemed too inefficient. Instead, the
compiler occasionally emits "time slice" instructions into CSP/k
programs. These instructions may appear anywhere in most kinds
of statements. These time slice instructions occasionally (but
not always) cause an interrupt.

Since line number instructions and time slice instructions
are not very common, and do not always cause interrupts, the
overhead of time slicing is kept quite small.

With this implementation, the programmer cannot predict the
occurrence of interrupts. However, a particular CSP/k program
with a particular set of data will always have the same
interrupts and the same output. If the program is slightly
changed, even by adding a filler statement such as "I=I;" then
the interrupts will probably be different, and the output may be
different.

PROCESS QUEUES AND TIMING

The CSP/k processor uses queues for processes in essentially
the same way as described for single CPU systems in Chapter 8.
There is a ready queue and a queue for each of the conditions.
Each of these queues is managed using priority ordering with FIFO
within a given priority. Condition variables that do not allow
programmer-specified priorities are implemented by always using
the same priority; the resulting ordering is FIFO. If a process
is not currently running, it is on the ready queue or a condition
queue.

The queue of busy processes (waiting at BUSY statements) is
implemented as the last part of the ready queue. The priority of
a process in the ready queue is actually the process's wakeup
time. When a CSP/k program begins execution, the system clock is
set to zero, and all wakeup times for processes are set to zero.
When a process executes a BUSY statement, its wakeup time is set
to its specified delay time plus the current value of the system
clock. When a waiting process is unblocked by a SIGNAL

statement, its wakeup time is set to the current value of the system clock. The processes that have a wakeup time equal to the current (simulated) system clock time are at the front of the queue. They will be executed until all of them are waiting for a condition or for a time delay via the BUSY statement. When this occurs, the system clock is moved forward to the next wakeup time and the next processes in the queue are executed.

Thus the system clock stays at the same value until all processes are either waiting on condition queues or on the ready queue because of a BUSY statement. When this state is reached it means that all possible computation at that value of the system clock has been completed. The system clock then advances to the next value at which any computation is possible.

After a CSP/k program terminates, the utilization of each process that used the BUSY statement is printed. A process's utilization is defined as the proportion of time the process was delayed by BUSY statements versus the final value of the system clock. This is computed by using a field in the process descriptor to accumulate the sum of all parameters to BUSY statements executed by the process. At the end of execution this sum is divided by the final value of the system clock to give the utilization.

The source level CSP/k constructs that cause queues to be manipulated or inspected are EMPTY, WAIT, SIGNAL and BUSY. EMPTY examines the specified condition queue to see if it contains any processes. WAIT inserts the currently running process into the specified condition queue, then removes and runs the first process from the ready queue. If the ready queue is empty then the system is deadlocked and is aborted. SIGNAL tests the condition queue to see if it contains at least one process. If so, the signaling process is inserted into the ready queue, and the first process on the condition queue is removed and made the running process. The BUSY statement inserts the currently running process into the ready queue, then removes the first process from the ready queue and runs it.

When a time slice occurs (due to line number or time slice instruction), the currently running process is inserted into the ready queue. The first process in the ready queue is then removed and made the running process.

All process switching, as just described, uses the process descriptor to store the information needed to restart a process or to order the queues by priority.

Before the processes of a CSP/k program begin execution, their descriptors are placed on the ready queue in a (seemingly) random order.

The implementation of the BUSY statement is simple and efficient, but the user must be wary of making false assumptions

about the properties of the BUSY statement. Take for example the
following program fragment:

```
X: PROCESS;
   CALL A;
   BUSY (2);
   CALL B;
   BUSY (2);
   END;
Y: PROCESS;
   CALL C;
   BUSY (3);
   CALL D;
   BUSY (1);
   END;
```

X and Y are processes executing concurrently; A, B, C, and D are
procedures that the processes use to perform their computations.
It is very easy for the user to think of the BUSY statements as
representing the simulated time taken by a segment of a process.
Many users may think that A and C operate concurrently from time
0 to 2, B and C operate concurrently from time 2 to 3, and B and
D operate concurrently from time 3 to 4. But what actually
happens is that A and C operate concurrently at time 0 until both
are complete, B then operates alone at time 2 and D operates
alone at time 3. Note that B does not operate concurrently with
either C or D.

MUTUAL EXCLUSION IN MONITORS

The CSP/k language specifies that only one process can be
executing in a particular monitor at a given time.   It allows
different monitors to execute concurrently, but does not require
this. The CSP/k processor allows only one monitor at a time to
execute, as this results in an efficient implementation (see
Chapter 8).

Essentially, the CSP/k implementation has a single CPU, which
is the simulator for the pseudo-machine.   Mutual exclusion of
processes in monitors is implemented by preventing interrupts
from occurring in a monitor. The only possible interrupts of the
pseudo-machine are by the line number and time slice
instructions, so the interrupts in monitors are eliminated at
compile time as follows.   During compilation of the code of a
monitor, emissions of time slice instructions are suppressed, and
a variant of the line number instruction which does not cause
interrupts is emitted.

Unfortunately, global procedures can be called from monitors,
as well as from processes. Both inter-process and intra-process
interrupts can occur in global procedures. To suppress these
when called from a monitor, the pseudo-machine has its interrupts

masked at run-time, analogous to the usual trick with traditional computer hardware.

The CSP/k processor could allow different monitors to execute concurrently, by using the logic described for a multiple CPU kernel in Chapter 8. However, this change would cost extra execution time at monitor entry and exit and at WAIT and SIGNAL statements.

MEMORY ALLOCATION

In a block-structured language such as SP/k, Algol-60 or Pascal, the space for variables is typically allocated using a stack. The SP/k pseudo-machine uses a stack, and allocates new space on the stack whenever a procedure is entered. This space is freed (popped off the stack) when the procedure returns. The space for a particular procedure invocation is called its activation record. The pseudo-machine uses a set of pointers, called display registers, that point into the stack and locate activation records. At any point during execution, these registers locate the activation records for the executing procedure, for its surrounding procedure, for the next surrounding procedure, and so on out to the main procedure.

The implementation of CSP/k uses these display registers in the following way. (We will simplify somewhat to shorten the presentation.) Each process has its own set of display registers. The first few of these registers is identical from process to process and locates the global variables and the variables of each of the monitors. These few registers never change once they are set. The remainder of the process's display registers are used just as in SP/k, and each process executes essentially like a separate SP/k program.

Each process has its own stack on which it allocates space when it enters procedures and monitor entries. In SP/k there is a single stack and as long as it does not overflow, there is no problem. If it does overflow then there is no more available space and the execution is aborted. In CSP/k the available space for process stacks is allocated among the processes before they begin execution. The compiler attempts to make a reasonable estimate of each process's required space. It inspects the sequence of calls (direct and indirect) from a process and finds the sequence that requires the most space. It uses this space as its estimate. This estimate is always sufficient, but may be pessimistic (too large).

The algorithm used for estimating this space depends on the fact that in CSP/k procedures (and processes) can only call procedures (and entries) that have been previously defined in the program text. The algorithm is very simple and is executed as a part of the semantic pass. For a particular entity E (process, procedure or entry) the algorithm computes the estimated space requirements of E as the space for its activation record plus the maximum of the estimated space requirements of entities called by E. Since all of the called entities have already been processed, their estimated space requirements are already available.

Two problems were ignored in stating this algorithm. First, each procedure needs a certain amount of space to evaluate expressions; since this amount is small and is not easy to estimate, a standard, generous amount is added to the size of each activation record. Second, if procedures are recursive (they call themselves directly or indirectly), the algorithm fails. This second problem can be solved by the programmer by explicitly giving an estimate of stack size in the source program. If any of the compiler's estimates of stack sizes are observed to be too pessimistic, the programmer may choose to give his own estimates.

After a program's execution, the actual stack space used by each process is printed by the CSP/k processor. (These amounts include the space for the process descriptor, which is about 250 bytes in Release 1.0 of the CSP/k processor. This amount is added to the estimated stack space requirement for a process.)

APPENDIX 6

SIMULATING PROGRAMS FOR Z7 PERIPHERAL DEVICES

This appendix gives the CSP/k programs that simulate the peripheral devices of the Z7 machine, as well as the monitors that interface with these programs. We include this material for two reasons: to show how software processes can be used to simulate hardware processes, and to resolve any ambiguities in the informal descriptions presented in Chapter 6.

The various CSP/k programs are similar in structure, and use a common naming convention for their variables. The devices are called READER, PRINTER, CONSOLE, and DRUM. The interface monitor for each device is called device_SYNC. The processes simulating the devices each have an outermost loop that calls the entry device_COMMAND to obtain a command, executes the command, and finally calls the entry device_READY to signal completion.

Each device has a BIT variable called device_FREE that indicates whether the device is prepared to accept a command. The device also has a CONDITION variable called device_AVAILABLE that is signaled when the device becomes ready to accept a command (i.e., when device_FREE changes state from false to true), and a CONDITION variable called device_START that is signaled when a command is received (i.e., when device_FREE changes state from true to false). The array device_PARAMETERS is used to pass parameters between the process requesting service and the simulated device.

The major I/O devices each contain a BUSY statement referencing the variable device_TIME. DRUM_TIME is the number of time units per page transfer. PRINTER_TIME is the number of time units per word printed. READER_TIME is the number of time units per word read.

In the sections that follow, the descriptions accompanying the programs are not intended to be comprehensive, but rather to clarify certain aspects of the design. The statement numbers allow the various program fragments to be assembled into a single program that simulates the hardware of the Z7 system.

THE CARD READER

The card reader must be able to differentiate between numeric data, which it places into user memory, and textual data, which it places into control memory. The easiest approach would be to require that each data item appear on a separate card. Since this would result in an extremely large input stream, we choose instead to precede each data item with a control character indicating whether a textual or numeric field follows.

The first character of the input stream is a control character, and thereafter a control character must immediately follow the end of each field. A blank control character indicates that the following field is numeric. A numeric field consists of zero or more blanks and/or card boundaries, followed by a number (which may not cross a card boundary), terminated by a blank or a card boundary. A non-blank control character indicates that the following field is textual. The remainder of the current card is ignored, and the contents of the next card up to but not including the delimiter character (which has the same value as the preceding control character) is returned as the text. The delimiter character terminates the field. In the example input stream shown in Appendix 8, the only non-blank control character is the slash ('/'). It is used to identify job control statements.

Note that for simplicity, the card reader and line printer interface monitors are each designed to be used by a single operating system process. An attempt to access either device from more than one process will result in severe concurrency errors. The console interface is much simpler, and does not share this restriction. (In fact, there is no process corresponding to the console; the interface monitor simply prints the text.) The drum interface will be described shortly.

```
93     READER_SYNC:MONITOR;
94          DECLARE(READER_START,READER_AVAILABLE)CONDITION;
95          DECLARE(READER_FREE)BIT;
96          DECLARE(READER_PARAMETERS(1:3))FIXED;
97          DECLARE(READER_TEXT)CHARACTER(80)VARYING;
98          DO;
99             READER_FREE=TRUE;
100            END;

101       DO_READER_IO:ENTRY(BUF_ADDR,BUF_LNTH,REM_LNTH,TEXT);
102            DECLARE(BUF_ADDR,BUF_LNTH,REM_LNTH)FIXED;
103            DECLARE(TEXT)CHARACTER(*)VARYING;
104            READER_FREE=FALSE;
```

```
105        READER_PARAMETERS(1)=BUF_ADDR;
106        READER_PARAMETERS(2)=BUF_LNTH;
107        SIGNAL(READER_START);
108        IF ¬READER_FREE THEN
109            WAIT(READER_AVAILABLE);
110        REM_LNTH=READER_PARAMETERS(3);
111        TEXT=READER_TEXT;
112        END;
113      READER_COMMAND:ENTRY(BUF_ADDR,BUF_LNTH);
114        DECLARE(BUF_ADDR,BUF_LNTH)FIXED;
115        IF READER_FREE THEN
116            WAIT(READER_START);
117        BUF_ADDR=READER_PARAMETERS(1);
118        BUF_LNTH=READER_PARAMETERS(2);
119        END;

120      READER_READY:ENTRY(REM_LNTH,TEXT);
121        DECLARE(REM_LNTH)FIXED;
122        DECLARE(TEXT)CHARACTER(*)VARYING;
123        READER_PARAMETERS(3)=REM_LNTH;
124        READER_TEXT=TEXT;
125        READER_FREE=TRUE;
126        SIGNAL(READER_AVAILABLE);
127        END;
128      END;

729    READER:PROCESS;
730        DECLARE(ADDR,LNTH,REM_LNTH)FIXED;
731        DECLARE(CHAR,CONTROL)CHARACTER(1)VARYING;
732        DECLARE(TEXT)CHARACTER(80)VARYING;
733        GET EDIT(CHAR)(A(1));
734        DO WHILE(TRUE);
735            CALL READER_COMMAND(ADDR,LNTH);
736            REM_LNTH=LNTH;
737            TEXT='';
738            DO WHILE((REM_LNTH>0)&(CHAR=' '));
739                GET LIST(MEMORY(ADDR));
740                ADDR=ADDR+1;
741                REM_LNTH=REM_LNTH-1;
742                GET EDIT(CHAR)(A(1));
743                END;
744            IF REM_LNTH>0 THEN
745                DO;
746                    CONTROL=CHAR;
747                    GET SKIP EDIT(CHAR)(A(1));
748                    DO WHILE(CHAR¬=CONTROL);
749                        TEXT=TEXT||CHAR;
750                        GET EDIT(CHAR)(A(1));
751                        END;
752                    GET EDIT(CHAR)(A(1));
753                    END;
754            BUSY((LNTH-REM_LNTH)*READER_TIME);
755            CALL READER_READY(REM_LNTH,TEXT);
756            END;
757        END;
```

THE LINE PRINTER AND THE CONSOLE

The line printer interface monitor has two entries, one to print numeric data and one to print textual data. Numeric data is printed in ten fields across the page. To print numeric data on the same line as textual data, the number must be converted to a character string, concatenated with the text, and printed using DO_TEXT_PRINTER_IO. A procedure to convert numbers to character strings is provided:

```
CALL NUM_TO_CHAR(NUMBER,TEXT,LNTH);
```

where the meanings of the parameters are:

    NUMBER: the number to be converted
    TEXT: the character string in which to store the result
    LNTH: the desired length of the result

The number will be converted to a character string of length LNTH, and will be right-justified in TEXT. If LNTH is too small then the first character of TEXT will be an asterisk.

```
129     PRINTER_SYNC:MONITOR;
130         DECLARE(PRINTER_START,PRINTER_AVAILABLE)CONDITION;
131         DECLARE(PRINTER_FREE)BIT;
132         DECLARE(PRINTER_PARAMETERS(1:3))FIXED;
133         DO;
134             PRINTER_FREE=TRUE;
135             PRINTER_PARAMETERS(3)=0;
136             END;

137     DO_NUMERIC_PRINTER_IO:ENTRY(BUF_ADDR,BUF_LNTH);
138         DECLARE(BUF_ADDR,BUF_LNTH)FIXED;
139         PRINTER_FREE=FALSE;
140         PRINTER_PARAMETERS(1)=BUF_ADDR;
141         PRINTER_PARAMETERS(2)=BUF_LNTH;
142         SIGNAL(PRINTER_START);
143         IF¬PRINTER_FREE THEN
144             WAIT(PRINTER_AVAILABLE);
145         END;

146     DO_TEXT_PRINTER_IO:ENTRY(TEXT);
147         DECLARE(TEXT)CHARACTER(*)VARYING;
148         PUT SKIP EDIT(TEXT)(A(120));
149         PRINTER_PARAMETERS(3)=0;
150         END;

151     PRINTER_COMMAND:ENTRY(BUF_ADDR,BUF_LNTH,FIELD);
152         DECLARE(BUF_ADDR,BUF_LNTH,FIELD)FIXED;
153         IF PRINTER_FREE THEN
154             WAIT(PRINTER_START);
```

```
155         BUF_ADDR=PRINTER_PARAMETERS(1);
156         BUF_LNTH=PRINTER_PARAMETERS(2);
157         FIELD=PRINTER_PARAMETERS(3);
158         END;

159      PRINTER_READY:ENTRY(FIELD);
160         DECLARE(FIELD)FIXED;
161         PRINTER_PARAMETERS(3)=FIELD;
162         PRINTER_FREE=TRUE;
163         SIGNAL(PRINTER_AVAILABLE);
164         END;
165      END;

166   CONSOLE_SYNC:MONITOR;
167         DO;
168             END;

169      DO_CONSOLE_IO:ENTRY(TEXT);
170         DECLARE(TEXT)CHARACTER(*)VARYING;
171         PUT SKIP EDIT(TEXT)(A(120));
172         END;
173      END;

210   NUM_TO_CHAR:PROCEDURE(NUMBER,TEXT,LNTH);
211      DECLARE(NUMBER,LNTH,J)FIXED;
212      DECLARE(TEXT)CHARACTER(*)VARYING;
213      DECLARE(NEG)BIT;
214      DECLARE(DIGITS)CHARACTER(127)VARYING;
215      IF NUMBER=0 THEN
216         DIGITS='0';
217      ELSE
218         DO;
219             DIGITS='';
220             J=NUMBER;
221             NEG=FALSE;
222             IF J<0 THEN
223                 DO;
224                     J=-J;
225                     NEG=TRUE;
226                     END;
227             DO WHILE(J¬=0);
228                 DIGITS=DIGIT(MOD(J,10))||DIGITS;
229                 J=J/10;
230                 END;
231             IF NEG THEN
232                 DIGITS='-'||DIGITS;
233             IF LENGTH(DIGITS)>LNTH THEN
234                 DIGITS='*'||DIGITS;
235             END;
236      DO WHILE(LENGTH(DIGITS)<LNTH);
237         DIGITS=' '||DIGITS;
238         END;
239      TEXT=DIGITS;
240      END;
```

```
758      PRINTER:PROCESS;
759         DECLARE(ADDR,LNTH,FIELD,I)FIXED;
760         DO WHILE(TRUE);
761            CALL PRINTER_COMMAND(ADDR,LNTH,FIELD);
762            DO I=1 TO LNTH BY 1;
763               PUT EDIT(MEMORY(ADDR))(COLUMN(FIELD*12+1),F(12));
764               ADDR=ADDR+1;
765               FIELD=MOD(FIELD+1,10);
766               END;
767            BUSY(LNTH*PRINTER_TIME);
768            CALL PRINTER_READY(FIELD);
769            END;
770         END;
```

THE DRUM

In contrast to the card reader and line printer, the drum is designed to be used by more than one operating system process. The CONDITION variable DRUM_DONE is used to signal a waiting process that its I/O is complete. DRUM_DONE is signaled when the BIT variable DRUM_IDLE changes state from false to true. Just as with the other devices, the CONDITION variable DRUM_AVAILABLE is used to signal a waiting process that it can use the drum.

This implementation of the drum uses FIFO scheduling of requests. No check is made that MEMORY_ADDRESS is a page boundary. A read from drum occurs if OP_TYPE is non-zero.

```
174      DRUM_SYNC:MONITOR;
175            DECLARE(DRUM_START,DRUM_AVAILABLE,DRUM_DONE)CONDITION
176            DECLARE(DRUM_FREE,DRUM_IDLE)BIT;
177            DECLARE(DRUM_PARAMETERS(1:3))FIXED;
178            DO;
179               DRUM_FREE=TRUE;
180               DRUM_IDLE=TRUE;
181               END;

182         DO_DRUM_IO:ENTRY(OP_TYPE,DRUM_PAGE,MEM_ADDR);
183            DECLARE(OP_TYPE,DRUM_PAGE,MEM_ADDR)FIXED;
184            IF ¬DRUM_FREE THEN
185               WAIT(DRUM_AVAILABLE);
186            DRUM_FREE=FALSE;
187            DRUM_IDLE=FALSE;
188            DRUM_PARAMETERS(1)=OP_TYPE;
189            DRUM_PARAMETERS(2)=DRUM_PAGE;
190            DRUM_PARAMETERS(3)=MEM_ADDR;
191            SIGNAL(DRUM_START);
192            IF¬DRUM_IDLE THEN
193               WAIT(DRUM_DONE);
194            DRUM_FREE=TRUE;
195            SIGNAL(DRUM_AVAILABLE);
196            END;
```

```
197        DRUM_COMMAND:ENTRY(OP_TYPE,DRUM_PAGE,MEM_ADDR);
198            DECLARE(OP_TYPE,DRUM_PAGE,MEM_ADDR)FIXED;
199            IF DRUM_FREE THEN
200                WAIT(DRUM_START);
201            OP_TYPE=DRUM_PARAMETERS(1);
202            DRUM_PAGE=DRUM_PARAMETERS(2);
203            MEM_ADDR=DRUM_PARAMETERS(3);
204            END;

205        DRUM_READY:ENTRY;
206            DRUM_IDLE=TRUE;
207            SIGNAL(DRUM_DONE);
208            END;
209        END;

771    DRUM:PROCESS;
772        DECLARE(DRUM_MEM(0:159,0:19))FIXED;
773        DECLARE(OP_TYPE,DRUM_PAGE,MEM_ADDR,I)FIXED;
774        DO WHILE(TRUE);
775            CALL DRUM_COMMAND(OP_TYPE,DRUM_PAGE,MEM_ADDR);
776            IF OP_TYPE=0 THEN
777                DO I=0 TO PAGE_SIZE-1 BY 1;
778                    DRUM_MEM(DRUM_PAGE,I)=MEMORY(MEM_ADDR+I);
779                    END;
780            ELSE
781                DO I=0 TO PAGE_SIZE-1 BY 1;
782                    MEMORY(MEM_ADDR+I)=DRUM_MEM(DRUM_PAGE,I);
783                    END;
784            BUSY(DRUM_TIME);
785            CALL DRUM_READY;
786            END;
787        END;
```

GLOBAL VARIABLES AND CONSTANTS

Below are the global variables and constants used by the Z7 hardware. Different system configurations and device speeds can be tested by altering their values. Since CSP/k only allows constants in array declarations, these parameters cannot be changed blindly. For example, if MEMORY_SIZE is changed, then the size of the global array MEMORY must also be changed. If DRUM_PAGES or PAGE_SIZE are changed, then the size of the array DRUM_MEM (found in the DRUM process) must be altered.

```
1 Z7:PROCEDURE OPTIONS(CONCURRENT);
2    DECLARE(TRUE,FALSE)BIT;
3    DECLARE(MEMORY_SIZE,DRUM_PAGES,PAGE_SIZE,ACTIVE_JOBS)FIXED;
4    DECLARE(CPU_TIME,DRUM_TIME,PRINTER_TIME,READER_TIME)FIXED;
5    DECLARE(SEGMENT_TABLE_ADDR,CORE_STATUS_ADDR)FIXED;
6    DECLARE(MEMORY(0:799))FIXED;
7    DECLARE(DIGIT(0:9))CHARACTER(1)VARYING;
```

```
 8     SYSTEM_INIT:MONITOR;
 9          DO;
10              TRUE='1'B;
11              FALSE='0'B;
12              MEMORY_SIZE=800;
13              DRUM_PAGES=160;
14              PAGE_SIZE=20;
15              ACTIVE_JOBS=5;
16              CPU_TIME=1;
17              DRUM_TIME=25;
18              PRINTER_TIME=5;
19              READER_TIME=5;
20              DIGIT(0)='0';
21              DIGIT(1)='1';
22              DIGIT(2)='2';
23              DIGIT(3)='3';
24              DIGIT(4)='4';
25              DIGIT(5)='5';
26              DIGIT(6)='6';
27              DIGIT(7)='7';
28              DIGIT(8)='8';
29              DIGIT(9)='9';
30              END;
31          END;

        ...  (Z7 hardware and software goes here)  ...

788    END;
789 /*END OF Z7*/
```

APPENDIX 7

THE Z7 CPU

The Z7 CPU is simulated by a CSP/k process that interprets the Z7 user language, a simple stack-oriented machine language. In this appendix, we first describe the structure of the CPU: its instruction cycle and the way in which its virtual memory facilities are implemented. Then, we describe the user language. In Appendix 8, we give some example user jobs.

CPU STRUCTURE

The CSP/k process that simulates the Z7 CPU consists of an outer loop that first calls an entry in the monitor CPU_SYNC to obtain a user job, then processes the instructions of that job until a trap occurs, and finally calls another entry in CPU_SYNC to signal completion.

The processing of instructions by the Z7 CPU is divided into two phases. During the first phase, the operation code of the instruction is fetched from user memory at the address specified by the instruction pointer, and the instruction pointer is incremented. During the second phase, the instruction is executed in accordance with the semantics that will be described in the next section. The variable CPU_TIME is used in a BUSY statement to specify the number of time units per instruction.

All memory references by the CPU are in the form of virtual addresses, as described in Chapter 7. These references take place via a set of procedures that read from and write to the data segment, and read from the program segment. These procedures use the page tables to perform address mapping, generating page fault traps if necessary. Should either phase of instruction processing be interrupted by a page fault, that phase will be restarted from the beginning. Some instructions reference several pages during a phase, so several page faults are possible; as many as three pages may have to be simultaneously resident for a phase to complete.

The CSP/k code for the CPU is straightforward but rather long. The interface monitor, CPU_SYNC, occupies lines 32-92 in the listing of the hardware. The CPU itself runs from line 241 to line 728. For this reason, we do not list these programs here. All of the simulating programs for the Z7 hardware can be obtained from the Computer Systems Research Group, University of Toronto.

THE INSTRUCTION SET

The Z7 user language is stack-oriented. Most instructions implicitly reference the stack, taking values from it (these values may be interpreted either as virtual memory addresses or as numeric operands) and returning values to it. The stack can be used in another way, as well: space for variables can be allocated in it, and these locations can be explicitly referenced during program execution. The example user jobs in Appendix 8 are written in a block-structured manner, and use the stack in both ways.

There are sixteen different Z7 instructions, varying in length from one to three words. The instructions are:

OP CODE   MNEMONIC and FORMAT

```
    0         BRANCH <addr1> <addr2>
    1         ENTER <addr>
    2         RETURN
    3         REPEAT
    4         EXIT
    5         PUSH <value>
    6         FETCH
    7         STORE
    8         ADD
    9         SUBTRACT
   10         MULTIPLY
   11         DIVIDE
   12         STOP
   13         GET
   14         PUT
   15         ALLOCATE <value>
```

In the paragraphs that follow, the semantics of the various instructions are specified. Instructions with similar functions are grouped together. We use a simple notation to describe the instructions. The variables I and J are registers local to the CPU. A left arrow (<-) denotes a stack operation. IP is the instruction pointer; recall that during the first phase of instruction processing it is incremented to point to the word following the operation code. Explicit memory references consist of a segment name and an offset. STACK_PTR always addresses the word beyond the top of the stack; it is implicitly manipulated by most of the instructions.

The arithmetic operations, ADD, SUTRACT, MULTIPLY, and DIVIDE, use the top two entries of the stack as operands. The result of the operation is placed on the stack.

```
ADD:
    J <- stack;
    I <- stack;
    stack <- I+J;

SUBTRACT:
    J <- stack;
    I <- stack;
    stack <- I-J;

MULTIPLY:
    J <- stack;
    I <- stack;
    stack <- I*J;

DIVIDE:
    J <- stack;
    IF J = 0 THEN
        trap 12;
    ELSE
        DO;
            I <- stack;
            stack <- I/J;
        END;
```

STOP, GET, and PUT each produce traps. (The traps for GET and PUT are issued during the first phase of instruction processing.) The operating system responds to a GET or PUT trap by providing a data segment address (IO_ADDR) to the CPU. In the case of a GET instruction, the CPU places the contents of this address on the top of the stack. In the case of a PUT instruction, the entry on the top of the stack is placed at the specified address.

```
STOP:
    trap 3;

GET:
    stack <- memory(data segment,IO_ADDR);

PUT:
    memory(data segment,IO_ADDR) <- stack;
```

ALLOCATE increases the stack pointer by the amount specified, in order to reserve space for variables. The instruction pointer must be incremented to the word following <value>.

```
ALLOCATE <value>:
   STACK_PTR = STACK_PTR + <value>;
   IP = IP + 1;  /* Bypass <value> */
```

PUSH, FETCH, and STORE each involve data transfers. PUSH places its operand on the top of the stack. FETCH removes the top entry from the stack, treats it as an address, and places the contents of that address on the top of the stack. STORE removes the entry on the top of the stack and places it at the address specified by the second entry on the stack.

```
PUSH <value>:
   stack <- <value>;
   IP = IP+1;  /* Bypass <value> */

FETCH:
   I <- stack;
   stack <- memory(data segment,I);

STORE:
   J <- stack;
   I <- stack;
   memory(data segment,I) = J;
```

ENTER, BRANCH, EXIT, RETURN, and REPEAT each affect the flow of control of Z7 programs. The ENTER instruction causes a transfer to a specified address and places two addresses on the stack. The first of these is the address of the instruction following ENTER; the second is the address to which control is transferred. These two addresses can be used by the EXIT, RETURN, and REPEAT instructions. The BRANCH instruction results in a conditional transfer to one of two specified addresses, depending on the value of the top of the stack. If this entry is greater than zero, control transfers to <addr1>. Otherwise, control transfers to <addr2>. Again, two addresses are placed on the stack. EXIT causes a transfer to the instruction following the most recent ENTER or BRANCH instruction. This is accomplished by removing the top two entries from the stack and transferring control to the address specified by the second entry. (The first entry is discarded; it is an address for use by the REPEAT statement.) The RETURN instruction is a conditional EXIT. If the value of the first stack entry is greater than zero, then two more entries are removed from the stack, and control is transferred to the address specified by the second. This will be the address of the instruction following the most recent BRANCH or ENTER instruction. Finally, the REPEAT instruction causes a conditional transfer of control to the location transferred to by the most recent BRANCH or ENTER instruction; in other words, the place where the current code segment was entered. If the value of the top entry on the stack is greater than zero, then control is transferred to the address specified by the next entry on the stack. This address is returned to the stack.

```
ENTER <addr>:
    stack <- IP+1;  /* Address of following instruction */
    IP = <addr>;
    stack <- IP;  /* Address transferred to */

BRANCH <addr1> <addr2>:
    I <- stack;
    stack <- IP+2;  /* Address of following instruction */
    IF I > 0 THEN
        IP = <addr1>;
    ELSE
        IP = <addr2>;
    stack <- IP;  /* Address transferred to */

EXIT:
    I <- stack;  /* Discard first address */
    IP <- stack;

RETURN:
    I <- stack;
    IF I > 0 THEN
        DO;
            I <- stack;  /* Discard first address */
            IP <- stack;
        END;

REPEAT:
    I <- stack;
    IF I > 0 THEN
        DO;
            IP <- stack;
            stack <- IP;
        END;
```

We conclude this appendix with a list of useful facts about the Z7 virtual memory hardware:

The CPU performs limited validity checking on SEGMENT_TABLE_ADDR (the address of the start of the segment table), CORE_STATUS_ADDR (the address of the start of the core status table), segment table entries (which point to page tables) and page table entries (which point to pages). In each case, the CPU makes certain that the corresponding table or page will fit between the specified address and the end of user memory. However, these addresses need not fall on page boundaries.

While Chapter 7 only discusses recovery from I/O and page fault traps, the Z7 executive may attempt to recover from any trap returned by the CPU. For example, segment table faults (CPU traps 41, 42 and 43) can be used to implement pageable page tables.

Shared program segments can be implemented by setting several segment table entries to point to the same page table.

The value of TIMER is decremented following the instruction fetch phase. Retries caused by page faults do not affect it.

APPENDIX 8

Z7 JOBS

This appendix gives an example job stream for the Z7 machine. Since the absolute decimal code required by the Z7 is not easy to read, the programs are first given in an assembler language commented by statements in a high-level language from which the assembler code could have been compiled.

In Appendix 9, a simple Z7 operating system is used to process these example jobs. The first job computes and prints prime numbers. Output should be 17 13 11 7 5 3. The second job computes and prints the first 40 Fibonacci numbers. The third job reads data cards containing temperatures in Farenheit and prints the corresponding Celsius temperatures. There are 8 data cards; the first contains a 7 indicating that 7 temperatures follow. Output should be -5 7 11 -16 23 37 18. The fourth job promptly divides by zero. The fifth (and last) job reads data cards and prints them along with their factorials. There are 4 data cards; the first contains a 3 indicating that 3 numbers follow. Output should be 3 5 120 9 362880 0 1.

Note that the entry point for each of these example jobs is the fifth from last word: the ALLOCATE instruction corresponding to the BEGIN statement.

```
#JOB PRIMES                          #JOB PRIMES
PR        EQU       0                ARRAY PR 100
I         EQU       100              VARIABLE I
M         EQU       101              VARIABLE M
N         EQU       102              VARIABLE N
COUNT     EQU       103              VARIABLE COUNT
SAVE      .                          BLOCK SAVE
          PUSH      COUNT            COUNT=COUNT+1
          PUSH      COUNT
          FETCH
```

```
         PUSH      1
         ADD
         STORE
         PUSH      PR              PR(COUNT)=N
         PUSH      COUNT
         FETCH
         ADD
         PUSH      N
         FETCH
         STORE
         EXIT                      END
NULL     .                         BLOCK NULL
         EXIT                      END
TEST     .                         BLOCK TEST
         PUSH      I               I=I+1
         PUSH      I
         FETCH
         PUSH      1
         ADD
         STORE
         PUSH      I               RETURN I-COUNT
         FETCH
         PUSH      COUNT
         FETCH
         SUBTRACT
         RETURN
         PUSH      M               M=(PR(I)*(N/PR(I)))
         PUSH      PR
         PUSH      I
         FETCH
         ADD
         FETCH
         PUSH      N
         FETCH
         PUSH      PR
         PUSH      I
         FETCH
         ADD
         FETCH
         DIVIDE
         MULTIPLY
         STORE
         PUSH      M               M=N-M
         PUSH      N
         FETCH
         PUSH      M
         FETCH
         SUBTRACT
         STORE
         PUSH      M               REPEAT M
         FETCH
         REPEAT
         EXIT                      END
```

```
FIND          .                           BLOCK FIND
              PUSH        N                N=N+1
              PUSH        N
              FETCH
              PUSH        1
              ADD
              STORE
              PUSH        I                I=0
              PUSH        0
              STORE
              ENTER       TEST             ENTER TEST
              PUSH        M                IF M THEN SAVE ELSE NULL
              FETCH
              BRANCH      SAVE      NULL
              PUSH        7                REPEAT 7-COUNT
              PUSH        COUNT
              FETCH
              SUBTRACT
              REPEAT
              EXIT                         END
PRINT         .                           BLOCK PRINT
              PUSH        PR               PUT PR(COUNT)
              PUSH        COUNT
              FETCH
              ADD
              FETCH
              PUT
              PUSH        COUNT            COUNT=COUNT-1
              PUSH        COUNT
              FETCH
              PUSH        1
              SUBTRACT
              STORE
              PUSH        COUNT            REPEAT COUNT-1
              FETCH
              PUSH        1
              SUBTRACT
              REPEAT
              EXIT                         END
MAIN          .                           BLOCK MAIN
              PUSH        COUNT            COUNT=0
              PUSH        0
              STORE
              PUSH        N                N=2
              PUSH        2
              STORE
              ENTER       SAVE             ENTER SAVE
              ENTER       FIND             ENTER FIND
              ENTER       PRINT            ENTER PRINT
              EXIT                         END
              ALLOCATE    104              BEGIN MAIN
              ENTER       MAIN
              STOP
```

```
#JOB FIBONACCI                              #JOB FIBONACCI
X           EQU         0                   VARIABLE X
Y           EQU         1                   VARIABLE Y
FIBNUM      EQU         2                   VARIABLE FIBNUM
COUNT       EQU         3                   VARIABLE COUNT
LOOP        .                               BLOCK LOOP
            PUSH        FIBNUM              FIBNUM=X+Y
            PUSH        X
            FETCH
            PUSH        Y
            FETCH
            ADD
            STORE
            PUSH        FIBNUM              PUT FIBNUM
            FETCH
            PUT
            PUSH        X                   X=Y
            PUSH        Y
            FETCH
            STORE
            PUSH        Y                   Y=FIBNUM
            PUSH        FIBNUM
            FETCH
            STORE
            PUSH        COUNT               COUNT=COUNT+1
            PUSH        COUNT
            FETCH
            PUSH        1
            ADD
            STORE
            PUSH        40                  REPEAT 40-COUNT
            PUSH        COUNT
            FETCH
            SUBTRACT
            REPEAT
            EXIT                            END
START       .                               BLOCK START
            PUSH        X                   X=1
            PUSH        1
            STORE
            PUSH        Y                   Y=1
            PUSH        1
            STORE
            PUSH        X                   PUT X
            FETCH
            PUT
            PUSH        Y                   PUT Y
            FETCH
            PUT
            PUSH        COUNT               COUNT=2
            PUSH        2
            STORE
            ENTER       LOOP                ENTER LOOP
            EXIT                            END
```

```
        ALLOCATE   4              BEGIN START
        ENTER      START
        STOP


#JOB CELSIUS                      #JOB CELSIUS
M       EQU        0              VARIABLE M
K       EQU        1              VARIABLE K
I       EQU        2              VARIABLE I
TEMPF   EQU        3              ARRAY TEMPF 20
TEMPC   EQU        23             ARRAY TEMPC 20
INPUT   .                         BLOCK INPUT
        PUSH       TEMPF          GET TEMPF(I)
        PUSH       I
        FETCH
        ADD
        GET
        STORE
        PUSH       I              I=I+1
        PUSH       I
        FETCH
        PUSH       1
        ADD
        STORE
        PUSH       M              REPEAT M-I
        FETCH
        PUSH       I
        FETCH
        SUBTRACT
        REPEAT
        EXIT                      END
CONVERT .                         BLOCK CONVERT
        PUSH       K              K=TEMPF(I)
        PUSH       TEMPF
        PUSH       I
        FETCH
        ADD
        FETCH
        STORE
        PUSH       TEMPC          TEMPC(I)=K-32
        PUSH       I
        FETCH
        ADD
        PUSH       K
        FETCH
        PUSH       32
        SUBTRACT
        STORE
        PUSH       TEMPC          TEMPC(I)=TEMPC(I)*5
        PUSH       I
        FETCH
        ADD
        PUSH       TEMPC
        PUSH       I
        FETCH
```

```
            ADD
            FETCH
            PUSH        5
            MULTIPLY
            STORE
            PUSH        TEMPC           TEMPC(I)=TEMPC(I)/9
            PUSH        I
            FETCH
            ADD
            PUSH        TEMPC
            PUSH        I
            FETCH
            ADD
            FETCH
            PUSH        9
            DIVIDE
            STORE
            PUSH        TEMPC           PUT TEMPC(I)
            PUSH        I
            FETCH
            ADD
            FETCH
            PUT
            PUSH        I               I=I+1
            PUSH        I
            FETCH
            PUSH        1
            ADD
            STORE
            PUSH        M               REPEAT M-I
            FETCH
            PUSH        I
            FETCH
            SUBTRACT
            REPEAT
            EXIT                        END
MAIN        .                          BLOCK MAIN
            PUSH        M               GET M
            GET
            STORE
            PUSH        I               I=0
            PUSH        0
            STORE
            ENTER       INPUT           ENTER INPUT
            PUSH        I               I=0
            PUSH        0
            STORE
            ENTER       CONVERT         ENTER CONVERT
            EXIT                        END
            ALLOCATE    43              BEGIN MAIN
            ENTER       MAIN
            STOP
#DATA                                  #DATA
    7       23      45      52             7       23      45      52
    3       75      100     65             3       75      100     65
```

```
#JOB ZERO DIVIDE                        #JOB ZERO DIVIDE
A           EQU         0               VARIABLE A
B           EQU         1               VARIABLE B
BOMB        .                           BLOCK BOMB
            PUSH        A               A=A/B
            PUSH        A
            FETCH
            PUSH        B
            FETCH
            DIVIDE
            STORE
            EXIT                        END
MAIN        .                           BLOCK MAIN
            PUSH        A               A=999
            PUSH        999
            STORE
            PUSH        B               B=0
            PUSH        0
            STORE
            ENTER       BOMB            ENTER BOMB
            EXIT                        END
            ALLOCATE    2               BEGIN MAIN
            ENTER       MAIN
            STOP


#JOB FACTORIAL                          #JOB FACTORIAL
M           EQU         0               VARIABLE M
N           EQU         1               VARIABLE N
FACT        EQU         2               VARIABLE FACT
FACTORIAL.                              BLOCK FACTORIAL
            PUSH        FACT            FACT=FACT*N
            PUSH        FACT
            FETCH
            PUSH        N
            FETCH
            MULTIPLY
            STORE
            PUSH        N               N=N-1
            PUSH        N
            FETCH
            PUSH        1
            SUBTRACT
            STORE
            PUSH        N               REPEAT N-1
            FETCH
            PUSH        1
            SUBTRACT
            REPEAT
            EXIT                        END
```

```
PRINT       .                           BLOCK PRINT
            ENTER       FACTORIAL       ENTER FACTORIAL
            PUSH        FACT            PUT FACT
            FETCH
            PUT
            EXIT                        END
ONE         .                           BLOCK ONE
            PUSH        FACT            PUT FACT
            FETCH
            PUT
            EXIT                        END
READ        .                           BLOCK READ
            PUSH        M               M=M-1
            PUSH        M
            FETCH
            PUSH        1
            SUBTRACT
            STORE
            PUSH        N               GET N
            GET
            STORE
            PUSH        N               PUT N
            FETCH
            PUT
            PUSH        FACT            FACT=1
            PUSH        1
            STORE
            PUSH        N               IF N THEN PRINT ELSE ONE
            FETCH
            BRANCH      PRINT       ONE
            PUSH        M               REPEAT M
            FETCH
            REPEAT
            EXIT                        END
NULL        .                           BLOCK NULL
            EXIT                        END
MAIN        .                           BLOCK MAIN
            PUSH        M               GET M
            GET
            STORE
            PUSH        M               PUT M
            FETCH
            PUT
            PUSH        M               IF M THEN READ ELSE NULL
            FETCH
            BRANCH      READ        NULL
            EXIT                        END
            ALLOCATE    3               BEGIN MAIN
            ENTER       MAIN
            STOP
#DATA                                   #DATA
    3       5       9       0               3       5       9       0
#END                                    #END
```

The absolute code for the example job stream appears below, in the form required by the Z7 hardware. The numeric parameters on each #JOB card specify the maximum number of instructions that the program should be allowed to execute, the maximum number of output operations, the priority of the job, and the maximum number of stack locations that will be required. Recall that a slash ('/') is used to delimit textual information.

```
/
#JOB PRIMES/   1791      6       0     123
       5     103     5     103     6       5       1       8       7       5
       0       5   103       6       8       5     102       6       7       4
       4       5   100       5     100       6       5       1       8       7
       5     100     6       5     103       6       9       2       5     101
       5       0     5     100       6       8       6       5     102       6
       5       0     5     100       6       8       6      11      10       7
       5     101     5     102       6       5     101       6       9       7
       5     101     6       3       4       5     102       5     102       6
       5       1     8       7       5     100       5       0       7       1
      21       5   101       6       0       0      20       5       7       5
     103       6     9       3       4       5       0       5     103       6
       8       6    14       5     103       5     103       6       5       1
       9       7     5     103       6       5       1       9       3       4
       5     103     5       0       7       5     102       5       2       7
       1       0     1      75       1     105       4      15     104       1
     130      12 /
#JOB FIBONACCI/        1123      40       1      13
       5       2     5       0       6       5       1       6       8       7
       5       2     6      14       5       0       5       1       6       7
       5       1     5       2       6       7       5       3       5       3
       6       5     1       8       7       5      40       5       3       6
       9       3     4       5       0       5       1       7       5       1
       5       1     7       5       0       6      14       5       1       6
      14       5     3       5       2       7       1       0       4      15
       4       1    43      12 /
#JOB CELSIUS/   549      7       3      54
       5       3     5       2       6       8      13       7       5       2
       5       2     6       5       1       8       7       5       0       6
       5       2     6       9       3       4       5       1       5       3
       5       2     6       8       6       7       5      23       5       2
       6       8     5       1       6       5      32       9       7       5
      23       5     2       6       8       5      23       5       2       6
       8       6     5       5      10       7       5      23       5       2
       6       8     5      23       5       2       6       8       6       5
       9      11     7       5      23       5       2       6       8       6
      14       5     2       5       2       6       5       1       8       7
       5       0     6       5       2       6       9       3       4       5
       0      13     7       5       2       5       0       7       1       0
       5       2     5       0       7       1      26       4      15      43
       1     109    12 /
#DATA/
       7      23    45      52       3      75     100      65 /
```

```
#JOB ZERO DIVIDE/        15        0        4       11
        5        0        5        0        6        5        1        6       11        7
        4        5        0        5      999        7        5        1        5        0
        7        1        0        4       15        2        1       11       12 /
#JOB FACTORIAL/         309        7        2       20
        5        2        5        2        6        5        1        6       10        7
        5        1        5        1        6        5        1        9        7        5
        1        6        5        1        9        3        4        1        0        5
        2        6       14        4        5        2        6       14        4        5
        0        5        0        6        5        1        9        7        5        1
       13        7        5        1        6       14        5        2        5        1
        7        5        1        6        0       27       34        5        0        6
        3        4        4        5        0       13        7        5        0        6
       14        5        0        6        0       39       72        4       15        3
        1       73       12 /
#DATA/
        3        5        9        0 /
#END /
```

APPENDIX 9

SIMPLE Z7 OPERATING SYSTEM

This appendix contains an extremely simple operating system
for the Z7 machine. The system has been used to process the
example jobs from Appendix 8, and the output that was produced is
included.

The system processes one user job at a time. In turn, each
user job is read into user memory, then executed, and finally
printed. The system operates in a completely sequential manner;
only one I/O device at a time can be in operation, and there is
no overlap between the CPU and the I/O devices.

There is a single address space whose two page tables (one
for each segment) begin at fixed locations. User input and
output areas are included in the address space of the data
segment. No page faults will occur in this system, nor is
spooling utilized. Memory is organized as follows:

```
000-039    Core Status Table
040-059    Segment Table (only address space 0 used)
060-074    Address Space 0 Segment 0 Page Table
075-094    Address Space 0 Segment 1 Page Table
100-399    Address Space 0 Segment 0
400-599    Address Space 0 Segment 1 Stack
600-699    Address Space 0 Segment 1 Input Area
700-799    Address Space 0 Segment 1 Output Area
```

The CSP/k program for the operating system follows:

```
788    OPERATING_SYSTEM:PROCESS;
789        DECLARE(PROG_START,PROG_LNTH,PROG_LIMIT)FIXED;
790        DECLARE(DATA_START,SCRATCH_START)FIXED;
791        DECLARE(INPUT_START,INPUT_LNTH,INPUT_LIMIT,INPUT_PTR)
               FIXED;
```

```
792        DECLARE(OUTPUT_START,OUTPUT_LNTH,OUTPUT_LIMIT,OUTPUT_PTR)
             FIXED;
793        DECLARE(TRAP,PROG_ENTRY,TRAP_ADDR,IO_ADDR,STACK_LIMIT,
             STACK_PTR,OP_CODE,TIMER)FIXED;
794        DECLARE(REM_LNTH,CPU_LIMIT,CPU_PRIORITY,I,J)FIXED;
795        DECLARE(CONTROL_CARD,STARS)CHARACTER(80)VARYING;
796        STARS='****************************';
797        STARS=STARS||STARS;
798        PROG_START=100;
799        PROG_LNTH=300;
800        DATA_START=400;
801        INPUT_START=600;
802        INPUT_LNTH=100;
803        OUTPUT_START=700;
804        OUTPUT_LNTH=100;
805        SCRATCH_START=95;
           /*INITIALIZE CORE STATUS TABLE*/
806        CORE_STATUS_ADDR=0;
807        DO I=0 TO 39;
808           MEMORY(CORE_STATUS_ADDR+I)=0;
809           END;
           /*INITIALIZE SEGMENT TABLE*/
810        SEGMENT_TABLE_ADDR=40;
811        MEMORY(SEGMENT_TABLE_ADDR+0)=60;
812        MEMORY(SEGMENT_TABLE_ADDR+1)=15;
813        MEMORY(SEGMENT_TABLE_ADDR+2)=75;
814        MEMORY(SEGMENT_TABLE_ADDR+3)=20;
815        DO I=4 TO 19;
816           MEMORY(SEGMENT_TABLE_ADDR+I)=0;
817           END;
           /*INITIALIZE PAGE TABLE*/
818        J=100;
819        DO I=60 TO 94;
820           MEMORY(I)=J;
821           J=J+20;
822           END;
823        CALL DO_READER_IO(SCRATCH_START,1,REM_LNTH,CONTROL_CARD);
824        DO WHILE(SUBSTR(CONTROL_CARD,1,4)¬='#END');
825           IF SUBSTR(CONTROL_CARD,1,4)='#JOB' THEN
826              DO;
                    /*READ #JOB CARD AND PRINT HEADER*/
827                 CALL DO_TEXT_PRINTER_IO(STARS);
828                 CALL DO_TEXT_PRINTER_IO(' ');
829                 CALL DO_TEXT_PRINTER_IO(CONTROL_CARD);
830                 CALL DO_TEXT_PRINTER_IO(' ');
831                 CALL DO_TEXT_PRINTER_IO('    CPU LIM  OUTPUT LIM
                      ||'   PRIORITY   STACK LIM');
832                 CALL DO_READER_IO(SCRATCH_START,4,REM_LNTH,
                      CONTROL_CARD);
833                 CPU_LIMIT=MEMORY(SCRATCH_START+0);
834                 OUTPUT_LIMIT=MEMORY(SCRATCH_START+1)+OUTPUT_START
835                 CPU_PRIORITY=MEMORY(SCRATCH_START+2);
836                 STACK_LIMIT=MEMORY(SCRATCH_START+3);
837                 CALL DO_NUMERIC_PRINTER_IO(SCRATCH_START,4);
838                 CALL DO_TEXT_PRINTER_IO(' ');
```

```
839                           CALL DO_TEXT_PRINTER_IO('OBJECT PROGRAM:');
840                           CALL DO_TEXT_PRINTER_IO(' ');
                              /*READ AND PRINT PROGRAM SEGMENT*/
841                           CALL DO_READER_IO(PROG_START,PROG_LNTH,REM_LNTH,
                                 CONTROL_CARD);
842                           PROG_LIMIT=PROG_START+PROG_LNTH-REM_LNTH;
843                           CALL DO_NUMERIC_PRINTER_IO(PROG_START,PROG_LIMIT-
                                 PROG_START);
844                           CALL DO_TEXT_PRINTER_IO(' ');
845                           CALL DO_TEXT_PRINTER_IO('EXECUTION BEGINS.');
846                           CALL DO_TEXT_PRINTER_IO(' ');
847                           END;
848                   IF SUBSTR(CONTROL_CARD,1,5)='#DATA' THEN
849                       DO;
                              /*READ INPUT DATA*/
850                           CALL DO_READER_IO(INPUT_START,INPUT_LNTH,REM_LNTH,
                                 CONTROL_CARD);
851                           INPUT_LIMIT=INPUT_START+INPUT_LNTH-REM_LNTH;
852                           END;
853                   ELSE
854                       DO;
855                           INPUT_LIMIT=INPUT_START;
856                           END;
                          /*INITIALIZE PRIOR TO STARTING EXECUTION*/
857                   PROG_ENTRY=PROG_LIMIT-PROG_START-5;
858                   IO_ADDR=-1;
859                   STACK_PTR=0;
860                   OP_CODE=-1;
861                   TIMER=CPU_LIMIT;
862                   TRAP=0;
863                   INPUT_PTR=INPUT_START;
864                   OUTPUT_PTR=OUTPUT_START;
                      /*EXECUTE TO COMPLETION*/
865                   DO WHILE(TRAP<3);
866                       TRAP=CPU(0,PROG_ENTRY,TRAP_ADDR,IO_ADDR,STACK_LIMIT,
                             STACK_PTR,OP_CODE,TIMER);
867                       IF TRAP=1 THEN
868                           DO;
                                  /*SERVICE GET TRAP*/
869                               IO_ADDR=INPUT_PTR-DATA_START;
870                               IF INPUT_PTR=INPUT_LIMIT THEN
871                                   TRAP=51;
872                               ELSE
873                                   INPUT_PTR=INPUT_PTR+1;
874                               END;
875                       IF TRAP=2 THEN
876                           DO;
                                  /*SERVICE PUT TRAP*/
877                               IO_ADDR=OUTPUT_PTR-DATA_START;
878                               IF OUTPUT_PTR=OUTPUT_LIMIT THEN
879                                   TRAP=52;
880                               ELSE
881                                   OUTPUT_PTR=OUTPUT_PTR+1;
882                               END;
883                       END;
```

```
                /*PRINT OUTPUT*/
884             CALL DO_NUMERIC_PRINTER_IO(OUTPUT_START,OUTPUT_PTR-
                    OUTPUT_START);
                /*PRINT TRAILER*/
885             CALL DO_TEXT_PRINTER_IO(' ');
886             CALL DO_TEXT_PRINTER_IO('          TRAP      CPU OPS'||
                    ' OUTPUT OPS   INPUT OPS   LAST ADDR');
887             MEMORY(SCRATCH_START+0)=TRAP;
888             MEMORY(SCRATCH_START+1)=CPU_LIMIT-TIMER;
889             MEMORY(SCRATCH_START+2)=OUTPUT_PTR-OUTPUT_START;
890             MEMORY(SCRATCH_START+3)=INPUT_PTR-INPUT_START;
891             IF(OP_CODE>=0)&(OP_CODE<=15)THEN
892                 PROG_ENTRY=PROG_ENTRY-1;
893             MEMORY(SCRATCH_START+4)=PROG_ENTRY;
894             CALL DO_NUMERIC_PRINTER_IO(SCRATCH_START,5);
895             CALL DO_TEXT_PRINTER_IO(' ');
896             CALL DO_TEXT_PRINTER_IO(' ');
897             CALL DO_TEXT_PRINTER_IO(' ');
898             CALL DO_TEXT_PRINTER_IO(' ');
899             END;
900         CALL DO_TEXT_PRINTER_IO(STARS);
901         END;
902     END;
903 /*END OF Z7*/
```

The output produced by this operating system in processing the example jobs of Appendix 8 is shown below. The output for each job begins with a header showing the job card. Then the job's object code and output are printed. Following this is a trailer indicating the number of the trap that caused execution to be halted, the number of instructions executed, the number of output and input operations, and the address of the instruction causing the termination trap. After all of the user jobs have been processed, the operating system shuts down and the CSP/k processor prints process statistics. The line printer process was modified to print five fields per line for this example.

****

#JOB PRIMES

CPU LIM	OUTPUT LIM	PRIORITY	STACK LIM
1791	6	0	123

OBJECT PROGRAM:

5	103	5	103	6
5	1	8	7	5
0	5	103	6	8
5	102	6	7	4
4	5	100	5	100
6	5	1	8	7
5	100	6	5	103

6	9	2	5	101
5	0	5	100	6
8	6	5	102	6
5	0	5	100	6
8	6	11	10	7
5	101	5	102	6
5	101	6	9	7
5	101	6	3	4
5	102	5	102	6
5	1	8	7	5
100	5	0	7	1
21	5	101	6	0
0	20	5	7	5
103	6	9	3	4
5	0	5	103	6
8	6	14	5	103
5	103	6	5	1
9	7	5	103	6
5	1	9	3	4
5	103	5	0	7
5	102	5	2	7
1	0	1	75	1
105	4	15	104	1
130	12			

EXECUTION BEGINS.

17	13	11	7	5
3				

TRAP	CPU OPS	OUTPUT OPS	INPUT OPS	LAST ADDR
3	1791	6	0	151

****

#JOB FIBONACCI

CPU LIM	OUTPUT LIM	PRIORITY	STACK LIM
1123	40	1	13

OBJECT PROGRAM:

5	2	5	0	6
5	1	6	8	7
5	2	6	14	5
0	5	1	6	7
5	1	5	2	6
7	5	3	5	3
6	5	1	8	7
5	40	5	3	6
9	3	4	5	0
5	1	7	5	1

5	1	7	5	0
6	14	5	1	6
14	5	3	5	2
7	1	0	4	15
4	1	43	12	

EXECUTION BEGINS.

1	1	2	3	5
8	13	21	34	55
89	144	233	377	610
987	1597	2584	4181	6765
10946	17711	28657	46368	75025
121393	196418	317811	514229	832040
1346269	2178309	3524578	5702887	9227465
14930352	24157817	39088169	63245986	102334155

TRAP	CPU OPS	OUTPUT OPS	INPUT OPS	LAST ADDR
3	1123	40	0	73

****

#JOB CELSIUS

CPU LIM	OUTPUT LIM	PRIORITY	STACK LIM
549	7	3	54

OBJECT PROGRAM:

5	3	5	2	6
8	13	7	5	2
5	2	6	5	1
8	7	5	0	6
5	2	6	9	3
4	5	1	5	3
5	2	6	8	6
7	5	23	5	2
6	8	5	1	6
5	32	9	7	5
23	5	2	6	8
5	23	5	2	6
8	6	5	5	10
7	5	23	5	2
6	8	5	23	5
2	6	8	6	5
9	11	7	5	23
5	2	6	8	6
14	5	2	5	2
6	5	1	8	7
5	0	6	5	2
6	9	3	4	5
0	13	7	5	2

5	0	7	1	0
5	2	5	0	7
1	26	4	15	43
1	109	12		

EXECUTION BEGINS.

-5	7	11	-16	23
37	18			

TRAP	CPU OPS	OUTPUT OPS	INPUT OPS	LAST ADDR
3	549	7	8	132

****

#JOB ZERO DIVIDE

CPU LIM	OUTPUT LIM	PRIORITY	STACK LIM
15	0	4	11

OBJECT PROGRAM:

5	0	5	0	6
5	1	6	11	7
4	5	0	5	999
7	5	1	5	0
7	1	0	4	15
2	1	11	12	

EXECUTION BEGINS.

TRAP	CPU OPS	OUTPUT OPS	INPUT OPS	LAST ADDR
12	15	0	0	8

****

#JOB FACTORIAL

CPU LIM	OUTPUT LIM	PRIORITY	STACK LIM
309	7	2	20

OBJECT PROGRAM:

5	2	5	2	6
5	1	6	10	7
5	1	5	1	6
5	1	9	7	5
1	6	5	1	9

3	4	1	0	5
2	6	14	4	5
2	6	14	4	5
0	5	0	6	5
1	9	7	5	1
13	7	5	1	6
14	5	2	5	1
7	5	1	6	0
27	34	5	0	6
3	4	4	5	0
13	7	5	0	6
14	5	0	6	0
39	72	4	15	3
1	73	12		

EXECUTION BEGINS.

3	5	120	9	362880
0	1			

TRAP	CPU OPS	OUTPUT OPS	INPUT OPS	LAST ADDR
3	309	7	4	92

****

END OF EXECUTION.   239531 STMTS EXECUTED.   208 LINES OF OUTPUT

PROCESS NUMBER	STATEMENTS EXECUTED	MEMORY USED	MEMORY CLAIMED	LAST LINE EXECUTED	STATUS	UTILIZATIO IN PERCENT
1	230445	304	756	71	BLOCKED	40
2	3084	396	624	116	BLOCKED	27
3	2666	168	392	154	BLOCKED	31
4	6	12980	13208	200	BLOCKED	
5	3296	868	1064	DONE	TERMINATED	

The process numbers in the above statistics correspond to the CPU, reader, printer, drum, and operating system, in that order. The poor utilization demonstrates the need for concurrency in the system.

COLLECTED BIBLIOGRAPHY

Brinch Hansen, P. The nucleus of a multiprogramming system.
Comm. ACM 13,4 (April 1970), 238-241, 250.

Brinch Hansen, P. Structured multiprogramming. Comm. ACM 15,7
(July 1972), 574-577.

Brinch Hansen, P. Operating System Principles. Prentice-Hall
(1973).

Brinch Hansen, P. Concurrent programming concepts. Computing
Surveys 5,4 (December 1973), 223-245.

Brinch Hansen, P. The programming language Concurrent Pascal.
IEEE Trans. on Software Engineering SE-1,2 (June 1975), 199-
207.

Brinch Hansen, P. The Architecture of Concurrent Programs.
Prentice-Hall (1977).

Conway, R.W., Gries, D., and Wortman, D.B. Introduction to
Structured Programming Using PL/I and SP/k. Winthrop of
Prentice-Hall (1977).

Courtois, P.J., Heymans, F., and Parnas, D.L. Concurrent control
with readers and writers. Comm. ACM 14, 10 (October 1971),
667-668.

Czarnik, B. (editor), Tsichritzis, D., Ballard, A.J., Dryer, M.,
Holt, R.C., and Weissman, L. A student project for an
operating system course. CSRG-29, Computer Systems Research
Group, University of Toronto (1973).

Dijkstra, E.W. The structure of the T.H.E. multiprogramming
system. Comm. ACM 11,5 (May 1968), 341-346.

Dijkstra, E.W. Cooperating sequential processes. In Programming Languages (F. Genuys, editor), Academic Press (1968).

Dijkstra, E.W. Information streams sharing a finite buffer. Information Processing Letters 1,5 (October 1972), 179-180.

Dijkstra, E.W. A Discipline of Programming. Prentice-Hall (1976).

Greenblatt, I.E. and Holt, R.C. The SUE/11 operating system. INFOR, Canadian Journal of Operational Research and Information Processing 14,3 (October 1976), 227-232.

Hoare, C.A.R. Operating systems: their purpose, objectives, functions and scope. In Operating Systems Techniques (C.A.R. Hoare and R.H. Perrott, editors), Academic Press (1972), 11-19.

Hoare, C.A.R. Monitors: an operating system structuring concept. Comm. ACM 17,10 (October 1974), 549-557.

Holt, R.C. Some deadlock properties of computer systems. Computing Surveys 4,3 (September 1972), 179-196.

Holt, R.C. Structure of computer programs: a survey. Proceedings of the IEEE 63,6 (June 1975), 876-893.

Holt, R.C., Wortman, D.B., Barnard, D.T., and Cordy, J.R. SP/k: a system for teaching computer programming. Comm. ACM 20,5 (May 1977), 301-309.

Hume, J.N.P. and Holt, R.C. Structured Programming Using PL/1 and SP/k. Reston of Prentice-Hall (1975).

Kaubisch, W.H., Perrott, R.H., and Hoare, C.A.R. Quasiparallel programming. Software-Practice and Experience, Vol. 6 (1976), 341-356.

Knuth, D.E. The Art of Computer Programming, Volume 1 - Fundamental Algorithms. Addison-Wesley (1968).

Knuth, D.E. The Art of Computer Programming, Volume 3 - Sorting and Searching. Addison-Wesley (1973).

Liskov, B.H. The design of the VENUS operating system. Comm. ACM 15,3 (March 1972), 144-149.

Menzel, R.G. Concurrent SP/k: a language supporting concurrent processes. M.Sc. Thesis, Department of Computer Science, University of Toronto (July 1976).

Ritchie, D.M. and Thompson, K. The UNIX time-sharing system. Comm. ACM 17,7 (July 1974), 365-375.

Sevcik, K.C., Atwood, J.W., Clark, B.L., Grushcow, M.S., Holt, R.C., Horning, J.J., and Tsichritzis, D. Project SUE as a learning experience. <u>Proc</u>. <u>FJCC</u> <u>1972</u>, <u>Vol</u>. <u>39</u>, 331-337.

Shaw, A.C. and Weiderman, N.H. A multiprogramming system for education and research. <u>Proc</u>. <u>IFIP</u> <u>Congress</u> <u>1971</u>, 1505-1509.

Teorey, T.J. and Pinkerton, T.B. A comparative analysis of disk scheduling policies. <u>Comm</u>. <u>ACM</u> <u>15</u>,3 (March 1972), 177-184.

Wirth, N. MODULA: a language for modular multiprogramming. <u>Software</u> - <u>Practice</u> <u>and</u> <u>Experience</u> <u>Vol</u>. <u>7</u>,1 (January-February 1977), 3-35.

INDEX

Priority
    conditions, 71, 97, 103, 184-185
    dynamic for processes, 160
    in long term scheduler, 137
    of PDP-11 hardware, 152
    of readers vs. writers, 89
    queue, 60, 80, 142-144, 146, 148, 152, 201
    user-specified in Z7, 126
Private semaphore, 28
Procedure, 10-11, 54, 59, 173
Process, 3, 8, 11, 63, 72, 77, 109, 181-183
    chemical, 3
    CSP/k feature, 63, 77, 181, 188
    data space requirement, 72, 76
    descriptor, 140, 146, 148-150, 202, 204, 205
    header in CSP/k, 63, 72, 76
    queues for CSP/k, 201, 202
    statistics, 76-78
    types of, 9
Process/device communication, 141
Process/process communication,
    see Interprocess communication
Processor, 10-11
Producer/consumer relationship, 34, 70, 100, 118
    example program, 74
    with large messages, 100-101
Producer process, 74, 100
Program
    SP/k, 167
    segment, 128
Pseudo-machine, SP/k, 200, 203
Pure procedure, 11, 12
PUT statement, 167
    field width, 197
PUTDOWN routine, philosophers, 86

Quantum, 127
    exercise, 138
    see also Time slicing
Queues, 24, 55-57, 73, 100, 138, 140, 146, 148
    exercise, 80
    FIFO, 142-143
    of busy processes, 201
    of processes, 201-202
    management, 142-144
    priority, 60, 143-144
    ready, 7, 202
    updating shared, 21
QUEUES program, 57
Quit statement, 17
Quotes, 165

Race conditions, 19-22
Railroad in Peru and Bolivia, 47
Randomness of concurrency, 199

Z, in picture format item, 178
Z7
    computer, 109
    console, 114, 208
    CPU, 128, 215
    drum, 114, 212
    evolution, 136
    instructin set, 216
    memory, 129
    operating system, 109, 231
    printer, 113,210
    reader, 112, 208
    user language, 216